ECOLOGIES OF ECSTASY

ECOLOGIES OF ECSTASY

MYSTICISM, PHILOSOPHY, AND VEGETAL LIFE

SIMONE KOTVA

Columbia University Press *New York*

Columbia University Press
Publishers Since 1893
New York   Chichester, West Sussex
cup.columbia.edu

Copyright © 2026 Columbia University Press
All rights reserved

Library of Congress Cataloging-in-Publication Data
Names: Kotva, Simone author
Title: Ecologies of ecstasy : mysticism, philosophy,
and vegetal life / Simone Kotva.
Description: New York : Columbia University Press, [2026] |
Includes bibliographical references and index.
Identifiers: LCCN 2025030880 (print) | LCCN 2025030881 (ebook) |
ISBN 9780231213967 hardback | ISBN 9780231213974 trade paperback |
ISBN 9780231560122 epub | ISBN 9780231564779 pdf
Subjects: LCSH: Spiritualism (Philosophy) | Philosophy and religion
Classification: LCC B841 .K675 2026 (print) | LCC B841 (ebook)
LC record available at https://lccn.loc.gov/2025030880
LC ebook record available at https://lccn.loc.gov/2025030881

Cover image: Vanna Bowles, "Person täckt av murgröna" (Person covered in ivy),
from *Orädd resa* (Intrepid journey), 2021. Photo © Peter Olsson, 2025.

GPSR Authorized Representative: Easy Access System Europe,
Mustamäe tee 50, 10621 Tallinn, Estonia, gpsr.requests@easproject.com

*To the Community at Redwoods Monastery
and Sister Veronique—in memory.*

Consider the lilies of the field, how they grow; they neither toil nor spin, yet I tell you, even Solomon in all his glory was not clothed like one of these.

—Matthew 6:28–39

Men would condemn such a [mystical] state, saying it makes us something less than the meanest insect; and so it does, not by obstinacy and firmness of purpose, but by powerlessness to interfere with ourselves.

—Jeanne Guyon, *Spiritual Torrents*

By its existence alone, the lily of the field sings the glory of the heavens, the goddesses and gods—in other words, the elements that it contemplates in contracting.

—Gilles Deleuze, *Difference and Repetition*

As for us, we are like plants.

—Simone Weil, *Waiting on God*

CONTENTS

Preface xi

1 Spiritual Exercises Across Species 1

2 A Natural History of Contemplation 45

3 Vegetal Mysticism 81

Interlude. Francis in Ecstasy 111

4 Let Nature Be Aroused! 119

5 The Plant in Us 159

Epilogue. Ecologies of Ecstasy 197

Acknowledgments 207
Notes 211
Bibliography 237
Index 251

PREFACE

The book you hold in your hands is the result of a spiritual exercise I began practicing several years ago. The connection between spiritual exercise and the theme of this essay—communication across species—was not at all evident when I started. At that point I was writing my first book, on philosophy and spiritual exercises. I had been teaching philosophy and theology for a few years and had a personal as well as professional interest in mysticism. Curious about what I was researching, I decided to commit to a daily practice. I was doing so within the context of Western Christian mysticism broadly and Catholicism specifically, which teaches, at the core of its spiritual tradition, a wordless prayer of the heart called contemplation. As such, I had little thought for anything but my inner life.

It was not until I was about a year and a half into my practice that things began to change. The changes began with my skin. During prayer, my skin would start to become hypersensitive. Tears would flow. The feeling was an erotic sensation, though not sexual. Odd things then happened to my sense of interiority: to my sense of "me," "mine," and "self." I would be left with a nearly continuous, buzzing sensation in which I experienced "self" diffused and spread out over the whole surface of my body. It was as if my skin *was* my "self," and "I" was nothing but the sensations received by the cutaneous covering holding my body together. I also started to become aware of things around me in new ways. I began *sensing* with intensity. I felt myself *feeling*, in a new way. The experience is difficult to describe. Plants were particular catalysts, but the sensation could come over me in all sorts of contexts: when doing the dishes or picking up shopping. But even when I was not around plants, I would find myself experiencing the world in a way that seemed, to me, more plantlike than human. I say "plantlike" because I felt more full of energy than usual but at the same time more passive. After a while, such experiences became a new normal for me. They would fluctuate in intensity but were always present to some degree. With practice, I learned how to tune into them easily and sustain awareness of them for long periods at a time.

Searching for ways to describe my experiences, Aristotle's vegetative soul came to mind. According to Aristotle, humans share with plants nutritive or purely sensitive activities. This resonated with my experience, but it also raised questions. Through my research I had come to learn what to expect from the mystical prayer I was practicing, but experiences of vegetal life were not among them. In fact, they seemed to contradict the tradition I knew. Was not contemplation the highest activity, reserved for humans? Had not Aristotle claimed it brought humans close to gods? And had not Christian mystics, in their turn, presented it as the path to mystical union with God? Why, then, was contemplation making me feel like a plant? The search for answers led me down a new path of research. Eventually, I shifted my focus from philosophy as spiritual exercise, to thinking about contemplation and creaturely life, and eventually to the relationship among mysticism, philosophy, and vegetal life.

Initially, I had no trouble finding literature on Western Christian mysticism and vegetal life. It was not difficult to find studies of the cosmos, creation, and nature in Western Christian mysticism. What proved more difficult to establish was an account of the vegetal in the sense I had come to perceive it: as the nutritive or sensitive life of not only plants but also of human animals. Then I stumbled across Michael Marder's work on vegetal life. In Marder's work, what he calls "plant-thinking" is not species-thought. The vegetal indicates not the life of a kingdom or indeed a species but the form of life: a type of activity common to creatures. Marder also points to the etymology of nature in Greek, where *phusis* derives from a verb, "to grow," that is cognate with one of the words for plant (*phuton*). Yet *phusis* does not refer to plants as a species. "That which grows and changes," or that which metamorphoses, is the open-ended way of rethinking nature from the perspective of crossing species and entities that emerges from Marder's philosophy of vegetal life.[1] Adventuring through the literature that has been emerging around Marder's work, I was struck in particular by the way Jeffrey Nealon defined Aristotle's vegetative soul as "what we share with other entities."[2] I also found that mindfulness and contemplation were appearing in the new philosophical literature devoted to vegetal life. Contemplation has begun to play a minor but striking role, invoked as a way of describing not only spiritual exercises but also vegetal life.

This helped me make sense of my own experience, where plants were significant but not exclusive catalysts of intense affectivity during contemplation. It also helped me make sense of mystical literature, which, as I had been learning, not only compared contemplation to being like a plant—sunflowers were a favorite among some mystics—but also to minerals and animals. The medieval mystic Richard of Saint Victor, for instance, compared contemplation to bird's flight: A soaring eagle was a common metaphor for contemplation in medieval and later mysticism. Contemporary philosophies of vegetal life became helpful as I attempted to piece together these metaphors. I came to recognize that what was at stake for mystics was not so much plants (or animals or minerals) as what they shared in common: spontaneity but also sensitivity—and the relationship between spontaneity and sensitivity, which seemed central to contemplation. One way of thinking about what I was calling "vegetal mysticism" was in terms of both plants and humans (as well as minerals, bacteria, fungi, and sharks . . .). Although humans are not plants, humans (like all animals) participate in plantlike activities simply because they are embodied. Vegetal life is most clearly seen (at least by humans) in plants, but for humans and other animals there are plenty of bodily activities that are not brain dependent. Skin, for instance, practices an incessant awareness of the world. Marder even argues that when we shift our awareness to our skin, we may be learning how to be attentive in the manner of the vegetal life that sustains our waking thoughts. Skin and its sensitivity were prominent in my own experience practicing spiritual exercises in the tradition of Western Christian mysticism. Partly in response to Marder, my writing of this book developed into a story of vegetal life told from the perspective of mystics cultivating sensory perception, sensitivity, and affect in different ways. I came to think of it as a graft of mystical and vegetal being. In my book, this graft also appears as a cross-disciplinary entwinement connecting philosophy to theology in fresh ways.

"Attention" and especially "attentiveness" were words that kept recurring, both in mystical literature and in contemporary philosophies responding to vegetal life. In this book, readers will find that contemplation is often glossed as a form of consciousness that is active yet unintentional (for this reason, some writers I cite prefer describing it as "unconscious awareness," but the basic sense is the same), meaning that I will be considering sensation a form of awareness and one of the means by which life metamorphoses, dies, decays, and emerges into new forms.

For my own part, the practices I have experienced are impossible to separate from everyday intimacies. Like speculative fiction, Indigenous knowledge practices, and other arts of attention, the contemplation I practice has facilitated living in solidarity with Terran kin, without too much killing. Whether this was the experience also of the historical mystics I describe within these pages, I will never know. But the significance of vegetal life in mystical literature suggests that, at the very least, experiences similar to mine may not have been an isolated phenomenon. If so, we have in the figures and texts I will be describing a tradition of practical knowhow with strong bearing on the present. Solidarity between entities is impossible without practices of attentiveness. It is my hope that the mystical literature retold in this book will contribute to the ongoing work of charting the arts of noticing entanglements: entanglements among discourses, histories, and disciplines but also among creatures, species, and things.[3]

Multiple stories entwine in this book: stories of historical mystics articulating the human-divine relationship through imagery and practices pertaining to vegetal life and stories of philosophers responding to vegetal life with gestures toward practical contemplation.

The relationship between these stories and my motivations for reading them together is introduced in chapter 1. Here, I outline the literature addressing vegetal life in Western Christian mysticism, giving particular attention to the link between vegetal life and femininity and the subsequent queering of this link in recent studies engaging critical plant studies. This is followed by a brief introduction to critical plant studies and the philosophies of vegetal life with which I will be in dialogue for the rest of the book. I am particularly interested in the way Michael Marder draws tentative connections between vegetal life and spiritual exercises. I observe how Marder invites a closer study of spiritual practices not—or not only—insofar as mystical literature figuratively favors vegetal life but to the extent that mystical practices provide means of recognizing shared participation in vegetal life. Having established this as my starting point, I then glance further back at the history of twentieth-century continental philosophy. I show how the entwining I am attempting in this book is anticipated in the philosophy of Gilles Deleuze, whose notion of "vegetable contemplation" is introduced together with responses from critical plant studies and theology.

Subsequent chapters interweave stories from the history of Western Christian mysticism with perspectives from recent philosophy and theology. My scope is the period c. 300–1700 typically addressed by scholars of mysticism, a period Bernard McGinn separates into three overlapping but distinct "layers": early, medieval, and early modern. My chapters follow this division, although loosely, and I make no pretence at providing an exhaustive account of the phenomena I describe. Rather, my aim has been to think through some of the theological and philosophical claims made among contemporary writers interested in vegetal life, and my reading of mystical literature has been guided accordingly.

Chapter 2, "A Natural History of Contemplation," addresses vegetal life in the monastic ideal of early Christian mysticism.

Plotinus opens and closes this chapter. Despite Plotinus's standing outside the history of Western Christian mysticism proper, his influence on mystical theology is profound, and his ideas have continued to reverberate down the centuries, most recently in the work of Michael Marder. Drawing on Marder's readings of Plotinus, I show the relationship between nature's contemplation and contemplative *practice*. Contemplative practices in Christianity are then my next topic. I follow the relationship between nature (*phusis*) and contemplation (*theoria*) in the monastic practice of *phusike theoria*, "contemplation of nature," that emerged in the deserts of Egypt and the Middle East. I focus on Egypt and Evagrian monasticism while indicating the connection to a wider tradition represented by Syriac monastic Christianity and engage with the work of Douglas Christie in order to do so. I find Christie's concept of "contemplative ecology" especially promising, as its semantic ambiguity—suggesting that environments may be engaged in contemplative activities—introduces back into early Christian mysticism an extended notion of contemplation as a multispecies activity. In this chapter I also introduce the theme of heresy and dissent. In the fourth century, contemplative practices began coming under suspicion from church authorities. While my concern is neither to verify nor defend Christian orthodoxy, I am fascinated with the implications of dissent. It suggests a trenchant rebellion against a culture bent on denying nature, a notion that will become relevant in subsequent chapters.

In chapter 3, "Vegetal Mysticism," I turn to medieval mysticism and develop an interpretative approach based on recent rethinking of classic texts. I begin with what is perhaps the most well known of medieval mysticism's vegetal metaphors: *viriditas*, "greenness," Hildegard of Bingen's name for not only green sap but for life—and the Holy Spirit. I read Hildegard's *viriditas* alongside the interpretations of Marder and of Liz Herbert McAvoy and Sarah Ritchey. While entire books could be dedicated to *viriditas* and its reception, what I tease out in this chapter is the relationship between vegetality and mystical practices of uniting to God. From Hildegard I turn to Gertrude of Helfta, and I look to the reading of grafting metaphors in her mysticism by McAvoy and others. I show how mystics' grafting—of themselves to Christ but also of Christ to the mystic—is read as a sexual practice but also one that queers human sexuality and instead models the human-divine relationship on asexual reproduction. In order to make a closer study of how mysticism relates to vegetal life, in the final part of the chapter, I look to Marguerite of Porete. Marguerite is important because she taught a method of mystical self-annihilation that influenced subsequent mystics such as Meister Eckhart. While self-annihilation is often viewed, by commentators, as a sign of Marguerite's hatred of nature, I draw on Amy Hollywood's insightful scholarship to foreground the crucial role of nature, its demands and entanglement with God, in Marguerite's *The Mirror of Simple Souls*. Mystics' appreciation for nature was one reason for their possible condemnation as heretics; indeed, Marguerite was burned at the stake. For this reason, rather than see self-annihilation as a means of escaping the world, I argue for its relevance as a means of stepping away from the interests of the self qua self-interested human. I show how Hollywood's interpretation of Marguerite thus shares many concerns and conclusions with recent "vegetal" readings of medieval mystics, especially Marder's.

Bridging the gap between the medieval period and the late seventeenth century, there follows a brief interlude on Franciscan spirituality: "Francis in Ecstasy." Through a reading of Giovanni Bellini's fifteenth-century painting *St. Francis in Ecstasy*, I suggest that while ecstasy today is often connected with an interior state, in medieval theology it was also seen as a natural activity. Drawing art-historical readings of Bellini's painting into conversation with theology and philosophy, I study the striking appearance of a visual rhyme between the posture of Francis and the shape of a tree and a rock, offering a vegetal interpretation of Francis's famous nature mysticism.

Nature, negative theology, and heresy come together in chapters 4 and 5, which concern the practice of self-annihilation as taught by a mystic often compared to Marguerite: the early modern French Catholic Jeanne Guyon. Chapter 4, "Let Nature Be Aroused!" situates Guyon in a countercurrent to Cartesian rationalism shared with nonconformist Christians, utopian mystics, and women spiritual reformers. Guyon's name has been associated chiefly with Quietism, a Catholic heresy; Guyon, although never formally condemned of Quietism, was interrogated over eighty times and spent ten years under house arrest or in prison. Following feminist scholarship on Guyon, I draw attention to the subversive virtue ascribed to passivity and silence in Guyon's mysticism, where such "activities" are viewed not as submission to power but as nondiscursive tactics of resistance to clerical authority. I also, however, draw attention to Guyon's own understanding of passivity, which is presented in terms not of gender but of nutritive activities (what Guyon calls "nature") common to all creatures. Recalling the vegetal mysticism of the previous chapter, I propose a new reading of mystical passivity in light of what I interpret as Guyon's sense for vegetal life. I also consider Guyon's immediate precursors and sources of inspirations, such as the French Discalced Carmelites but especially Francis de Sales, Jane de Chantal, and the Visitandines.

Situating Guyon's mysticism in the context of Natasha Meeker and Antónia Szabari's idea of a "vegetal modernity" sprouting in the seventeenth and eighteenth centuries, I make the case for a vegetal mysticism also in early modernity. While scholars of early modern mysticism have succeeded in redeeming corporeality in important ways, my argument is that the body redeemed by mystics like Guyon is experienced as sustained by vegetal activities: Here, the exercises called spiritual are multispecies activities. Following Michel de Certeau, the important work of the Guyon scholar Marie-Florine Bruneau, and, more recently, the work of Bo Karen Lee, I point to the significance of Guyon's mysticism as a "low anthropology" that challenges species supremacism through experiential techniques aimed at arousing the senses and cultivating interspecies vulnerability through intense experiences of the sensitive life. I then propose ways in which Guyon's "low anthropology" might be grafted onto concepts germinating in critical plant studies.

In chapter 5, I continue to be accompanied by Guyon, now grafting her work with philosophies of vegetal life. Thinking with Guyon's influential manual, *A Short and Easy Method of Prayer* (1685), I propose a new way of understanding the practice of contemplative prayer. Rather than see Guyon's emphasis on passivity and silence as disembodying the mystic, I show how her account of passivity, in fact, is interpreted as a letting-go of the body's natural inclinations—but also of the inclinations of vegetal life. Ruminating on the curious role of breath, air, and atmosphere in Guyon's imagery, I make connections to the same themes in the philosophies of Luce Irigaray and Emanuele Coccia. Uniting their recent work on plants and contemplation is a rethinking of passivity through a deep, detailed consideration of what kind of activity constitutes vegetating. Here, breathing has come to describe not an organismic activity but an interrelated, multispecies process of creating atmosphere through receptivity, and I relate this to Guyon's understanding of contemplation as breath and God as air. By grafting Guyon with Irigaray and

Coccia, I detect a tacit liberation of spiritual life from organismic frameworks. Finally, I provide a theological perspective by returning to the engagement with Gilles Deleuze's "vegetable contemplation."

The epilogue, "Ecologies of Ecstasy," is less summary than opening. Picking up again the threads of personal practice I have introduced here, I provide more detail on my experience and the choices I made when settling on the historical and theoretical context for this book. I then look forward to the nineteenth and twentieth centuries and situate my book within a much wider and more complex narrative of modern Western mystics for whom vegetal life was a source of wisdom and resilience. While the graft I cultivate in *Ecologies of Ecstasy* comes to a natural hiatus after the death of Guyon in 1717, similar cross-disciplinary readings of later mystics are possible and are already being tended.

ECOLOGIES
OF ECSTASY

1

SPIRITUAL EXERCISES ACROSS SPECIES

This is a book about Western Christian mysticism, but it is also about ethics in a more-than-human world, about what humans share with other entities. At first blush, nothing could seem more exclusive to human beings than mysticism. Indeed, in Western traditions of philosophy and theology, the word for spirit can also mean mind, and it is common to associate spirituality with belief or faith. Yet this association lends to the whole subject an anthropocentric bias completely at odds with the meaning of the word, which comes from *spiritus*, the Latin for breath.[1]

Breathing is not subject to faith, nor is the exchange of gases with the atmosphere the preserve of human interiority. All lifeforms breathe; most even do so without lungs, since they are plants or fungi. The perspective I take in this book is that spiritual activity is best understood as a multispecies activity, one in which all life participates, only some of which is human. I ask what would happen, what kind of reorientation might take place, when the *vegetal* is given priority in our narratives of mysticism. The vegetal, I will argue, is not species-thought but is the name for activities that go on wherever there is life. It has a central role in explaining how consciousness works before and beyond brain-dependent activity, conceptual thinking, and the constraints of subjectivity. And vegetal life is also significant to the history of mystical literature and the literary representation of *contemplation*, to the loss of distinction between self and world, and to the idea of mystical union that rests upon it.

I suggest that one way of understanding the loss of self prominent in mysticism is to read it through contemporary philosophies of vegetal life and critical plant studies. In recent years, the recognition of the vegetal in postmodern critiques of subjectivity has intimated this possibility, from Elaine P. Miller and Jeffrey Nealon, through Emanuele Coccia, to Luce Irigaray, Michael Marder, and others. In different ways, but with a shared understanding drawn from plant biology, these writers describe a way of knowing that is receptive, lacking distinction between subject and object, existing in total communion with the environment—even as itself contemplative. Writes Coccia, in *The Life of Plants: A Metaphysics of Mixture*: "The plant is the purest observer when it comes to contemplating the world in its totality."[2] Alternatively, the sensible qualities of vegetal milieus bring humans, in Irigaray's expression, "from concentration to contemplation [and] a sort of ecstasy."[3] To what extent, though, do these metaphors bear the weight of an entanglement with contemplative *practices*? And if such entanglement is evident, what might it indicate about the *ethics* at stake for writers turning to vegetal life today? This is the guiding question of my book. It has led me to investigate not only uses of vegetal metaphors in Western Christian mysticism but also parallels between how philosophers and scientists understand plant intelligence, on the one hand, and how historical mystics understood the practice of contemplation, on the other. To this I have added the insights of Pierre Hadot and Gilles Deleuze, who in the 1960s first recognized the connection between vegetal life and contemplation, relating it to mystical and philosophical practices, as well as to the philosophy of vital matter. My inquiry thus draws together discourses from separate disciplines, converging around a central theme shared among philosophy, theology, and plant theory: What happens to agency in a more-than-human world? The philosophical study of plant intelligence shares a concern or ethos similar to mysticism. In both cases, we detect a resistance to the self-possessed subject. It is in the abandonment of self so frequently stressed by historical discussions of contemplation that I see a fruitful point of contact between the mystical and the vegetal. In this chapter, I propose to sketch only how mysticism might be rethought through an encounter with past and contemporary philosophies of the vegetal. I will then provide narratives of how the mystical and vegetal have entwined throughout the history of Western Christian mysticism.

THROUGH MYSTICAL AND VEGETAL BEING

In one sense, the entwinement of mystical and vegetal being has already been well underway for some time. Western Christian mysticism has long been known to evidence "cosmism" or the "tendency to aspire to God through the contemplation of creation and its wonders."[4] Animal life is significant in Christianity and has been given the most attention by scholars,[5] but the importance of plants has also been recognized. Plants and horticultural activities figure prominently in the Hebrew and Greek scriptures not only as part of the world described but also as metaphors for God and spiritual ideas.[6] As Thomas Arentzen, Virginia Burrus, and Glenn Peers have pointed out recently, while Christian theology did not make a special place for plants in its understanding of the world, spiritual practices tell a different story: "Ancient and medieval Christians retained an openness to and sense of connection with vegetal life, and especially tree life, that sometimes far exceeded the strict limits of their theological orthodoxies."[7] In ancient and medieval mysticism, vegetal growth is symbiotic (rather than merely symbolic) in its link to mysticism, providing a "sensitive imagining of asceticism in, under, and within nature."[8] Sarah Ritchey recently coined the term "spiritual arborescence" in order to describe an otherwise easily overlooked aspect of medieval Christianity in particular: its penchant for trees.[9] Arboreal diagrams were used as memory aids and in devotional imagery; alternatively, the reader was to climb a pictured tree in the imagination, following the path of the hermit striving for God. Dendrite or tree-sitting asceticism originated in Eastern Christianity, but the practice is also attested in Europe, where the trees in question "are more than speculative objects."[10] Dendrite saints, like the eleventh-century German ascetic Edigna of Puch, lived for years in trees, performing miracles and ministering to their communities.[11] During this period, an increasing number of hermits and ascetics "sought solace and spiritual testing among the uncultivated trees of the dwindling thirteenth-century wilderness."[12] Gardens, like trees, were similarly significant: "From the earliest days the archetypal symbol of the garden has been associated with the image of paradise, that ideal blessed state to which human kind has sought to regain access."[13] In vernacular Catholicism, Mary was thought to recline in a garden, and some enclosed gardens were planted in order to reflect "Mary's Garden."[14] In general, medieval formal gardens were often configured with spiritual symbolism in mind, relating it to paradise but also to the Garden of Eden, Gethsemane, and Solomon's garden in the Song of Songs. Here, according to Bernard of Clairvaux (1090–1153), the Bride rests in ecstasy in the arms of her Bridegroom, both reclining on a bed of herbs.[15] With roots going back to Jewish mysticism and ancient monasticism,[16] Bernard's mystical garden supplied countless later mystics with an array of metaphors through which to articulate and express their visions, teachings, and experiences. The Song of Songs and its vegetal imagery continued to be significant in Western Christian mysticism. In the European, Catholic tradition with which I am mostly concerned, we will see these and other vegetal themes maintaining their importance well into the eighteenth century.

Taking refuge among trees, whether materially or metaphorically, has been a prominent feature in the long history of Christian mystical literature. Vegetal milieus played an important role in the lives and writings of women mystics. The medieval abbess Hildegard of Bingen (1098–1179) named the Holy Spirit *viriditas*, "greenness," to indicate the connection between vegetal and divine life, and female monastic communities in northern Europe crafted multimedia collages, representing miniature walled gardens, as a form of devotional exercise.[17] Women mystics often identified with the Bride of the Song but also pictured their own heart as an interior garden. This link between vegetal life and women's devotional practice was recognized by feminist historians and became the basis for an influential feminist rereading of mysticism. Grace Jantzen observed how "flourishing" emerged in women's mysticism as a distinctive metaphor for the human-divine relationship.[18] Building on the work of the feminist philosopher Luce Irigaray, Jantzen proposed a close relationship between women and vegetal life and suggested that female "flourishing" provided a counternarrative to male-coded mysticism focused on personal salvation, death, and the afterlife. Irigaray had envisioned the possibility of "another kind of subjectivity," one that consciously addressed the plant, "both to criticize the negative way in which it has traditionally been used to characterize the ontological status of women, and, increasingly to subvert the traditional metaphor in the productive notion of efflorescence."[19] According to Jantzen's reading, vegetal life in mysticism seemed to address the experiences of female-coded lives. Within studies of women's mysticism, vegetal imagery comes to take on an added layer of meaning. Historically, nature often was gendered, typically a "she." In women's mysticism where vegetal life figures prominently, this identification seems both reinforced and subverted, as women mystics take refuge in the qualities associated with the vegetal—principally, passivity—while finding in these qualities new ways of resisting those normative values threatening to suppress both women and nature.

However, vegetal life in Western Christian mysticism is not confined to a representation of gender, nor are women mystics alone in invoking vegetal imagery. The theme is quite widespread, across texts by both men and women throughout the history of Christian mysticism. As Barbara Newman, an important commentator both on the conception of nature and on women's mysticism, puts it, female-coded imaginaries of divine-vegetal life for this reason cannot be interpreted satisfactorily according to a simple gender binary.[20] Michael Marder, the contemporary philosopher of plant life with whom I will be engaging throughout this book, makes a similar observation. Like Jantzen, Marder has also been influenced (as we shall come to in a later chapter) by Irigaray, whose reclaiming of the association between plants and femininity echoes in Jantzen's notion of "flourishing." However, Marder also expresses resistance to Irigaray's focus on sexuate difference. In *Through Vegetal Being: Two Philosophical Perspectives*, a book structured as a dialogue with Irigaray, Marder therefore asks: "How do you propose to think about the sexuality of plants? What is its relevance to human sexuate difference?" He continues:

> What I have in mind is the fluidity, pliability, and plasticity of vegetal sexuality, where many plants are hermaphrodites, others can change from masculine or feminine (and vice versa) in their lifetimes, while still others reproduce asexually. Without a doubt, sexuate difference belongs to the phenomenon of embodiment and to life itself. But is it such a linear process, whereby one is recalled to (or one recalls) one's own sexuate being, as a living body, upon contact with plants? Does the vegetal world open sexuate difference, through which we attempt to encounter it, to sexuate differences that are more diverse still than what Freud referred to as the "polymorphous perversity" of the human infant?[21]

Irigaray does not respond directly to this question, noting only that "the vegetal world is not sexuate as we are."[22] Marder instead pursues these questions elsewhere, especially in his recent writing on Christian mysticism, *Green Mass: The Ecological Theology of Hildegard of Bingen*. In Marder's work on Hildegard, attention to plant life disrupts, rather than confirms, assumptions about human subjectivity. Here, Marder allows the plasticity of vegetal sexuality to foreground the vegetal metaphors in historical women's mysticism. Moreover, he also indicates the ways in which mysticism itself pushes back against a gendered narrative of vegetal life. For Marder, mysticism appears to rest on a radical letting-go of self-identity. To unite with God is to abandon the self, and it is this state, rather than a gendered experience of embodiment, to which vegetal imagery is linked in *Green Mass*. Marder's appearance in the recent work by the feminist historian of mysticism Liz Herbert McAvoy points in similar directions. Commenting on the problems of a gendered vegetal nature, inevitably a "she," McAvoy describes a reciprocal process of feminizing and vegetalizing. On the one hand, women mystics invoke plants "not only to provide a vocabulary with which to articulate their visionary insights but also to posit an alternative imaginary in which renewal, growth and flourishing take up a primary position, and place a spirituality identified with the 'feminine' at central stage." Yet the vegetal and *its* configurations also challenge the "feminine" system of the mystics, issuing in a form of femininity that is not womanish. Vegetal life provides women mystics not only with images of fruitful passivity but also with diverse sexual difference. What does the sexual plasticity of vegetal life do to the vegetal metaphors sprouting from women's mysticism? Do they reinforce a species-specific image of femininity, or do they, rather, introduce a "place of *process* where abundance is the result of action and *intra*-action"?[23]

In this book, I read vegetal imagery as that which both invites and challenges analogies of female-coded systems of configurations in mysticism, opening the latter toward an ethic that foregrounds not a *human* womb-matrix but *vegetal* metamorphosis. I will be thinking not only with women mystics but also Desert Fathers and male monastics, especially in chapter 2. That being said, the emphasis on vegetal imagery in women's mysticism is striking, and the majority of my stories center around women. Chapter 3 turns to the celebrated example of vegetal imagery in medieval women's mysticism, exploring its possible relation to the mysticism of Marguerite of Porete (1250–1310). In chapters 4 and 5, I offer an extended reading of the French mystic Jeanne Guyon (1648–1717), a pivotal figure confronting modernity, writing at a time of interreligious tensions, missionary violence, and crisis in the history of Western Christianity. Nevertheless, I follow Marder and others in arguing that this connection between women's mysticism and vegetal life is not one of gender essentialism, and I think with contemporary philosophies of vegetal life in order to do so. Key to contemporary philosophies of vegetal life has been a queering of identity through an engagement with the science of plant intelligence and the study of non-neural consciousness. My contention is that, in Western Christian mysticism, the vegetal entangles with contemplative practices leading to ecstasy and mystical union rather than, fundamentally, with the experiences of gendered bodies.

CONTEMPLATIVE ECOLOGY REDUX

In this book, I will be making a case for the ecological significance of contemplative practices. Why *contemplative* practices in particular? Contemplation holds an elevated yet ambiguous place in Western Christian mystical literature as a practice that is viewed both as the zenith of human achievement and, at the same time, a natural and spontaneous activity. In the standard medieval definition of contemplation, formulated during the twelfth century by Richard of St. Victor, contemplation is distinguished from thinking and meditating:

> Thinking, slow footed, wanders hither and thither along by-paths, caring not where they will lead. Meditation, with great mental industry, plods along the steep and laborious road keeping the end in view. Contemplation, on a free wing, circles around with great nimbleness wherever the impulse takes it. Thinking crawls along, meditation marches and sometimes runs, contemplation flies around and when it wills, it hovers upon the height. Thinking is without labor and bears no fruit. Meditation labors

and has its fruit. Contemplation abides untoiling and fruitful. Thinking roams about; meditation investigates; contemplation wonders.[24]

According to this approach, contemplation was a practice that followed "thinking" and "meditation," that is, came after what we might call study and reflection. While thinking, meditation and contemplation are all considered metaphorically, by Richard, as physical activities, in the case of contemplation this activity is modeled on the "untoiling" flight of birds, meaning spontaneous effort. Similar analogies are not unusual in mystical literature. Ultimately, they can be traced back to the words of Jesus in Matthew 6:26: "Look at the birds of the air; they neither sow nor reap nor gather into barns, and yet your heavenly Father feeds them." But Jesus also invokes plants: "Consider the lilies of the field, how they grow; they neither toil nor spin, yet I tell you, even Solomon in all his glory was not clothed like one of these" (Matthew 6:28–29). Comparisons between contemplation and plant life are not uncommon in mystical literature. The influential seventeenth-century spiritual reformer Francis de Sales (1567–1622), an author we will be returning to in a later chapter, suggested that, when contemplating, a person is like a sunflower turning to the "Sun of Righteousness."[25] Jeanne Guyon, with whom I will be lingering in detail in this book, takes the analogy still further, asserting that contemplation renders a person "something less than the meanest insect," claiming that a vegetal state was a perfection rather than an embarrassment of human nature.[26]

What do such statements suggest regarding the relationship between contemplation and vegetal life? In Western Christian contemplative practice, words, thoughts, and sense of self were to be negated or "annihilated." Yet the affections were to be aroused, with the understanding that God might be enjoyed in this life in a natural repose that would ideally be continual for the practitioner. Contemplative practices were thus linked *both* to the *via negativa*, or "path of negations," of mystical theology *and* to an affirmation of nature. Historically, such practices were especially popular among monastic and lay communities, but they often met with resistance from church authorities. Some forms of mysticism were condemned as heretical, and many mystics—including Meister Eckhart, Teresa of Ávila, John of the Cross, and Ignatius of Loyola—were suspected of heresy.[27] Despite their long history in Western Christian mysticism, contemplative practices became increasingly contentious, leading to their being eventually maligned in the eighteenth century. After the "crisis" of Western Christian mysticism at the end of the seventeenth century, contemplative practices enjoyed continued popularity among Pietist and nonconformist communities, such as Quakers and Methodists, while playing a minor role in Catholic and more mainstream Protestant spiritualities, until their widespread revival in the twentieth century.[28]

Without going further into the historical theological debates regarding contemplation (some of which we will be addressing in subsequent chapters),[29] I note a few of the ways key aspects of contemplative practices have since been rethought, especially by recent scholars. The idea first presented itself in Thomas Merton's early reflections on the remarkable practice known in early Christian asceticism as *phusike theoria*, "contemplation of nature," or "natural contemplation."[30] More recently, the work by Douglas Christie, Bruce Foltz, Jacob Holsinger Sherman, and others has situated contemplation in relation to contemporary concerns.[31] Christie in particular has opened the question of a "contemplative ecology" in early monasticism, drawing attention to the cultivation of sensory perception as a key theme. Christie takes his point of departure in the ascetical tradition of the fourth and fifth centuries but observes that "the cultivation of this kind of contemplative awareness" finds expressions in later mysticism as well as in other religious traditions and in contemporary poetry, art, and environmental movements.[32] The work by Christie especially, to develop a "contemplative ecology," and the wider contemplative turn in recent philosophy of religion, forms the immediate backdrop to chapter 2.

In chapters 2 through 5, feminist approaches of different kinds become particularly important. Feminist theory has helped theologians rethink contemplative practices in the context of women's spirituality, by arguing that it has been studied, until recently, mainly from the perspective of a male-coded and/or heterosexual self that casts agency in terms of autonomy, self-assertion, and willpower. In relation to philosophy more broadly, feminist approaches to mysticism (both ancient and modern) have been recognized as significant for the way they have shifted the discourse around mysticism from extraordinary and/or interior psychic events to the everyday and to corporeality.[33] Rather than assimilating or imitating the autonomous, individualistic self, themes of passiveness and self-annihilation are seen as ways of *resisting* these ideals.[34] The reclaiming of mystical negation and "nothingness"—key notions in contemplative practices in Western Christian mysticism—has been important also for queer and decolonial readings. Writing from the perspective of queer theory, Kent Brintnall argues that in mysticism "the subject's relation to itself, to its sense of its power and prerogatives" is "radically challenged," or, as he puts it, that there is "something to be gained by adopting practices that . . . will 'ruin in [us] that which is opposed to ruin.'"[35] It has also been claimed that mystical "nothingness" resonates with the "ontological quandary" of the colonized, where nothingness "is the space or state of ultimate indeterminacy," in which the self is experienced not as "internally undifferentiated" but "*displaced . . .* internally incoherent, fractured, contradictory and always in a state of becoming."[36] "Displacement" is the literal meaning of "ecstasy," from the Greek *ekstasis*, meaning "movement outward," and it leads not to a negation of agency or to a glorification of inferiority but to a refiguring of subjectivity in terms of becoming, dependency, and vulnerability (the sense that one is not the self-sufficient author of one's existence).[37] According to such readings, mystical or contemplative negation must be understood as an attempt to reclaim agency in a nonpossessive mode that would resist the cultures of violence that identify agency narrowly with the possession and acquisition of power.

Along similar lines, the feminist and environmental theologian Catherine Keller views the *via negativa* as crossing paths with an "ecological relationalism."[38] One common way of interpreting mystical "nothingness" has been to emphasize its connection to world-renunciation and thus its assumed antipathy to ecology. For Keller, however, what is expressed in the *via negativa* of mysticism is not the negation of nature but the negation of species hierarchies, hierarchies that mysticism rethinks by foregrounding relations. Environmental theology has drawn attention to mystical theology in a number of ways during the past decades. As the ecotheologian James W. Perkinson writes, in the mystic's ecstasy "there is insight only on the outside of the subject's own consciousness."[39] The work of Keller speaks to themes that have been discussed in ecofeminist theology for decades. Already in the 1990s, Sallie McFague hinted at the importance of contemplative traditions for ecology when she drew Iris Murdoch and Simone Weil into conversation with environmental ethics, proposing an "attention epistemology" rooted in mystical theology.[40] Following McFague's influential work, ecological theology has been marked by a renewed and vibrant interest in contemplative traditions and ways of life. In turn, this interest in spiritual traditions has facilitated encounters between mystical theology and critical animal studies and new materialist and posthumanist philosophies.[41] In this book, I will be grafting histories of Western Christian mysticism with critical plant studies, rather than with new materialism, animal studies, or posthumanist philosophies. However, I will also be weaving my reading together with perspectives from the philosophy of Gilles Deleuze, whose work intersects with several new approaches to mystical theology, not least that of Keller. In *Cloud of the Impossible: Negative Theology and Planetary Entanglement*, Keller describes Deleuze's philosophy as a "generative atheism . . . close to pantheism," which aids her "decomposing of the anthropocentric perspective," allowing Keller to "ply the human otherwise."[42] While Keller engages extensively with Deleuze, in this book Deleuze's thought instead provides a road-opener for navigating the twists and turns taken by one particular concept—contemplation—in critical plant studies.

Cultivating impulses from theology and philosophy toward solidarity across species, this book is a cross-disciplinary graft. By studying examples from the contemplative tradition of Western Christian mysticism, I will be entwining the vegetal and the mystical in fresh ways. Shifting the discussion of vegetal life in mysticism from gendered bodies to practical contemplation, I narrate ecology from the perspective of a vibrant but suppressed current in Western Christian mysticism. Here, my own experiences practicing contemplation has very much helped me see the relevance of the reading I develop. What I offer is an essay that also carries aspects of the spiritual manual, insofar as my interest in contemplative practices is as much pragmatic and experimental as it is theological and philosophical. As a result, the mystical theology that appears in these pages may be somewhat unfamiliar, even for many theologians. Over the past decades, ecotheologians have labored hard to narrate the enchanted materialism of mystics. Less attention has been given to what mystics *did* in order to *experience* the world differently. What practices were at stake? This question has also shaped my book.

RETHINKING THE VEGETAL

For a graft between mystical theology and philosophies of vegetal life to be fruitful, the concept of "the vegetal" needs to be approached with some care. One of the risks of speaking about the vegetal is that one thinks it is a matter of privileging plants above other species or, alternatively, because of the way vegetal life is foregrounded in this book, of encouraging species envy. As Jeffrey Nealon points out in *Plant Theory: Biopower and Vegetable Life*, there is a risk of species chauvinism in the recent critical literature on plants.[43] While many writers now turning their attention to vegetal life do focus on plants, however, in most cases the philosophical questions underpinning the movement are much broader. Michael Marder, the philosopher behind the new discourse, argues that it is not a question of focusing on the plant kingdom to the exclusion of other creatures. He reflects how "'plants' stand for a tendency of living and thinking that promotes growth, decay and metamorphosis."[44] In Marder's work, "plant-thinking" emerges from a rethinking of the premodern idea of the vegetative or nutritive soul. According to Aristotle, plants have a soul that corresponds to the power of growth, nutrition, and reproduction. Animals possess an appetitive soul in addition to the vegetative soul, while humans possess a rational soul as well as an animal and intellective soul.[45]

This idea, which was dominant in Western philosophy and theology before modernity, figures in different ways in the work engaging with Marder or otherwise indebted to his approach. In Nealon's *Plant Theory*, despite some superficial disagreements with Marder, Aristotle's "vegetative" or "vegetable" soul is an important touchpoint. Thinking with Aristotle on the question of the vegetal, Nealon argues that the vegetal should be understood not as the vegetable kingdom but rather as "what we share with other entities."[46] At the same time, as Nealon also explains, the idea of a vegetable soul is not neutral, nor ought it to be reclaimed uncritically according to premodern usage. Historically, souls were arranged by hierarchy, with the vegetative viewed as inferior and the rational as superior. Plants were deemed lesser than humans, but so too were those parts of human behavior that were thought to express vegetative qualities, such as sensibility, emotions, and intuition. Moreover, the vegetative was also gendered, with female sexuality compared to vegetal life, while male sexuality was thought to correspond to reason and the mastery of emotions.[47] In Marder's *Plant-Thinking: A Philosophy of Vegetal Life*, the interest in a concept like the vegetative soul thus coalesces around a demand to dismantle hierarchies. We see a critical rethinking, rather than a reviving, of an ancient idea. Instead of interpreting the vegetative in a hierarchical way, the suggestion is to view life from the perspective of shared activities. An attempt is made to allow the perspective of vegetal life to critique Western metaphysics, to envisage "the outlines of a method drawn from the plants themselves and of a discord rooted . . . in these vegetal beings."[48]

Marder sees the vegetal taking the place of Being in metaphysics and operating as a resistance to species chauvinism.[49] Marder's argument starts from the Greek *phusis*, a word often translated as "nature." Unlike "nature," however, which comes from a Latin word meaning "that which is born," thus linking nature to specific forms of animality, *phusis* is related to a word for plant, *phuton*, and simply means "that which grows." Marder proposes that we rethink the vegetal as *phusis*, in its literal sense: not as the plant kingdom but as the world of growth. What he calls "plant-thinking" is "not species thought."[50] This perspective, which has been developed recently by philosophers engaging with Marder, shifts the emphasis from the vegetal as a consideration of specific life forms (lilies as opposed to sparrows) to a consideration of the form of life (what lilies have in common with sparrows). What is "vegetal" is not, then, that which bears flowers but that which metamorphoses spontaneously, the way a plant does, but also the way a bird or a mushroom does—or a crystal.

While considerable attention has by now been given to the ramifications of the vegetal turn in philosophy, art, and literature, the consequences for theology are only beginning to receive notice. Marder intimates a close connection between theology and vegetal life, and it is this connection I will be returning to and thinking through at various points in the book. In *Plant-Thinking*, Marder notes an ancient tradition, stretching back to Greek philosophy, of viewing affinities between plants and the divine. Both were thought, Marder points out, to live in "flawless harmony and repose," free from the "constant alteration, unrest, and metamorphosis" of animals.[51] Marder is interested in these affinities, which he sees as invitations but also as challenges. They are challenges because, as he reflects, "we would do well to remember that, like that of the gods, the freedom of plants (from consciousness and from self-relatedness, from need and from the *conatus*) is not purely negative: if it appears to be so, this is due to the insufficiency of language, be it rigorously conceptual or raw and colloquial, but in any event hopelessly mired in anthropocentric references and projections."[52] When writers compare the life of gods to the life of plants, they tend to idealize the vegetal: The actual activities constituting nutritive life are forgotten, ironically excised from the definition of vegetal life. Nonetheless, comparisons between plant life and divine life appear as invitations to Marder because they help unsettle the habit of assuming that the "intellective" part of human life is superior. In *Plant-Thinking* Marder explains the hazards of valorizing the sleep of reason by idealizing the vegetal life as divine in the sense of remote and removed from Terran life. He also suggests an alternative, the "vegetalizing" of the divine from the perspective of plant science and vegetal life. One possibility that opens from Marder's work, and one that most interests me in this book, is the notion that spiritual practices—especially contemplation—offer ways of recognizing the "plant in us," as Marder puts it.[53]

In *Through Vegetal Being: Two Philosophical Perspectives*, Marder proposes that because vegetal life sustains human bodies, it is possible to cultivate awareness of vegetal life not only by attending to plants but also by cultivating awareness of what he calls bodies' "unconscious attention" of environments, or their "vegetal mindfulness." This "vegetal mindfulness" is already practiced by the body's cells as they constantly sense their environment. The vegetal mindfulness most readily accessible to human consciousness is for Marder rooted in the skin. "If we wish to discover vegetal mindfulness in ourselves," he writes, "we should look no further than our bodies' unconscious attention to the surroundings. Like the leaves of plants, our skin senses humidity and temperature, light gradients and vibrations. Without knowing it, we pay attention to the world on the surface, from the porous, essentially open, cutaneous remembrance that keeps our living bodies enact and, at the same time, communicate with whatever lies beyond them."[54] Nealon's *Plant Theory* ends with a similar appeal to practices of noticing. Nealon gives a specific image of paying attention to actions, just as they are: "The question for politics . . . is not really what we humans *should* do (as if our good intentions could immunize us against inflicting more harm), but . . . maybe we need to pay closer attention to what our doing does . . . which is to say, examining how the mesh of life is altered by x or y practice, rather than securing the best theoretical or epistemological ground for our political actions."[55] While Nealon writes from the perspective of political philosophy, however, Marder seems to have developed his notion of practicing vegetal life in relation to traditions of spiritual exercise. In *The Philosopher's Plant: An Intellectual Herbarium*, he is drawn to the Buddhist practice of awakening awareness of the skin through the cultivation of sensory perception. At stake for Marder is the need to guard "vigilantly against the reduction of plants (or of any other living beings for that matter) to symbols by moderating the theoretical impulse with practical contemplation and by letting them grow, leaving them be, freeing them from the noise of *logos*."[56]

I will be returning to Marder's understanding of "practical contemplation" in a later chapter (where I will also be expanding on its relationship to the philosophy of Luce Irigaray). For the moment, I want to note that Marder's shift toward "practical contemplation" is invoked as a necessary means of resisting the reduction of the vegetal to literary trope or abstraction. Marder turns toward practical contemplation when looking for ways in which to integrate philosophical reflection on vegetal life with a practice of becoming attentive to vegetal life—by cultivating awareness of the "unconscious attention" without which acts of conscious attention would not be possible. For Marder, it is through such spiritual exercises that "we grow a little plantlike" and disrupt the division between humans and nonhumans, culture and nature. "To be initiated into this essentially superficial way of breathing," remarks Marder, "supplementing the activity of the lungs, we must seek guidance from vegetal respiration. Totally exposed to the atmosphere, which they replenish with oxygen, plants breathe throughout their entire extension and, most of all, through the leaf. Inhaling with the skin, perceiving the world with our whole bodies, we grow a little plantlike."[57] Subsequently, in Marder's more recent work on Western Christian mysticism, the practice of becoming plantlike is found also in the work of a Christian mystic. In *Green Mass*, Marder explains how he sees "[Hildegard] vegetalizing theology in much the same way as I've attempted to vegetalize the Western philosophical canon." By "vegetalizing," Marder has in mind a process whereby life is rethought from the perspective of the vegetal, that is, from "unconscious attention" to environments. For Marder, to vegetalize means to appreciate a mode of acting and thinking that is wakeful yet that resists identification with Kant's self-possessed Enlightenment subject, in control of their will and their environment. In other words, Marder thinks of vegetalizing as a way of attuning agency to those states that are involuntary but essential to life, those that are neither active nor passive but rather exist in the middle, "in order to save the middle."[58] Having already hinted that spiritual practices bring such vegetalizing out of abstraction, it is no surprise that *Green Mass* develops the notion further. In a felicitous turn of phrase, Marder suggests that mysticism's *via negativa*, the "path of negations," is also *via vegetativa*, a "vegetal path." Interestingly, the contemplative life is not woven into the narrative of *Green Mass*, which focuses instead on Hildegard's creativity as a writer and composer. This leaves open several questions. If the path of negations is also a vegetal path, then how—if at all—does it relate to the practice of contemplation, considering that the *via negativa* was not a merely literary trope in Western Christian mysticism but a way of life? Marder suggests a profound relation, yet *Green Mass* is not concerned, or not concerned directly, with contemplation as a practice. At the same time, it initiates a graft between vegetal life and practical contemplation.

What I have set out to do in this book is to cultivate a graft between vegetal and mystical life in ways that will provide fresh and strange fruit. I will be situating Marder's proposed *via vegetativa* in a longer history of contemplative practices and their entwinement with vegetal life. I will be developing Marder's suggestion regarding practical contemplation as the cultivation of sensory perception. "Contemplation," although used frequently, is not always the word of choice by mystics, however, and at times I will be discussing other terms, such as mystical union, interior prayer, silent prayer, and ecstasy, among others. I do so only insofar as they are used by authors to describe an epistemic passiveness rooted in deep experiences of sensation that are not disembodied. I will thus not be discussing the related but distinct question of contemplating God in the afterlife. It is, rather, in the embodied receptivity and affectability so frequently stressed by mystics that I see a fruitful point of contact between the mystical and the vegetal.[59]

Meanwhile, scientific research on plant intelligence also suggests parallels with the language used, in the history of Western Christian mysticism, to describe contemplative practices. Critical plant studies is influenced, to a large extent, by recent scientific interest in plants; it is a "broad framework for re-evaluating plants and human-plant interactions informed by principles of agency, ethics, cognition and language."[60] Scientific research on plants has demonstrated sophisticated modes of knowing that expand notions of agency and cognition from organisms to non-neutral life.[61] Although Charles Darwin observed that plants possessed complex behavior, the question of intelligence was long resisted in the West. Research on plant intelligence was pioneered by Anthony Trewavas, who at first fought an uphill battle to defend his contention that plants were intelligent, but his research slowly gained recognition and is now accepted by many in the field. Trewavas's position, however, rests on an explosive redefinition of intelligence, one that moves away from the focus on brains. Trewavas's research shows that plants forage for food, communicate, sense the world, make choices, and remember what has happened to them. In other words, plants fulfill the criteria for intelligent behavior. For Trewavas, this suggests that brains are not necessary for intelligent behavior and that thoughtful responses are not exclusive to mammals with brains but go all the way down and are common to life as such. Moreover, plants' lack of a brain may have certain unexpected advantages, epistemologically speaking. As the biologist Daniel Chamovitz demonstrates in *What a Plant Knows: A Field Guide to the Sense of Your Garden—and Beyond*, brainless consciousness can do things we cannot. Unlike animals, plants lack a nervous system with which to interpret environmental stimuli. This means that, while plants sense the world, they do not process it; they possess the hardware, as it were, but lack the software to interface with what they sense through images, concepts, language, and ideas. This is a drawback if one wants to write poetry about a summer's day. But it is an advantage if one wants to have a direct experience of a summer's day, unmediated by conceptual representations. Plant awareness, though more simple in terms of its construction than mammalian perception, is, for that very reason, more directly in touch with the elements. As Chamovitz puts it evocatively, plants are "free from ... subjective constraints."[62]

Although the scientific literature on plants typically does not describe plants as "contemplative,"—indeed, Chamovitz distances his work repeatedly from mysticism—there are many suggestive overlaps with the imagery associated with contemplation by the mystics I consider in this book, according to whom contemplation is wordless and (often) silent but also, and importantly, without thought and sense of self. In contemplation, there is sensory awareness but no mediating process of reflection and no "noise" from reason, meaning that what the senses perceive is intuited directly and all at once, rather than grasped by reason and imagination. In *Plant Behaviour and Intelligence*, Trewavas describes plant intelligence in similar terms, without, however, making any claims to mysticism. Nonetheless, the parallels are interesting. Trewavas notes that simple organisms lacking nervous systems are capable of sophisticated behavior, and he redefines intelligence as awareness of environments, rather than in relation to specific organs or neural activity. For our purposes, the most interesting aspect of his argument comes toward the end of *Plant Behaviour*, when Trewavas addresses his findings in relation to the broader question of intelligence and consciousness. Citing Lynn Margulis and Carl Sagan, Trewavas writes: "Not just animals are conscious but every organic being, every autopoietic cell is conscious. In the simplest sense, *consciousness is an awareness of the outside world*."[63] Consciousness, Trewavas argues, does not stop at plants qua trees and flowers but is indistinguishable from evolving life. Trewavas rejects the idea that non-neural intelligence is reducible to reflex responses, that is, the idea that a cell, for instance, is responding a certain way as a result of a mechanical process. Evolution, Trewavas argues, would never have happened if behavior were predetermined; even amoeba "can never do exactly the same thing twice." Trewavas argues that scientists should expand the definition of consciousness along the lines opened by research on plants, as a direct awareness of environments, while acknowledging that "[plant intelligence] is a form of consciousness that we cannot at present access."[64] Research on plant intelligence thus intersects with a wider current in contemporary biology addressing consciousness across and between species.[65]

The idea of consciousness inaccessible to humans yet sustaining human life and thus—paradoxically—accessible to humans on some level (cells also are aware of their environments) finds a particularly close parallel in the history of Western Christian mysticism. As the historian of Neoplatonism Kevin Corrigan has shown, early Christian mysticism inherited a tradition of Greek, predominantly Neoplatonic, philosophy that maintained the idea of intelligible biology, that is, the idea that all life is aware in some way.[66] Moreover, early Christian mystics, like their Neoplatonist cousins, tended to view life in terms of contemplation, or *theoria*, a word that in Greek philosophy had a surprisingly wide range of meaning. On the one hand, *theoria* was modeled on the cultural practice of spectating at shrines, religious festivals, or during travels for the sake of learning (the English "theater" is derived from the same root word). On the other hand, *theoria* bore a relationship to the Presocratic idea of the world possessing a soul and *nous*, "mind."[67] In consequence, as Corrigan explains, it was not surprising that the two ideas would come to merge, as indeed they did in the work of the most influential Neoplatonist, Plotinus, whose idea of nature contemplating we will be returning to at various points in this book. Meanwhile, early Christian theologians expressed similar ideas, arguing that the whole of creation related to God ecstatically, participating in a common activity of contemplating God. The father of mystical theology in the West, Pseudo-Dionysius, states explicitly that matter is not evil but rather is engaged in contemplating God: "If it be objected that matter . . . leads souls toward evil, how could that be true when many material creatures turn their gaze toward the Good?"[68] A hundred years earlier, Evagrius of Pontus, an equally significant figure for Western Christian mysticism, wrote: "My book . . . is the nature of created things, and it is always at hand when I wish to read the words of God."[69] Necessarily, for contemplation to have this cross-species meaning, it was important to emphasize its distinctness from "human" knowledge; otherwise, rocks and trees could not be said to contemplate. As Augustine Casiday puts it, for the early monastic tradition in the West, "anoetic prayer" thus best describes what authors had in mind when writing about contemplation. In early Christian mysticism, representations—*noemata*—were acutely problematic, and Pseudo-Dionysius connects contemplation with *anoesia*, or "lack of representational thought." Creatures were thought to reveal God and nature was to be contemplated, and yet, when grasped by the intellect, contemplation of nature prohibited unmediated awareness of things in their true being. Thus nature needed to be contemplated without representations, that is, in the manner of nature's own contemplation of God. In this way, contemplation "[reinforced] the attitude of attentive openness toward God."[70] Openness to God thus meant a deliberate attempt to cultivate awareness in ways that differed from conventional human awareness. Interestingly, it may also have involved, as in Buddhist spiritual practices, exercises of attending to sensory perceptions, such as breathing. This is evident in the premodern Christian recommendation to pray with the breath in order to remain undistracted.[71]

Intersecting with these notions of contemplation is the plant scientist Daniel Chamovitz's discussion of "anoetic consciousness." While Chamovitz's usage of the term is strictly scientific, the meaning he gives to the concept aligns, nonetheless, with many classical definitions of contemplation and the higher stages of prayer. What Chamovitz has in mind is a state of awareness unmediated by representations and "subjective constraints."[72] The notion of a consciousness liberated from subjective constraints opens to further comparisons with the contemplative tradition, where self-annihilation and abandonment of self are significant themes. Without claiming that the contemplative tradition's anoetic prayer is the same thing as the anoetic consciousness of vegetal life, the similarities are too striking not to investigate further. At the very least, they indicate that vegetal metaphors in mysticism speak to meanings beyond the figurative. Since we will be lingering with these notions in detail in chapters 3 and 4, I will not discuss them further at this point. For now, suffice it to say that there are many structural homologies between contemplative practices in Western Christian mysticism and the new approach to plant intelligence and vegetal minds in the contemporary critical theory that draws on plant science.

These structural homologies and their ramifications for what Marder calls a practical contemplation of vegetal life provides the opening for the narratives related in subsequent chapters of this book. Both the contemplative tradition and critical plant studies depend on a creative rethinking of intelligence, or better yet, *agency*, outside the conventional boundaries of subjectivity, reason, and self-determination. It is in the abandonment of self so frequently stressed by some mystics, as well as in a tendency toward "cosmism," that I see the possibility for a graft. There are, however, many currents within Western Christian mysticism, and it should be stressed that what I am narrating is not a general account. Nonetheless, the epistemic role of passiveness combined with a regard for matter's intelligence are striking motifs recurring in many different texts. This perspective is especially helpful when dealing with the broader question of what role the vegetal plays in mysticism. Typically, studies of mysticism focusing on the vegetal have been interested principally in the role of plants—trees and flowers—thus overlooking the perspectives articulated in recent years by critical plant studies. I will be working, instead, with an expanded notion of the vegetal grafted from contemporary philosophies of vegetal life. In this book, the vegetal is a way of describing those spontaneous, imperceptible activities that sustain life; while plants instance vegetal life, they are not sole carriers. This allows me, in turn, to read mystical-vegetal life in new ways. Although Christian mystics *do* invoke plants frequently, what they point to is not species specific. When describing contemplative practices, mystics like to draw on metaphors referring to plants but also to animals, minerals, elements (water, fire, air, and earth), and any number of aspects of life including *human* activities like digestion, sensory perception, and breathing. This is especially true of the mystic with whom this book culminates, Jeanne Guyon. I argue that Guyon's thinking consistently favors the vegetal without showing any marked preference for plants. I have also found it to be true in earlier currents of contemplative practice, where the vegetal is conveyed by allusions to plants but also by the pairing of contemplation with *phusis*, nature, or "the world of growth." In order to make this point, however, the foregrounding of an expanded notion of the vegetal is paramount.

 Cultivating the graft of mystical and vegetal life thus fulfills a double task. On the one hand, there is the rethinking of mysticism through vegetal being, a rethinking that will be of interest to theologians and philosophers of religion. On the other hand, there is the rethinking of vegetal being through mysticism and practical contemplation, a labor that will resonate with readers interested in contemporary philosophies of vegetal life and the broader question of multispecies thought and the work of "giving voice to other beings."[73] Practices in an epoch where interspecies solidarity on Terra has become all the more urgent and necessary cannot be imagined without ecologies. The contemplative practices I will be narrating offer one way of cultivating the everyday attentiveness and sensory perceptions needed in order to notice relations between creatures and things and live among entities without too much violence. At either end of this task, however, is the same question: the question of an almost imperceptible yet creative (not to say creating) *knowing* and of upending epistemological hierarchies through the practice of such knowing. And here my graft reveals itself to be birthed from a previous strange fruit, this one created sotto voce in twentieth-century continental philosophy and allowed to pass, like the vegetal life it so often invokes, almost unnoticed. However, in recent years it has reentered critical plant studies especially through the significance of Gilles Deleuze. Deleuze's work shows how contemplation and vegetal life have already been entwined in fundamental ways that offer affordances for fresh grafts. In this previous entwinement, contemplation is reimagined, seeing it emerging from non-neural life in ways that intersect with the critical project of this book.

VEGETABLE CONTEMPLATION: THEORIZING *THEORIA* FOR TERRAN LIFE

For the purposes of the creative grafting that this book attempts, it will be important to work with a concept of lively matter that is not based on a new dualism separating activity from passivity, recognizing instead that what we call life is always mixed with passiveness, modes of passiveness that compose every action, even as these modes compose the spontaneous generation of life from itself. The significance of passivity for matter's liveliness has been intimated in engagements with a significant figure in the philosophy of vitalism, Gilles Deleuze. Through Deleuze's influence on critical plant studies, the way of understanding contemplation that I advance here will be seen to resonate with earlier approaches.

Deleuze is often invoked, with Félix Guattari, as a resource for critical plant studies. In Deleuze and Guattari's *A Thousand Plateaus*, the authors insist on the importance of the vegetal, telling readers at the outset to "follow the plants" and introducing the book through the celebrated image of the rhizome. The rhizome—an underground stem capable of producing both shoots and roots—interests Deleuze and Guattari because of its decentralized, asexual mode of reproduction, which, they argue, suggest life's tacit resistance to its own organizing structures. "We're tired of trees," the authors declare provocatively. "We should stop believing in trees, roots, and radicles. They've made us suffer too much. Nothing is beautiful or loving or political aside from underground stems and aerial roots, adventitious growths and rhizomes."[74] Plants, for Deleuze and Guattari, are important, and yet, they suggest, plants have been misunderstood. *A Thousand Plateaus* argues that vegetal life has been forced into an organismic mold. Trees then become the noblest plant because of their resemblance to an upright, human organism. The provocation to stop believing in trees is an encouragement not to disregard trees' existence but to dismantle the idealized tree by giving attention to the nonorganismic ways of plants. What is at stake in this reaction to trees is not plants as such but rather the way plants have been anthropomorphically compared to humans and to human ways of thinking and acting. As Hannah Stark explains, the rhizome, for Deleuze and Guattari, is "a way of being in the world.... For them there is something about plant being itself, which mobilizes the principles of the rhizome: connection, heterogeneity, multiplicity, rupture and cartography. Plants, whether or not they are rhizomes in the conventional botanical sense, have the capacity to form a rhizome assemblage with the soil, nutrients, wind, water and climate that constitute their environment." Although the idea of "becoming-animal" is more prominent in *A Thousand Plateaus*, Deleuze and Guattari also stress the idea of becoming-vegetal; in this way, they provide an early and striking anticipation of the contemporary turn to the vegetal. Stark also points out the affinities between Deleuze and Guattari's understanding of ecology and the closely related field of multispecies ethics. Despite some differences between Deleuze and Guattari's approach and those of contemporary philosophers, multispecies research and *A Thousand Plateaus* "share a common interest in the project of challenging human exceptionalism and the categories on which it rests: self/other, human/animal, human/nonhuman. In this way they all work to undermine the fiction that the human is bounded and coherent and suggest a much closer proximity to otherness than we might imagine."[75] The rhizome, for Deleuze and Guattari, becomes a way of thinking about the porosity of species boundaries. Rhizomes reproduce without sex and genetic filiation. Deleuze and Guattari wonder if this is not a useful way of understanding "true Nature spanning the kingdoms of nature." Rather than arrange relations according to species and genetic relationships, creatures of all types form configurations ("assemblages") that are vital without being in and of themselves genetic. Stark brings up the equally celebrated image, in *A Thousand Plateaus*, of the "assemblage" truffle, tree, fly, and pig, in which species relate without filiation in "unnatural participations" that nonetheless constitute nature.[76] In rhizome-assemblages, an animal "becomes" a plant, who "becomes" an insect, and so forth. It is as an image of the unnaturalness of nature that rhizomes speak most closely to critical plant studies.

An alternative perspective is offered by Jeffrey Nealon's chapter on Deleuze and Guattari (but principally Deleuze) in *Plant Theory*. Here, Nealon addresses the rhizome but also looks at Deleuze and Guattari's joint reflections on plants more broadly. Nealon, like Stark, considers the rhizome as a significant concept for thinking of vegetal life today, although he also expresses reservations. Nealon's hesitation regards not Deleuze and Guattari's rhizome so much as its use in scholarship. While Deleuze and Guattari, he argues, characterize the rhizome as vegetal life, Nealon thinks this point is often missed by those who invoke the rhizome. "The primary difficulty," he explains, "is this: plant-based rhizomatics has in the present scholarly context become a metaphor for everything and anything ... ironically enough, rhizomatics has become a template for discussing virtually everything *except* plant life." To show what he means, Nealon points to Deleuze and Guattari's understanding of "becoming." The rhizome, for Deleuze and Guattari, is a process of becoming, but this concept, Nealon argues, is often misinterpreted as a "freeing motion" *from* one entity (a human) to another (an animal or a plant or a mineral, and so on). Nealon points out that for Deleuze and Guattari it is rather the opposite: "Becoming is primarily a process of inventing and inhabiting territory otherwise (rather than a preexisting thing freeing itself from its present stratification by becoming 'like' something else)." He argues that a better way of characterizing what Deleuze and Guattari intend by "becoming" is to take seriously their admonition to the reader that they "follow the plants." Rhizomatics, Nealon argues, too often models the rhizome on a miraculous idea of transmogrification that is not to be confused with the vegetal metamorphosis Deleuze and Guattari associate with the rhizome. Put differently, Nealon argues that Deleuze and Guattari do not see becoming opposed to being in the way movement might be opposed to stasis or animal to plant. Rather, becoming is a "'mode of resolution' within a field of being rather than the undermining or outflanking of reification."[77] In turn, being is not a backdrop to becoming but emerges together with individuation; passivity and activity, here, are impossible to separate. Nealon prefers this account of rhizomatic becoming to the idea of the rhizome as "a metaphor for how everything is connected in an underground way," arguing that it is more faithful both to Deleuze and Guattari's thought and to plant life.

Interestingly, another reason why Nealon voices his critique of rhizomatics and clarifies Deleuze and Guattari's vegetal understanding of becoming is because he thinks it helps us understand another equally significant but typically overlooked concept of vegetal life in their philosophy: "vegetable contemplation." Deleuze and Guattari's curious notion of vegetable contemplation appears in various places, including *What Is Philosophy?*:

> Sensation is pure contemplation, for it is through contemplation that one contracts, contemplating oneself to the extent that one contemplates the elements from which one originates. Contemplating is creating, the mystery of passive creation, sensation. Sensation fills out the plane of composition and is filled with itself by filling itself with what it contemplates: it is "enjoyment" and "self-enjoyment." . . . Plotinus defined all things as contemplation, not only people and animals but plants, the earth, and rocks. These are not Ideas that we contemplate through concepts but the elements of matter that we contemplate through sensation.[78]

As Nealon points out, the idea predates Deleuze's collaboration with Guattari and is in fact one of the earliest and most persistent concepts to accompany Deleuze throughout his work. It appears, initially, in Deleuze's very first book and then again in *Difference and Repetition*:

> By its existence alone, the lily of the field sings the glory of the heavens, the goddesses and gods—in other words, the elements that it contemplates in contracting. . . . What organism is not made of elements and cases of repetition, of contemplated and contracted water, nitrogen, carbon, chlorides and sulphates, thereby intertwining all the habits of which it is composed? Organisms awake to the sublime words of the third *Ennead*: all is contemplation! Perhaps it is irony to say that everything is contemplation, even rocks and woods, animals and men . . . even our actions and our needs.[79]

As Nealon reads it, what Deleuze means by "contemplation" in these and other passages is comparable to something like the premodern understanding of a vegetable soul. While Nealon admits that the language is "a little odd," he recognizes that what Deleuze is describing is the "power of becoming," rather than an anthropomorphic idea of a soul in rocks and trees. Furthermore, Nealon connects this idea of contemplation to Deleuze and Guattari's understanding of becoming as inseparable from being. In *Difference and Repetition*, Deleuze argued that by privileging activity and thus imputing traditional conceptions of human subjectivity to matter, the vitality of life had been organized according to human models of what it means to act. As a result, the liveliness of nonorganismic life was overlooked, effectively written out of life. Not only nonorganismic life, however, but those aspects of the human organism that are not willed: pure sensation. According to Nealon, Deleuze's argument is that while matter is lively, it is not driven by a will; rather, it is lively in the sense of being spontaneous, which means that it is also passive: "Deleuze insists that humans, rocks, and lilies of the field are all composed of countless subroutines, passive syntheses that make 'agency' or organic identity possible . . . there is *a* life before there is *my* life or *your* life."[80] For Nealon, when Deleuze describes life as a process of "contemplation" what is meant is thus not a voluntary or spectatorial activity such as a philosopher might perform when focusing their attention on a concept; rather, contemplation is the spontaneous affect that makes volitional activities (such as attention) possible.[81] At the same time, the language of contemplation is far from arbitrary. In ancient Greek philosophy, contemplation was the highest form of poetic or creative activity in which a philosopher might participate. By naming life "contemplation," contemplation is equated with creativity, yet creativity is also rethought in terms of nutritive or vegetal life: Rather than our concepts, "our 'habits' or 'contemplations' contract a territory for living out of the chaos of being."[82] This reflects what Deleuze writes in *Difference and Repetition*, that contemplation precedes "our actions and our needs,"[83] shaping these in ways that give form to thought. Hence contemplation is identified with sensation, although Deleuze resists a mechanistic understanding of our actions and needs as predetermined. If actions were predetermined, life would never change, yet life is, for all its apparent monotony, at bottom nonidentical repetition.

The "mystery," as Deleuze and Guattari put it in *What Is Philosophy?*, is thus not actions but passivity and the ability of life to create *without* a will. Put differently, what is mysterious is not the grasping of an idea by a philosopher's thought but the contraction of the elements by their skin. Vegetal life expresses this "mystery." In *What Is Philosophy?* Deleuze and Guattari go on to reflect that although "not every organism has a brain, and not all life is organic," because there is sensation, there must be a "faculty of feeling that coexists with embryonic tissues."[84] As Nealon also recognizes, Deleuze and Guattari here come very close to the theory of a contemporary scientist of plant intelligence like Anthony Trewavas, although the language used in *What Is Philosophy?* necessarily is quite different. The line of thought, however, is related to what we saw earlier in the discussion of plant consciousness: Consciousness, awareness, does not depend on a brain, and the extent of conscious life can be appreciated by attending to plants. For his part, Nealon sees in Deleuze's philosophy, not least in the idea of "vegetable contemplation," a more helpful articulation of vegetal life than that which emerges from the image of the rhizome. For Nealon, the contemporary discourse around plants is born from attention to the neglected and forgotten "silent" creatures that plants are, but a study of their ways yields realizations also about humans and other animals. Nealon points out that a philosophy focused on plants to the exclusion of other creatures winds up being inattentive to the very life it seeks to describe. The obscure, apparently "passive" nature of plants in relation to human perception is significant. The main task for a philosophy of vegetal life is to balance attention to plants with attention to what plants practice in common with other species and life forms: "If we really are approaching the end of the world—with catastrophic climate change, ecological disaster, and maybe even human extinction looming very close by—it might be time to start diagnosing the world not as a static or dynamic backdrop for the myriad (im)possibilites of individual lives but as the ecological territory that cuts across all strata of life as we've known it . . . which is to say by the practices of emergence and transformation."[85] In this sense, for Nealon, the concept of contemplation conveys an important aspect of vegetal life, despite its apparent incongruity with Deleuze's otherwise atheistic philosophy.

Another aspect of "vegetable contemplation" can be articulated in theological terms. Nealon views vegetable contemplation as insightful for plant theory but also as "a little odd,"[86] a view that can be linked to a wider ambivalence regarding the role played by contemplation in Deleuze's philosophy. With some notable exceptions, the reception of contemplation in Deleuze's thought has tended either to overlook or dismiss its possible relationship to Western Christian mysticism.[87] The notable exception is the work of Jacob Holsinger Sherman. Sherman views contemplation as *the* theological element in Deleuze's philosophy, the element that, when developed, helps "preserve what is most valuable in Deleuze—his project of cosmological and metaphysical re-enchantment."[88] Sherman adopts the idea from Peter Hallward, who argued that it was possible to extract a form of mysticism from Deleuze's philosophy. Hallward, however, explored that affinity in order to launch a vigorous attack on what he calls Deleuze's "subtractivist" philosophy: For Hallward, mysticism equates to world-renunciation and the "subtraction" of self from the world. The mystical tendencies in Deleuze's thought amounts, on Hallward's reading, to a regrettable desire to flee life, leaving Deleuze "no more a thinker of this world" than any other Western Christian mystic.[89] As Sherman reflects, Hallward's Deleuze is one who, by emphasizing contemplation, seeks "union with the dark eternal flux of pure becoming, casting aside all our relations, bodies, projects, and political aspirations."[90] Sherman then invites a reading of the theological Deleuze that would be "more discerning still." While commending Hallward for identifying a cryptotheological element to Deleuze's thought, he questions Hallward's interpretation of it as escapist and nihilistic. Rather than excising the theological element from Deleuze's thought in order to grasp its relevance for a world of entangled life, Sherman argues that Deleuze's political relevance is inseparable from his gestures toward contemplation. The affirmation of contemplation, its remarkably consistent place in Deleuze's oeuvre, is cryptotheological but also cryptoecological.

Sherman claims that Hallward's nihilistic view of contemplation originates from a dualistic ontology in part maintained and promoted by theologians in the West, especially after the early modern period.[91] Mystics that were practicing oneness with the world and attentiveness to lively matter were held in suspicion, yet their methods survived in contemplative practices that were later revived in the twentieth century. Sherman questions Hallward's portrait of mysticism by arguing that, when looked at carefully, "Deleuze intends his divine line of flight to deliver the world from a reductive naturalism to a more robust, ecstatic, even enchanted materialism."[92] In turn, Sherman sketches an outline of Deleuze that opens toward the vibrant materialisms discernible in contemplative traditions. For Sherman, mystical literatures articulate "the infinite becomings, the strange alliances, and the cosmic planes that animate Deleuze's own project" while also reinstating, in ways that perhaps are obscured (Hallward is right) in Deleuze's thought, the "redemptive relationships of responsibility and care, community, open traditions, living memory and hope."[93] In other words, Sherman points toward the same themes of politics and lively matter that emerge from Nealon's *Plant Theory* and its engagement with contemplation in Deleuze. These similarities are striking. Yet it is not my purpose to propose that a theological reading of contemplation is superior to the one now emerging from critical plant studies. Rather, I observe convergent ways of reading from disparate currents. What motivates the cross-disciplinary "grafting" in this book is the desire to allow mysticism to vegetalize thought but also to vegetalize mysticism from the perspective of plant-thinking. It is from the perspective of vegetable contemplation that I propose to unmoor spirituality from at least one part of its anthropocentric bias: the focus on self and interiority.

From the perspective of this book, a concept of contemplation as vegetal life but *also* as spiritual practice helps unmoor the spiritual from species thought. It promises to do so through a clarification of the nature of passivity in contemplation. Following Deleuze and others, a new way of characterizing contemplation as a creaturely or multispecies disposition emerges; following contemporary theologies of mysticism, a reclaiming of mystical passivity takes form. It will become important to the argument I am developing here that contemplation is a *habit*, that is to say, that contemplation is passive in the way an unconscious or spontaneous action is passive, meaning that the passiveness of contemplation is less like inertia and more like sensing, a comparison we also find frequently in mystical literature. The graft I am cultivating between mystical and vegetal being can be seen to rest on a previous graft, this one cultivated in continental philosophy, in the reclaiming of contemplation through an attention to vegetal life in the cryptotheology of Deleuze. While this earlier graft only gestures toward the subject of my book—the contemplative tradition in Western Christian mysticism—it poses an invitation to engage a closer study of the vegetal life hiding in contemplative practices. I will thus be drawing theological and philosophical perspectives on vegetal life into dialogue, a dialogue returning, however, to the concept and practice of contemplation. In the debates surrounding the vegetal, theorizing *theoria* for Terran life is a neglected topic but one where several disciplines and discourses appear to intersect. What might fruit and bloom were this intersection cultivated into a graft? This is the question I am asking in the chapters that follow.

ECSTASY FROM THE PERSPECTIVE OF ECOLOGIES

Before the ecstasy of the mystic, vegetal life contemplates. The "spiritual life" has perhaps often been misunderstood, as if it designated a separate realm or substance into which the human ascends in order to escape the world. In contemplation, however, the spiritual life becomes indistinguishable from *life*. In Latin, the word "contemplation," whose etymology relates to the space (*templum*) set apart for augury and "the observation and interpretation of natural signs (such as the behavior of birds or celestial phenomena),"[94] implies secession in its sense of designating a place apart and receptivity in its sense of describing an ability to be affected by the environment.[95] I propose that contemplative life is best figured as a practice of cultivating sustained affectability and receptiveness. Contemplation is thus less like an escape from the world of becoming and more like a recognition of co-becoming.

The approach I take to mysticism thus queries the conventional interpretation of contemplation as a solitary or introspective affair but also the assumption that it is as an exclusively *human* activity. In other words, I do not take a psychological approach to contemplative life, but neither do I follow the approaches of Michel Foucault and Peter Sloterdijk, who have understood mysticism in terms of subjectivity and "anthropotechnics." I will be making reference instead to alternative readings by feminist historians, plant theorists, and continental philosophers seeking to unburden "life" from traces of subjectivity. Although theologians have been engaging with animal studies, posthumanism, and new materialism for some time, the question of vegetal life is only beginning to enter the conversation of what it means to speak of spiritual traditions in a time of species extinctions. In this book, I want to show a vegetal or, better yet, more-than-human way of understanding the attentiveness at stake for both contemplative practices and the philosophies of vegetal life. To this end, I relate several stories from the long history of contemplative ecology in Western Christian mysticism, leading to a detailed account of Jeanne Guyon and early modern Catholic spirituality. If philosophies of vegetal life have looked to contemplation as a way of figuring, metaphorically, the activities of a non-neural, nonorganismic consciousness, Guyon sketches the practice of contemplation in the language of vegetal life and nonorganismic life: to contemplate, for Guyon, is to vegetate! The entwinement between vegetal and mystical raises several questions. To what extent does plant *theory* imply *theoria*, that is, contemplation? And how do we talk about, describe, and moreover help cultivate practices for recognizing what one commentator aptly names "a practice through which people might come to feel the pulsing vibrations of our plant-selves . . . our common enactments of liveliness"?[96] Such talk should resist drawing from history normative injunctions (*you must practice in this way!*), yet to ignore histories of the practicing is equally hazardous. My modest proposal is that, by studying Guyon and other figures from the contemplative tradition of Western Christian mysticism, one might be confronted with narratives that help situate an otherwise abstract hope into histories of lived experience, struggle, and solidarity. This would open the roads toward *theoria* not as theory merely but as way of life—as ethics in the literal sense of *ethoi*, "habits," practices.

Contemplative practices, however, are also paradoxes, paradoxical calls to silence, indecision, and nonconformity as a means of active resistance to the strategies of dominant regimes. Like every contemplative practice, Guyon's is a practice of attentiveness as well as of attention, aimed at cultivating concentration but also its opposite: a relaxed yet alert awareness in which an ability to notice and to respond spontaneously to suffering and demands for solidarity might be possible. Emerging from a time of rampant misogyny but also of violent ideological clashes between warring factions of Christian religion following the Reformation, Guyon was acutely attuned to the need for *common ground*. Scarred by the coercive methods of Catholic clergy, she found herself unable to enjoin practices that failed to let others be. In the mounting tensions of post-Reformation Europe, when Catholic but also Protestant missions were intensifying, Guyon chose to articulate her tactics in terms of listening, waiting, and letting-be. Opposed to the control exercised by clergy, religious rituals, and even doctrinal belief, Guyon looked instead to the spontaneous activities of the human body but also to the activities of animals and plants and the habits of rocks, water, air, and fire. Her notion of contemplation "as easy and natural as breathing" arose to protest the control of thought, speech, and sensation by systems of power. By articulating the spiritual life in terms of nondiscursive life, Guyon found a common ground with those for whom speech is not possible, not in order thereby to escape human society but rather to disarm its strategies of domination.

Plant theories allow for me to think more closely with the ethical implications of mysticism, while the history of mysticism attests to the ethics emergent from contemporary philosophies of vegetal life. Guyon's contemplative practice offers an example that brings to light the challenges of establishing and cultivating everyday habits of attentiveness. Guyon's manual, *A Short and Easy Method of Prayer* (1685), becomes a window onto the pragmatics of attentiveness. Thinking with Guyon's art of attentiveness, I will discuss what it means to notice connections between species, but I will also be noticing connections between spiritual practices and philosophical ideas. I will be grafting one of Guyon's books with the work of Luce Irigaray, Emanuele Coccia, and others. The potential for grafting circles around, on the one hand, Guyon's work and its ability to enfold a contemporary vegetal account of contemplation as "breath" and "breathing." On the other hand, grafting emerges from contemporary echoes of Deleuze's multispecies *theoria*. The writers I think with look to vegetal life and especially to contemplation, and the way the term "contemplation" is used gives rise to a constellation composed of old elements foraged from ancient philosophy and Western Christian mysticism but forming, together with contemporary philosophies of plant life, a fresh growth: *the practical contemplation of life*. What is important to this constellation is the widening of contemplation: While humans contemplate life, contemplation creates life through passive syntheses, indicating the need for practices of attending to the "plant in us."

This grafting process establishes common ground between species and entities but in combinations that are not reducible to an agreement or consensus. Marder writes that grafts are acts of transgressive creation: "The very fact that grafts can refer to animal or human tissues as well as to plant parts testifies to the word's and the practice's quiet rebellion against the strictures of identity."[97] As with the agronomic practice of grafting, this book yields strange results. Thinking through mystical and vegetal being has produced offspring that is monstrous, theologically speaking: a weird, human-divine-vegetal hybrid that refuses the categories laid down by orthodox texts and institutions. Yet it is precisely "our monsters" who "help us notice landscapes of entanglement, bodies with other bodies, time with other times." After all, "life has been monstrous almost from its beginnings."[98] The same is true of mysticism, which has always played a dangerous game historically, encouraging humans to unite with a more-than-human God. Like eukaryotic life, all mystical life is monstrous.

2

A NATURAL HISTORY OF CONTEMPLATION

When my baby was born, I remember thinking how contemplative my infant seemed. That is what I told the midwife, who noted it in my birth journal: "Baby appears contemplative." Contemplation speaks of mysticism, but it has a wide array of uses beyond either theology or philosophy. In one sense, contemplation would seem to have very little to do with the matter of life. It is common to picture contemplation as otherworldly: as a rarefied practice reserved for ascetics. Yet contemplation has a long history of being used in a variety of ways to describe activities that seem remote from asceticism. In this chapter, I am interested in the way contemplation has been called upon to make sense of the vegetal life that sustains so many earthlings. What is the significance of contemplation for an ethic of entangled life? Is there a historical precedent for the recent appearance of the language of mysticism in the vegetal turn, or does it belong solely to postmodernity? In what ways does contemplation intersect with the arts of noticing the crossings that weave together species on Terra?

What I call, in this chapter, the "natural" history of contemplation has been largely ignored by philosophers and theologians alike. Amid a growing literature on spirituality and ecology in

Western Christian mysticism, the significance of contemplation is overlooked or its relevance simply misunderstood. This is attributable, in part, to the psychological perspective that still persists in both philosophical and theological approaches to mysticism. Despite the work of feminist and environmental theologians on Christian spirituality, the tendency to view contemplative life in opposition to ordinary life remains remarkably persistent. Reading insights from the vegetal turn together with the history of contemplation means reexamining these assumptions. Above all, it means questioning the idea that contemplation is solely about the self and human identity.

Yet contemplation and vegetal life seem opposed, as supernatural to natural. One way of understanding mysticism has been to see it as the expression of humans seeking to renounce or transcend nature for a world beyond. In the history of Neoplatonic thought and Western Christian mysticism, the theme of renouncing nature in favor of the One or God is persistent. Contemplation is opposed to nature in the sense that it is presented as the opposite of "natural" awareness. Nevertheless, mysticism also *affirms* nature, drawing on a rich vocabulary of imagery, partly inherited from the Psalms. When, in this chapter, I write about the "contranatural" or "unnatural" I am referring to the fact that mystics often present contemplation as a deliberate disruption of nature. However, I will also argue that it is precisely this disruption that is of significance today, as philosophers and theologians seek to critique the abstract concept that "nature" so often has become. By presenting contemplation as contranatural, mysticism queries conceptualizations of life in ways that resonate with contemporary environmental philosophy. I will be showing that the mode of attention associated with contemplation, through which nature is reimagined as immediate life rather than an externalized object mediated through subjectivity, is of profound significance for the vegetalizing of thought in which this book participates. I will be focusing on the early history of contemplation, or *theoria*, as it appears in Neoplatonism and Western Christian mysticism before the tenth century (and I will also be engaging briefly with Byzantine and Syriac Christianity). The reader will find that this chapter bears a particularly close relationship to Gilles Deleuze's "vegetable contemplation," introduced in chapter 1. While the ancient understandings of *theoria* may seem remote from what we encounter in later mysticism and philosophy, the concepts at work here provide a framework that will help deepen our reading of texts discussed in subsequent chapters.

My task in this chapter is to think about contemplation as it once related to the elements and how it might, today, relate to vegetal life. In the history of Western Christian mysticism, the way that contemplation is pictured is as a brush with transcendence. But it is also seen as synaesthesia and attentiveness to symbiosis. For this reason, ancient figurations of *theoria* will become the first in a story of interlocking narratives seeking to show how a practice of attentiveness to the present slowly transforms the desire to seek God beyond the world, metamorphosing it into a continual contemplation of immanent spirit. I also demonstrate how the awareness sought by mystics in contemplation resonates with descriptions of plant intelligence. This helps show how a critique of metaphysics might be lived in contemplation as a practice, indicating the ethical significance of what Michael Marder calls "vegetal mindfulness." Vegetal mindfulness, however, does not signify a misanthropic rejection of the human and a nostalgia for the sleep of reason. Rather, it points to a recognition of the vegetal life already constituting a human animal and the need to diversify modes of attention to accommodate such recognition. This final point is one that will recur throughout the book, as I read contemplation across different historical periods. The connecting thread in these stories is an attempt to show, through a reading of historical examples, modes of attention that are open, receptive, and contiguous with the elements. My final point is that such attention is practiced across entities and that what is viewed as the peak of human experience in one context belongs to casual wayside flowers in another. It implies an ethic for more-than-human worlds.

GROWTH-THOUGHT: PLOTINUS AND MARDER ON VEGETAL CONTEMPLATION

Western Christian mysticism developed out of preexisting practices of contemplation, both philosophical and religious, with rich histories. The natural history of contemplation takes significant bearings from Neoplatonism. Neoplatonism synthesized diverse philosophies and ways of life, including currents influenced by local traditions and indigenous animisms as the result of Hellenistic colonial expansion. The remarkable vegetal imagery and attention to diverse life forms that characterizes Christian mysticism, though it develops in relation to Scriptural as well as philosophical traditions, is impossible to understand without some mention of its Neoplatonic cousin. Here, I will be focusing on Plotinus. Plotinus is important for emphasizing the role of contemplation; he is also significant for developing the idea that all species contemplate, an idea that is carried forward into Christian mysticism.[1] Plotinian Neoplatonism provides us with an important way to address the vegetal turn. This will help establish the philosophical as well as theological foundations of what, in the next chapter, I will be referring to as "vegetal mysticism."

Turning to Plotinus, however, one immediately comes up against the hierarchical structure of his philosophy. Neoplatonism privileges the One over the many, spirit over matter, reason over the senses, and humans over other life forms. Vegetal life, for Plotinus, is an obscure state in which reason is asleep, rather than awake, and Plotinus often disparages the body for exhibiting vegetative states. The connection between this way of thinking and its impact on Christian interpretations of Genesis 1:26 (in which humans are granted "dominion" over creation) is not difficult to draw, and many historians have charted it exhaustively.[2] Yet the vegetal in Plotinus's thought is more complex. Although Plotinus ranks the vegetal at the lower end of life, he nonetheless insists that it is intelligent. According to Plotinus, knowing or thought (*noesis*) is not exclusively human. Thought is active everywhere, whether as "soul-thought," "sense-thought," or "growth-thought" (*phutike noesis*).[3] Indeed, "growth" is how Plotinus characterizes life, choosing an image that is functional rather than species specific, and thus speaks to plants but also minerals and simply life as such. *Phusis*, the word for "nature" in Greek, derives from a verb "to grow" (*phuo*), and in Neoplatonic thought it refers to the world of change and becoming.[4] In Neoplatonism, life is understood as a continuum, in which all creatures express intelligence differently and all are directed to the Good. A remarkable attentiveness to vegetal life is intimated by Neoplatonism, even as it seems to undo the very premises for the multispecies ethic it intimates.

The strict hierarchy separating the One from nature emerges from Plotinus's idea of emanation. *Phusis*, "nature," is born of mind, or *nous*, itself the child of the One. When mind contemplates itself, it gives birth to nature, and when nature contemplates, it gives birth to itself. In *Ennead* 3.8, "On Nature, Contemplation, and the One," Plotinus suggests that "all things aim at contemplation ... not only rational but also non-rational animals, and nature in plants and the earth which produces them."[5] However, the contemplation performed by plants is lesser than that of humans. *Phusis* is a devolution from the One, whose movements it imitates imperfectly. Vegetal life, for Plotinus, participates in contemplation, but in an inferior manner. Vegetal contemplation is, writes Plotinus, "soundless, but ... clouded," more like sleeping than waking consciousness.[6] For this reason, Plotinus disparages the body and disdains the extent to which human nature is also vegetal. In the famous opening lines of Porphyry's *Life of Plotinus*, Plotinus is described as a person "ashamed of being in a body."[7] Indeed, Plotinus insisted that those who wanted to practice contemplation should chastise the body and avoid activities that could draw undue attention to bodily functions. A hierarchy that places the vegetal, that is, the life of matter, in a subservient role is thus very evident in Neoplatonism.

The consequences of this kind of thinking are well known, and recently they have been addressed with care by Michael Marder in *The Philosopher's Plant: An Intellectual Herbarium*. The trouble with Plotinus, argues Marder, is not only the hierarchy he imposes between the One and *phusis* but also the way in which *phusis* is made to conform to the One in those passages where Plotinus is defending the intelligence of nonrational Terran life. Although the intelligence of *phusis* is defended, the way that vegetal growth is presented seems to conform to an organismic rather than truly vegetal model. Nature's contemplation, after all, is for Plotinus an imitation of the One. Marder, however, asks whether vegetal life really is characterized by unity. As Elaine P. Miller has also pointed out, although the One is presented as a general term in Western philosophy, it is in fact zoocentric, modeled on the organismic unity and centralized structure typical of animals—specifically, human animals. The logic of Neoplatonist metaphysics attempts to measure *phusis* by the totalitarian standards of the One, a logic that plays itself out by imposing on *phusis* an ideal at odds with the vegetal foundations of Terran life. "So majestic are the qualities Plotinus finds in plants," observes Marder, "it may be hard to believe that he urges humans to uproot and to flee from the plant in us, which is to say, from everything we have in common with the vegetable mind." I will return to this idea of the vegetable mind soon; for now, I note that it is organismic logic that Marder detects lurking at the roots of the Great Acceleration. Ruthless destruction of species is possible only once it has become impossible to recognize "the plant in us and ourselves in the plant."[8] Any attempt to put the brakes on the Great Acceleration must seek to relearn the art of attuning to vegetal being.

Marder, however, shows that the totalitarian thinking undermining Plotinus's appreciation for vegetal being is also undermined, itself, by the plants Plotinus invites into his metaphysics. In Plotinian philosophy, plants "do not at all match the caricatured view of them as simple, barely living, and totally predetermined impassive things." Nor does *theoria* resemble the activity of looking at a spectacle, as it does for Aristotle and other Greek philosophers. "The contours of *theoria* had to be redrawn to accommodate the plants' contemplative reason," remarks Marder.[9] The remark gestures to a longstanding discussion about the nature of contemplation in Plotinian philosophy. As John Deck pointed out already in the 1960s, for Plotinus there exists

> another and better way in which knowledge ... can bring about results in the sensible world. It is the "automatic" producing of

sensible things.... He vigorously combats the notion that praxis [i.e., human ways of creating things through the application of skill], with the limitations that is implies, is the pattern of all "intelligent" making. He envisages a type of knowledge which flows immediately into action, or better, is immediately productive.... Nature simply contemplates, and the things of nature come to be.[10]

Plotinus introduces this idea in the passage from the *Enneads* quoted earlier, "On Nature, Contemplation, and the One." It begins with Plotinus asking his audience: "If, before attempting to be serious, we were actually to begin by playing and say that all things aim at contemplation and look to this foal, not only rational but also non-rational animals and nature in plants and the earth which produces them ... would anyone put up with the oddity of the statement?"[11] The most striking aspect of this passage is perhaps Plotinus's allusion to playfulness. The concept of vegetal contemplation is introduced as play, and Plotinus goes on to surprise his audience, a few lines further on, by proposing that something as aimless as playing might be all there is to contemplation. "Are we too, then contemplating right now when we are playing?" he asks rhetorically, before going on to answer in the affirmative: "Both we and all who play [meaning children] are contemplating."

This is a crucial suggestion, and it shows the extent to which Plotinus was, indeed, redrawing the contours of *theoria* to accommodate plants' contemplative reason. In the *Metaphysics*, Aristotle had pictured contemplation as a remote and abstract reflection on the world, one performed by adult humans and gods. Plotinus's innovation here is to suggest, through the analogy between vegetal life and child's play, a new criterion for contemplation, one based on what, today, we would call spontaneous rather than deliberate behavior. The passage leads to a long and involved discussion detailing how contemplation works *as nature*. He explains that contemplation is not (as his audience might presume) the activity of gazing at an external object; contemplation is, rather, the activity that allows for the gaze in the first place. Giving the example of an artist creating a wax model, he remarks that contemplation is not to be found in the mental effort that created the art but in the underlying biological effort sustaining the artist's body. Contemplation is the "something" that "must remain in [the artisan] in accordance to which, while still remaining in them, they produce their artefacts by means of their hands."[12] The discussion culminates in an imaginary speech delivered by *Phusis*, now personified as a woman, who admonishes the philosopher for comparing her contemplation to human craft, proposing instead the image of childbirth. The references to trees, plants, animals, children, spontaneity, "the earth itself," and now childbirth introduce the idea of a cross-species way of life rather than a description of a specific kind of creature.

The relationship between Neoplatonism and the philosophy of plants is important not only because Neoplatonism introduces an abiding species hierarchy but because it also provides the means of resisting those hierarchies from within the tradition. Neoplatonism shows that another contemplation is possible. This other contemplation is irreducible to the specialized activities of some adult philosophers; it is an activity expressed by diverse species. The vegetalizing of contemplation that comes to light in Plotinus plants a seed that makes it possible to imagine spirit sprouting from the bedrock of Terra and of vegetal life as spiritual Elder. For that sprouting to happen, however, the non-organismic must be foregrounded, and the stronghold of organismic thought surrendered. One result of reading Plotinus today, as the intelligence of plants is being studied seriously, is that we see how important it is to attend to Plotinus's concepts yet not settle for his interpretations. This is why Marder, in his reflections on Plotinus, finally remarks: "It falls to us to think with and against Plotinus, striving to be more Plotinian than the ancient thinker himself."[13] Marder's idea of plant-thinking, which takes impression from the *Enneads*, is part of that process of thinking with but also against Plotinus.

Marder's *Plant-Thinking: A Philosophy of Vegetal Life*, alludes to Plotinus's notion of an intelligence going all the way down into the Terra. Marder follows Plotinus in adopting the literal sense of the Greek term *phusis*, which, following a very ancient usage in Presocratic philosophy, refers not to the species of plants or even to the plant kingdom but rather to the world of growth; Marder's favored metaphor is metamorphosis. Following Plotinus, plant-thinking for Marder is contemplative. And rather than measure contemplation against human spiritual exercises, Marder, like Plotinus, attempts to invert the comparison, allowing plants to set the standard for contemplation, rather than humans. As he writes in *The Philosopher's Plant*, "since in plant life there is no separation between the subject and the object or, indeed, between practical living and theoretical activity, the plants' contemplation is identical to what they are and what they do according to their type of animating reason. In growing, they practically contemplative life."[14]

Throughout Marder's discussions of plant-thinking, "what [plants] are and what they do" is informed not only by ancient philosophy but also by recent scientific research on plant intelligence. According to Anthony Trewavas, plant intelligence is analogous to the swarm intelligence observed in social insect behavior.[15] For the plant neurobiologist Stefano Mancuso, "the definition of 'individual' that we use for animals has little relevance to the world of plants."[16] As Suzanne Simard comments, in the world of wild growth, plants and fungi work together in order to create "a facsimile of a neural network" in which "molecules moving among trees [are] like neurotransmitters."[17] This neural network is not a centralized organ like the human brain but a decentralized intelligence "that generates order from the bottom upwards."[18] For Marder, vegetal contemplation relates both to swarm intelligence and to anti-individualism. Marder calls the contemplative reason of plants "anarchic" and writes, in reference to Plotinus: "What eludes the attention of Plotinus [and others] is the nonorganismic life of plants that does not add up the unity of the One. It is not monarchy but vegetal anarchy that reigns there where parts are interchangeable with the whole. Neither political nor ontological hierarchies are sustainable on the grounds of the world-plant."[19]

In his contribution to *Through Vegetal Being*, Marder introduces the concept of "vegetal mindfulness." Vegetal mindfulness is like swarm intelligence; it is attentive by virtue of togetherness and contiguity rather than relation, hierarchy, or separation. The best a human can do is attempt to tune into vegetal mindfulness for brief periods, shuttling between human mindfulness and vegetal mindfulness. This can be done by silently attending to trees, but it can also be practiced by attending to one's skin: "If we wish to discover vegetal mindfulness in ourselves, we should look no further than our bodies' unconscious attention to the surroundings. . . . Without knowing it, we pay attention to the world on the surface, from the porous, essentially open, cutaneous membrane that keeps our living bodies intact, and, at the same time, communicates with whatever lies beyond them." Whether vegetal mindfulness takes place in the root systems of trees or on the surface of the human skin, it acts in way that reflects a continuous, absolute awareness of the elements. This tuning-into vegetal mindfulness is described by Marder in terms of a disruption and metamorphosis of self: "When I linger with plants . . . I am together with myself differently as well; I become myself, otherwise."[20] In this sense, plant intelligence manifests at a crucial juncture in Marder's rethinking of Plotinian contemplation; here, it is vegetal anarchy—rather than the One—that disrupts the sense of self in contemplation.

A brief look at the study of plant intelligence, then, reveals contemplation in a new light. In relation to the way of thinking I develop, vegetal anarchy will connect to mystical antinomianism. One striking feature of Western Christian mysticism, which we will be encountering in this and coming chapters, is the perceived social threat posed by contemplative practices. The use of vegetal imagery would seem innocent enough, even saccharine, yet when such imagery is used to describe contemplation, sometimes it was seen as threatening the social order of religious life. If the highest spiritual state is equivalent to a natural activity, then clergy, rituals, and sacraments are no longer necessary. Historically, accusations of heresy were directed at the perceived antinomianism practiced by those advocating direct awareness of God in this life. In this way, vegetal imagery in mysticism does not only indicate an important appreciation for flourishing, life, and natality, as many philosophers have already pointed out. I propose that we read it also as a tacit acceptance of the anarchic "plant in us." In other words, to shuttle between human and vegetal mindfulness in contemplation comes at the cost of unmooring the self from ideas of supremacy and exceptionalism. Christian mysticism dwells on the loss of a sense of self at length, and it is perhaps the most fundamental aspect of contemplation as a practice; it is also one of the motivations, I will argue, for the many analogies we find between contemplation and vegetal life. Reading mysticism alongside the vegetal turn, we will be developing an anarchic notion of contemplation.

Contemplation can be a practice reinforcing species hierarchies. But it can also be a practice of accepting the "plant in us." Vegetal mindfulness is, if not unavoidable, then certainly contained in the Neoplatonic roots of Western mysticism. The human who recognizes themselves as constituted by vegetal swarm-intelligence is less able to disdain the nonhumans with whom they share Terra. The notion of species supremacy is risked in contemplation. As Kevin Corrigan writes in his recent study of plants and animals in Neoplatonism, "hierarchical thinking has to be kept in tension with the anti-hierarchical immediacy of the Good's presence to everything."[21] Thus contemplation does not only offer an experience of human self-transformation but implies a multispecies ethic. I want now to show how these ideas come to fruition in the first layer of Christian mysticism, focusing on examples from the both the Western and Eastern traditions of early monastic life.

PHUSIKE THEORIA: MULTISPECIES CONTEMPLATION IN EVAGRIAN MONASTICISM

Christian mysticism emerged with the establishment of the monastic ideal in the deserts of Egypt, Syria, Judea, and Asia Minor during the late third and early fourth centuries: This ideal remained formative for the institutional context of mysticism until the end of the twelfth century. Although there are many differences between the approaches and texts I am narrating here (and I will only be touching on a few), common themes emerge between writers, mystics, and movements in distinct geographical and historical contexts. Among these, I am interested in the relationship between *phusis* and *theoria*, the world of wild growth and contemplation. As has been well documented, Christian monasticism was in part a response to the social, political, and economic unrest tugging at the seams of the Late Roman Empire. Urbanization, commercialization, and the overexploitation of environments and peoples led ascetics, as Douglas Christie puts it, to attempt to "repair the torn fabric of the world" by living differently and apart from towns, either as solitaries or in groups.[22] In *The Blue Sapphire of the Mind: Notes for a Contemplative Ecology*, Christie illustrates this with the most influential text in early Western Christian monasticism, *The Life of Antony*, which relates how the fourth-century Egyptian leaves his home in the Nile Valley to pursue years of contemplation in the desert. Here, Antony is described as wandering and contemplating and, while doing so, falling in love with a remote, mountainous site, spending much of his time alone. Though many ascetics chose a less solitary path than Antony, his story "became an emblem of the entire early Christian monastic quest."[23] Indeed, the *Apophthegmata*, a collection of anecdotes and sayings from the first desert ascetics, are full of life stories in which place, plants, animals, and critters are paramount in unfolding the contemplative vision.[24] "This fluid, reciprocal relationship between place and spirit, the interior and the exterior landscape, became a distinctive part of the world of early Christian monks," remarks Christie, and one that became hugely influential, remaining especially significant in Eastern Orthodox Christianity.[25]

The early Christian practice of contemplating nature can be said to express these developments and facilitate them. In the wake of the first Egyptian ascetics, Evagrius of Pontus (c. 345–399) insisted on "the contemplation of nature" (*phusike theoria*) as a core part of Christianity. The idea was inherited from

Hellenistic philosophy. The practice, very prominent in early Christian mysticism, is also found in Stoicism, Neoplatonism, and Epicureanism. Pierre Hadot has described it in detail in *Philosophy as a Way of Life: Spiritual Exercises from Socrates to Foucault* and *The Veil of Isis: An Essay on the History of the Idea of Nature*, where he calls it "physics as spiritual exercise." Writes Hadot: "For [ancient philosophers] physics is not only a discourse but also a practice. . . . [It] consists of contemplating the universe, thinking of the All, and harmonizing oneself with its movements. Here, the contemplative way of life is recommended, together with the effort to free oneself from individual passions, in order to turn toward the rational study of the world."[26] Hadot's understanding of "physics as spiritual exercise" is helpful when interpreting the relationship between *phusis* and *theoria* in early Christian monastic mysticism. Olivier Clément described *phusike theoria*, or "contemplation of nature," as an "attentive gaze, stripped of covetousness . . . which perceives each object . . . and honors it."[27] Evagrius, who is the basis for much of Clément's understanding of *phusike theoria*, is today most known, perhaps, for claiming that a true theologian is one who prays, but Evagrius also claimed that "if you seek prayer attentively you will find it; for nothing is more essential to prayer than attentiveness."[28] Evagrius's idea of *phusike theoria* has four characteristics. First is the emphasis on attentiveness to creation. Christie argues that "at its deepest level, the contemplative life was understood by the ancient monastic as a way of seeing (or to extend the metaphor as the monks often did, a way of listening or touching or tasting or smelling)." That way of seeing (or sensing) was characterized by receptivity, and a continual awareness, practiced throughout the day. It manifested as "an intense awareness of the present moment" but also as a heightened sense of process, chance, change, and becoming.[29]

Second, the contemplation of nature was understood as a return to a natural state. Immediately after introducing the concept of natural contemplation in his handbook to monks, the *Praktikos*, Evagrius writes: "The Kingdom of Heaven is *apatheia* of the soul along with true knowledge of existing things."[30] *Apatheia*, which Christian monasticism inherited from Hellenistic philosophy, means "without passion," and today it is often taken to indicate a rejection of natural inclinations. But a rejection of natural inclinations was not how *apatheia* was seen in Christian antiquity. Regarding the passions in Christian antiquity, Peter Brown noted that "they were not what we tend to call 'feelings': they were, rather, complexes which hindered the true expressions of feelings."[31] In the description just cited, Evagrius concludes his description of the Kingdom of Heaven by adding that the Kingdom is "true knowledge of existing things."[32] Evagrius's idea seems to have been that *apatheia*, far from being a rejection of nature, was in fact the opposite, a continual attentiveness to the physical world that leads to salvation not by liberating the mind from nature but by immersing it more deeply in the world. In the ascetic tradition that developed after Evagrius, "the inherent antagonism between body and soul surfaces *only* if one lapses into the contranatural state."[33] Here, "the 'natural' state of the human is one of virtue; salvation entails returning to this primal state, through a control of nature which has become distorted."[34] The point seems to be that humans tend to abuse nature by caring more about concepts of the "natural" than about their own, natural needs.

Third, and following on from the previous point, contemplation of nature was also related to negative or mystical theology. Evagrius urged that prayer should be amorphic, meaning free of mental forms or representations (*morphe*). Augustine Casiday recently coined a new term for this aspect of Evagrian asceticism, calling Evagrian prayer "anoetic."[35] *Anoesia* is used by Pseudo-Dionysius when discussing the "want of understanding" necessary to perform the sacraments in a contemplative state. According to G. W. H. Lampe, *anoesia*, in early Christian theology, referred both to God and to humans; specifically, it was used to describe contemplation "beyond ratiocination."[36] Evagrius emphasized the need to let go of language, concepts, and images when attempting to pray, an idea later developed in the fifth and sixth centuries by Pseudo-Dionysius in his account of mystical theology as an ascent to God through negations.[37] For Evagrius as for Pseudo-Dionysius, God is received in a state that lacks human specificity; God is contemplated through an apophatic "unsaying" and a path of negations. Not only the attributes of God are negated: Language itself, concepts, words, and images, and even the idea of self are abandoned on the path to contemplation. The result is that God is attended to by *anoesia*, a prayer "without concepts." Even the senses have ceased to convey impressions to the mind, which now experiences God directly, unmediated by concepts. On one level, this would seem to contradict Evagrius's emphasis on contemplating nature, since nature appears in images to the human mind. According to Casiday, however, on another level the anoetic nature of contemplating God in Evagrian mysticism follows from the Evagrian sense of *phusike theoria*. As Casiday explains, Evagrius's objection to *noesia*, or concept-thought, is not simply that it impedes communion with a God beyond language but also that it impedes communion with creatures. Representations (like passions) were seen as acutely problematic to the early monastics. Creatures reveal God but are then grasped by the intellect in ways that do harm, both to God and creatures. By insisting on the absence of concepts in contemplation, Evagrius was concerned to align the attitude of attentive openness toward God with a similar attitude toward creatures. In other words, the aim was to contemplate *phusis* with the same openness accorded God.

The fourth and final trait that I want to draw attention to regarding *phusike theoria* is that the practice involves what I interpret as a subtle but significant critique of species-thought. Behind *phusike theoria* was the aspiration to do without books and institutions by attending to Terra, not only because creation was considered the gift of God but because "we must know how to perceive the giver *according to the gift*."[38] The ability to perceive God was understood as possible only through an attunement to creaturely life: knowing God according to creation, the "gift" of God. The Hebrew Psalms but also early Christian liturgies depict creatures praising God, and this idea found support in the Neoplatonic tradition of intelligent life. Elizabeth Theokritoff reflects that although the image of creation rejoicing in God is metaphorical, "it is *not* an allegory or fable; it is saying something about the nature of behavior of created things . . . however different it may be from the way we normally perceive the behavior of the elements, the earth, and other creatures."[39] One might say that all earthlings become, in early Christian monasticism, co-contemplative or "syntheoric." The contexts for contemplation, in the Christian monastic ideal—the desert places sought out by ascetics like Antony—were also teachers of contemplation. The world of wild growth was an object of contemplation but also a swarm of contemplating subjects. To contemplate nature was to learn about God but also to learn with nature the way to contemplate God—a God whose Kingdom, in this mysticism, was not located in a remote realm but in acts of everyday attentiveness. As Christie explains, "Evagrius (and here he is joined by many of those who will follow him in the Eastern Christian tradition) views natural contemplation as a significant part of the larger contemplative project. Learning to see the created world this carefully and sensitively is no small part of what it means to become contemplative."⁴⁰

Here, contemplation *of* nature was also contemplation *by* nature, a double meaning reflected by Christie's interpretation, in this passage, of *phusike theoria* as "natural contemplation." Indeed, the Greek is ambiguous, with *phusike theoria* yielding two possible translations. It could mean "contemplation *of* nature" but also "contemplation *according to* nature," that is, "natural contemplation." Bearing in mind that "natural" (*phusike*) comes from the same word as *phusis* with its connection to the vegetal, another possible translation of *phusike theoria* would be "growth-contemplation" or "vegetal contemplation." In this sense, Evagrian monasticism resonates with plant-thinking. The relationship between *phusis* and *theoria*, vegetal growth and contemplation, in Christian mysticism extends beyond a subject-object relation. With the practice of contemplating nature, mystics intend something quite different to spectating the world from a position of spiritual superiority. In fact, conceptual thought is discouraged; the world is not to be "represented" during contemplation, and reading *phusis* is not the same as reading a scroll. The "book of nature" is knowledge of beings gained through attentiveness. Rather than project this knowledge into a supramundane realm or the afterlife, however, Evagrian monasticism suggests that it is given as the present moment and open to those patient enough to attend. More importantly, God is not remote from this process, and one way of interpreting Evagrius's description of the Kingdom of Heaven is to equate it with immediate knowledge of physical entities. While it is common to imagine this immediate knowledge as spiritual in the sense of invisible and abstract, Christie helps us see an alternative interpretation:

immediate knowledge gained through radical receptivity. The contemplative life is then one of *sensing*. Habits that have resulted in an inveterate insensitivity to physical entities are metabolized into new habits formed by attending to *phusis*.

The monastic ideal suggests that the spiritual life emerges from attentiveness to vegetal life, *phusis*. Who or what "God" is in this practice is not clear, but the notion that the heavenly Kingdom realizes itself through such attentiveness implies a certain resistance, intentional or not, to theological dualism. In the next section of this chapter, I want to look at the relation between natural contemplation and heresy and explore its connections to the theme of vegetal anarchy.

THE STRANGE FRUITS OF BECOMING-TREE: BYZANTINE AND SYRIAC ASCETICISM

In 431 CE, the belief that the Kingdom of Heaven was possible to attain in this life (along with several other practices and beliefs) were anathematized by the Council of Ephesus. The name "Messalianism" became attached to the first major, ecclesial persecution of mysticism. Messalianism was a movement of Syrian origin (the name is from the Syrian *mṣallyānā*, meaning "one who prays") that appeared in the 370s but quickly spread throughout the Late Roman Empire, eventually finding its way to Egypt. Although Evagrius of Pontus himself was not part of this movement, the similarities between his spiritual teachings and those of the famous heresy have been noted by several scholars.[41] Texts associated with Messalianism stress that God can be found in the present moment through an act of continuous prayer in this life, that sacraments were not essential, and that natural inclinations were not to be feared by those who had achieved sanctity. The practice of interior stillness or *apatheia* was particularly contentious. It implied that sanctity was possible in this life. Those accused of Messalianism were said to reject the role of priests and sacraments; they were also reported to flaunt sexual norms by claiming themselves free from sin and thus able to indulge in all manner of natural inclinations.

Columbia Stewart argues that, while the accusations brought against Messalianism were most likely exaggerated, it is true that Messalian spirituality employed "graphic and sensual metaphors" that would have "jarred theologically sensitive ears."[42] Evagrius's language is muted by comparison, yet the emphasis on finding God in this life through contemplation and on returning to—rather than rejecting—nature is striking. Helen Hunt describes what she calls Messalianism's synaesthesia: "It is typical of [Messalian] thought to attribute qualities to the body and soul which are usually associated with the other ... this reinforces the unity of the parts of the human person."[43] Similar arguments have been put forward for Evagrius's theology. For Hunt, Messalian spirituality was principally a question of uniting the *senses*; it was concerned with the sensitive life and with the integration of mind and body. What the Council of Ephesus saw as the antinomianism of this mystical current, Hunt instead proposes that we appreciate, today, as its ecstatic antidualism.

In the fifth century, Syria, like Egypt, lay at the outskirts of the Late Roman Empire, and its deserts were home to a flourishing tradition of ascetics, developing its own tradition of asceticism. Regarding *apatheia*, the parallels between Messalianism and Evagrian monasticism are obvious, but they extend also to the recognition of *phusis*, nature, as the revelation of God. The key figure here is Ephrem the Syrian (d. 373), contemporary with Evagrius and just as influential in the Syriac tradition that developed in his wake. In Ephrem's work, much of it poetic, creation is hymned in vivid and sensual language, and the movement of the spirit toward God is depicted with imagery borrowed from the physical world, not least plant life. In the opening verses of the *Hymn to Faith*, Ephrem writes: "The seed, swollen with moisture, bursts asunder its covering of soil and out peers the blade of wheat, full of symbols. So faith, whose bosom is filled with good fruits, is a blade bearing praise."[44] As one commentator remarks, in Ephrem's hymns, "nature is . . . replete with intimations of the presence of God."[45] Sebastian Brock has written at length about this aspect of Ephrem's work. Ephrem has an "awareness of the sacramental character of the created world" and of "the potential of everything in the created world to act as a witness and pointer to the Creator." In Ephrem's spirituality, writes Brock, "everything is imbued with significance," and spiritual teachings are almost invariably illustrated with material things or creaturely behavior. For Brock, this is what gives Ephrem's poetry its vivid quality, since it operates by means of the senses rather than by abstract argument. It is also, he argues, expressive of Ephrem's spiritual practice. As Brock notes, in Ephrem's hymns, the fact of nature's sacramentality is evident yet invisible to the untrained eye: "It requires the eye of faith on the part of each individual" to recognize this fact. In Ephrem's spirituality as in Evagrian monasticism, *ascesis* is important.[46] Ephrem writes frequently of the "eye of faith" beholding nature, a reference to the practice of natural contemplation. For this reason, Ephrem's hymns can be read as the result of one training the eye to see the world in ways that lead to an appreciation of the physical world itself as a witness to God, as itself contemplative.

This training of the eye through natural contemplation continued to be prominent in later Syriac asceticism. Isaac of Nineveh

(613–c. 700), whose role in the Syriac tradition was hugely significant, writes that "prayer is one thing, but contemplation (*theoria*) during it is quite another—even though they have their cause in each other, the former being the seed and the latter the load of sheaves—where the harvester is full of wonder at the sight he sees which cannot be described: out of the miserable bare seeds that he has sown, what glorious ears of corn have all of a sudden sprouted forth in front of him! as he gazes, he ceases from all motion." The idea of contemplation as an inexorable, natural movement "sprouting" from prayer is important in the Syriac approach to contemplation. As in the Evagrian tradition, contemplation is associated with a state of inner peace and stillness beyond words. Isaac's work is important for describing in detail the stages that lead from prayer (by which he means deliberate meditation or petition) to contemplation or "pure prayer" (an effortless and spontaneous activity). The point is that contemplation is something into which the ascetic is supposed to relax and to which they surrender. One must wait, like the farmer at the wheat field, for the time when contemplation is ready to "sprout"; it is useless to force things. For Isaac, contemplation is a vegetal process. It is described as a letting go of "natural free choice" and yet as a surrender to nature. What is at stake is not a rejection of the physical world but a state in which "what is endowed by nature no longer has authority over itself" but is "guided in a direction which it does not know."[47]

Meanwhile, in very different ways, Byzantine ascetics were living out their whole lives in trees, and these dendrite saints (from the Greek word for tree, *dendron*) were venerated as icons of spiritual perfection, situating their practices at "the borders of their humanness." In *Byzantine Tree Life: Christianity and the Arboreal Imagination*, Thomas Arentzen, Virginia Burrus, and Glenn Peers bring to life remarkable figures who, although relatively rare in the West, help render still more vibrant the idea I have been putting forward, namely, that in early Christian monasticism, contemplation was imagined as a participation in vegetal being. Arentzen, Burrus, and Peers study the long Byzantium, stretching from late antiquity to the fifteenth century. Like the present book, they engage with the recent recognition by philosophers that "it is not so much the animal as the (uncultivated) plant that is the human's excluded 'other' in Western thought." Michael Marder's work, too, is a point of contact for the authors, especially the way Marder argues that the concept of the plant having intelligence and agency "challenges the ... human-cantered ... premises of western metaphysics." This challenging of the premises of Western metaphysics is especially striking in the case of the dendrite saints, the subject of a fascinating chapter, "Becoming-Tree." Here, Arentzen, Burrus, and Peers focus on David of Thessaloniki, a fifth-century ascetic who became a famous tree-sitter. According to his brief vita, David's miraculous powers appeared after he had lived in an almond tree for several years. The authors draw special attention to some of the surviving iconography of David, which shows "a new hybrid man of wood, leaf, blossom, and fruit," half-tree, half-human. "He became more than he was before he climbed into the overstory," they reflect, suggesting that "David's image is a particular, sensitive imagining of asceticism in, under, and within nature."[48]

Byzantine Tree Life does not address the practice of contemplation as such; however, contemplation is implicit in any account of ascetic endeavor from this period. I would also suggest that the authors hint at a cross-cultural connection between tree-sitting and contemplation. As Arentzen, Burrus, and Peers remark, David was said to have come from the East, and they point out that tree-sitting may have originated in Syria, where there seems to have been a concentration of dendrite ascetics. If we read dendrite asceticism against the backdrop of Syriac asceticism, tree-sitting becomes understandable on an additional level, as the materialization of metaphor. What, in the writing of Ephrem and Isaac, is presented as an image (and one among many borrowed from vegetal life) becomes, in the actions of David, a spiritual direction: *Become vegetal!* As Arentzen, Burrus, and Peers argue, what takes place in dendrite spirituality is not only a practice of asceticism *in* trees but also a spiritual growing-together of humans *with* trees. *Byzantine Tree Life* compares this process to grafting, in relation to the striking iconography of David as half-human, half-tree. They point out that grafting was a ubiquitous practice in ancient Greece and Rome and that Paul uses it to describe the relationship between Christians and Christ; they also engage with contemporary plant theory and Marder's reflections on grafts.

Grafting, for Marder, is distinctive for the way in which it upends Western philosophy's ideas of identity, hierarchy, and organization. Unlike animals, plants are able to procreate by grafting, which gives to their growth a peculiar lack of individual identity. In a graft, life is facilitated by togetherness in a way that is different to sexual reproduction. Marder reflects that grafting, however, is not confined to what plants do; when humans perform surgical procedures, they are using a related survival strategy:

> When [surgical procedures] are successful, that is to say, when the organism does not reject the tissues grafted onto it, these operations disclose the vegetal character of corporeality: of flesh proliferating on flesh, of skin breathing through its porous superficies like a leaf, of the entire body put together thanks to additions and superimpositions, not as a closed *either/or* totality but

as a potential infinity of *and, and, and.* . . . The very fact that grafts can refer to animal or human tissues as well as to plant parts testifies to the word's and the practice's quiet rebellion against the strictures of identity.[49]

Thinking with this passage, Arentzen, Burrus, and Peers reflect on the iconography of dendrite saints. Dendrite saints like David are read as rebelling against the dichotomies separating humans from other creatures but also God from creation. In the practice of tree-sitting, the authors see anarchic grafting, one in which the already vegetal nature of a human animal is discovered by sharing the space of intimate contemplation with trees. The authors of *Byzantine Tree Life* reflect that "of course, such procedures are far from David's world" but suggest that, even so, "they allow us to look back and see, too, how profoundly both our world are made by them, how our bodies have always been open to the arboreal remaking and re-pairing by means of the other."[50] The insights of the Syriac tradition on the created world as exemplifying the activity of contemplation would support such a view. Indeed, the metaphors of contemplation as a vegetal activity move in this direction.

They also move mysticism still further in the direction of vegetal anarchy. In his Letter to the Romans (11:11–31), Paul uses grafting as a positive metaphor, yet in the ancient world grafting was also viewed with suspicion, something we will return to in the next chapter. It was common, for instance, to refer to grafting as "unnatural," and it is possible that Paul is playing deliberately with this meaning. What interests Arentzen, Burrus, and Peers is the ability of mysticism to reclaim the "unnatural" in a creative process of resistance and subversion. Through tree-sitting and grafting with trees, mystics claim nature yet do so by upending common assumptions regarding "nature." Nature becomes, for the dendrite ascetics, the anarchic commons where identity is formed in acts of monstrous union with vegetal kin, acts that seem to rebel against the strategies of orthodox texts and institutions. We will see these themes developing further in medieval mysticism.

VEGETAL ASCETICISM: GROWING MORE PLOTINIAN THAN PLOTINUS

Before we turn to medieval mysticism, however, I want to recall Plotinus and his idea of vegetal contemplation with which we began this chapter. In particular, I want to return to Michael Marder's suggestion that we read both with and against Plotinus. In *The Philosopher's Plant* Marder regards Plotinus very highly, but he also voices his concern with the tradition in which Plotinus's philosophy stands. We have already discussed Marder's critique of the way vegetal life is pictured by Plotinus; we have yet to discuss the way he characterizes the practice of contemplation according to Plotinus. For Marder, Plotinus's asceticism is problematic. He cites the *Enneads*: "[We must] reduce the body . . . so that it may be made clear that the real man is other than his outward parts."[51] By insisting that the body must be "reduced," Marder reflects, Plotinus contradicts his own idea of contemplation as a natural activity. Nonetheless, the idea of natural contemplation—of contemplation as vegetal life—is germinal to Marder's work. Marder suggests that instead of dismissing Plotinus we strive to be "more Plotinian" than the ancient philosopher.

The way I have portrayed them, figures like Evagrius, Ephrem, Isaac, and the dendrite saints, presents alternative views of ascetic practice that both draw on Neoplatonist and other

Hellenistic ideas while metamorphosing them in fresh ways. I have engaged with contemporary readers of asceticism, like Douglas Christie and Thomas Arentzen, in order to rethink assumptions about the spiritual life in this period. In the interest of providing a fuller picture of how *theoria* and *phusis* coevolve in the first millennium CE, however, I also want to give more space to Plotinian asceticism. I would like to turn, briefly, to Pierre Hadot's classic *Plotinus: Or, the Simplicity of Vision*, not only because it provides a remarkable analysis of asceticism but also because it centers that interpretation around a rethinking of vegetal life and the idea of "nature contemplating." *Plotinus* was an essay that, when it appeared in 1963, challenged the conventional assumption that Plotinus's asceticism was about escaping the world and also that Neoplatonism took a pessimistic view of matter. In this way, Hadot provides some very good reflections that, I think, complement Marder's insights and brings Plotinus into closer dialogue with the Christian material introduced in this chapter.

In *Plotinus*, asceticism is discussed with exceptional clarity by Hadot in two chapters, "Virtues" and "Gentleness." In the first, "Virtues," Hadot points out the discrepancy between modern and Plotinian understandings of asceticism. Modern notions picture *ascesis* against the backdrop of a struggle in which spirit overcomes body. In common with the Christian mystical tradition, Plotinus argued that contemplation (*theoria*) required training (*ascesis*). Plotinus uses *ascesis* and its cognates at least five times in the *Enneads*, suggesting that, in addition to a person's natural disposition, one who wishes to live the contemplative life will usually need training and preparation, involving periods of fasting and celibacy. Hadot grumbles that modern readers have taken this to indicate that Plotinus insisted on severe and austere practices as the requirement for contemplation in toto. Hadot suggests that this appearance, if not wholly deceptive, is misleading, an appearance created by the habit of citing Porphyry's remark that Plotinus was one who seemed ashamed of having a body. Yet a closer look at Porphyry's book, Hadot argues, indicates that Plotinus encouraged moderation rather than deprivation. Moreover, although *ascesis* plays a role in the *Enneads*, it is understood to be abandoned once contemplation has become habitual. "There will come a time," Hadot writes, citing Plotinus, "when contemplation will be continuous, and the body will no longer present any obstacle."[52]

While it is possible to interpret this to mean that Plotinus was anticipating a time when the body would be so utterly defeated as to provide no resistance to the mind, Hadot is not satisfied with such a reading. Here, Hadot grounds his argument largely on the passage that also interests Marder, *Ennead* 3.8, where Plotinus suggests that trees, rocks, and indeed all of *phusis* is engaged in contemplating.[53] Hadot reasons that if, as Plotinus claims when identifying contemplation with nature, contemplation is the *easiest* activity, then contemplation cannot at the same time be opposed to nature—the latter, on Plotinus's own reading, being represented by plant growth. No, the easiest activity must also be the most natural. Yet Hadot recognizes that Plotinus does emphasize training or *ascesis*. A person's natural disposition, Plotinus argues, is insufficient, and they will need specific types of practice in order to contemplate. Hadot, however, does not interpret this habituation as going against nature. Rather, what he sees in Plotinus's argument is an encouragement, directed at philosophers, to be *more* in tune with the body. The idea is that such attunement feels unfamiliar and "unnatural" if one is out of tune with one's body's natural needs. This is how Hadot interprets the language of ascetic "reduction" in Plotinus's asceticism: Rather than encouraging a person to rise above their natural state, Plotinus is suggesting the philosopher reduce themselves to nothing *but* their natural state.[54] At one point, Hadot explains this as a "conversion of attention" and contrasts it with the idea of contemplation as the acquisition of superhuman abilities. Comparing Plotinian contemplation to the very same Christian mystical tradition that we will be encountering in chapters 4 and 5, Hadot suggests that for Plotinus attention was "already identical [to] 'natural prayer.'" On this reading, which Hadot bases on other passages from the *Enneads*, contemplation is not an extraordinary event that takes a person out of the world but a state of continual attentiveness: "Virtue is the continuation of contemplation," writes Hadot. For Hadot, Plotinian contemplation—despite the often otherworldly language in which Plotinus clothes his accounts of the One—ends in events that are "no longer rare and extraordinary" but rather consists in "an extremely simple spiritual attitude."[55]

Precisely what that spiritual attitude is and how it is maintained—how it is continuous—is described in the essay's middle chapter, "Gentleness," a reflection on the life and person of Plotinus. Hadot begins by recognizing that readers "cannot help but feel a certain uneasiness" at Porphyry's description of Plotinus as someone "ashamed of being in a body." This, however, is potentially misleading. While it is true that Plotinus disparaged his physical habit, Hadot argues that it is clear from Porphyry's narrative that Plotinus's embarrassment was not a sign of disgust; in addition, "many features of this gloomy portrait have been exaggerated," as Hadot remarks.[56] By Porphyry's account, Plotinus was moderate, rather than world renouncing; he was at ease with food and wine and, although seemingly indifferent to suffering, not above feeling pain. Most importantly, Porphyry's biography describes Plotinus as being "present both to himself and to others," apparently maintaining a constant contemplative activity while also being attentive to those around him.⁵⁷ To Hadot, what Porphyry describes is the effect of one practicing what they teach: "It was as though the complete receptivity in which he established himself with regard to God allowed him, and even commanded him, also to remain in a state of complete receptivity and availability with regard to other people." Other people, but also other creatures; the point, for Hadot, is that "attention paid to the Spirit does not exclude attention to other people, to the world, and to the body itself." On the contrary, as Hadot reads Plotinus, in this kind of contemplation the body is *more* present than it was before spirit became the sole object of attention. "It is not the body he struggled against," comments Hadot. Thus "there is . . . no struggle against the self, no spiritual 'combat' in Plotinian asceticism . . . despite some of Plotinus' phraseology, his mysticism, in the form in which he lived it, does not appear to have been an escape mechanism."⁵⁸

Of course, such a view of contemplation makes sense only if Spirit names not some distant realm or separate substance but life, that is, *phusis*—the process of vegetal growth, change, and metamorphosis. Such, indeed, appears to be Hadot's reading of Plotinian contemplation, as he explains in a later interview: "My book *Plotinus* [argued] that there is something ineffable in human existence, but this ineffable is *within* our very perception of the world, in the mystery of our existence and that of the cosmos."⁵⁹ One can in consequence observe in Hadot's alternative reading of Plotinian asceticism a pragmatic relationship between the language of renouncing nature and contemplating nature.

It remains to note that Hadot's work on Plotinus is comprehensive, and I make no claims to present a full picture. What I have presented is one detail in a much larger argument. Yet later scholars have also been concerned to show that a world-renouncing attitude is misleading as a way of reading Plotinus's philosophy. Much Plotinus scholarship, although it tends to give less attention to contemplation than did Hadot, supports the core idea animating Hadot's *Plotinus* and points in a similar direction.[60] Recent commentaries on Plotinus leave behind the idea that nature is transcended in Plotinian philosophy, inviting instead a close dialogue with the natural sciences.[61] With respect to questions of how nature's contemplation relates to the philosopher's practice, we can see how not only in Plotinus's notion of vegetal life but also in his understanding of asceticism there are the seeds for growing "more" Plotinian. In this way, a reading of Hadot's *Plotinus* alongside Marder offsets the sense of a hidebound asceticism. In *Plotinus*, contemplation plunges the philosopher into the planet's growth-thought. For Hadot, only the person who has *not* succeeded in contemplating can give the appearance that this activity is somehow very arduous, a harrowing struggle to overcome the body, nature, and matter.

In consequence, there is always an anarchic movement to Plotinian contemplation, to use Marder's expression in a new context. For the philosopher, the activity of *theoria* is primary, in a double sense: both in the sense of being made continuous through habit (Plotinus's ability to contemplate even while chatting with students) and in the sense of being already continuous by virtue of the body's vegetative activities. At this point, though, the acquired and the instinctive converge. The habit of contemplating, initially a deliberate activity, through repetition loses itself imperceptibly in the body's ability to sense its environments, external as well as internal. This is an abandonment that is not answerable to an overarching One but to *phusis*, which is not an entity but an activity, the activity of continuous growth, change, and metamorphosis.

Finally, if one wishes to say—as Plotinus does—that this process is itself subject to growth, to practice through training, then one is not necessarily stepping back from an understanding of contemplation as natural. Simply knowing, as a philosopher, that nature contemplates, that one's body is already synthesizing environments passively through vegetal activities, is but half the story of contemplation viewed from the perspective of the human animal. One cannot in such cases rest content with spectating, because merely viewing the facts from afar precludes that contact which alone imparts attunement to nature's contemplation.

A NATURAL HISTORY OF CONTEMPLATION

In the ways sketched here, contemplation, *theoria*, in both Neoplatonism and early Christian mysticism, overlaps with a general notion of nature as *phusis*: the world of wild growth, spontaneity, and continual receptivity that is vegetal life. Yet it presents this "natural" activity as achievable through ascetic—that is, "unnatural"—practice. The result is a paradox.

What I have been calling, variously, natural contemplation or contemplation according to nature is a paradox because of the role played by habit. In the tradition of Neoplatonist philosophy and Western Christian mysticism, contemplation is a skill: It requires time and practice to learn. However, in the context of the philosophical and religious traditions I have been considering, contemplation is also natural: according to Plotinus's suggestion, the most natural activity of all, shared by rocks and trees. So the skill in question is unlike that of learning to speak a new language, sculpt with clay, or play a musical instrument.

Still, it is a skill, and like all skills, it demands a context of practice and repetition. New skills are acquired through repetition. Repetition, moreover, has the result of making any action feel natural to the one performing it. Once an action has become habitual through repetition, it is common, in philosophy and theology, to refer to it as "natural" or "second nature."[62] In most cases, though, "natural" is used figuratively. If it is said that a musician plays with natural ease, it is understood that, nonetheless, effort contributed to spontaneity.

In the case of contemplation, the natural is not figurative but actual. In this respect, it is true to say, with Hadot and others, that there really is no struggle with nature *qua* vegetal life in contemplation. At the same, it is equally true to observe, as the Western monastic tradition does so frequently, that the experience is one of struggling against "nature" in the sense of unhelpful conceptions of nature. If nature is vegetal life, the "nature" with which asceticism struggles stands for that which impedes attunement to vegetal life. In this scenario, what is experienced as disembodied is, in fact, another way of experiencing embodiment, a way that has become unfamiliar. Contemplation remains a renunciation of "nature," insofar as "nature" is perceived as excluded from contemplation, but it also clings to nature, insofar as nature is recognized—through contemplation—as the activity that makes contemplation possible.

We have seen that Plotinus's account of contemplation makes a significant break with Plato and Aristotle, yet in ways that are surprising. While Plotinus's account of plants as contemplative strikes today's reader as strange, what, historically, may in fact be the most inventive aspect of *Ennead* 3.8.1–4 is its account of contemplation as a natural—rather than spectating—activity. Here, *phusis* in the sense of vegetal life leads the way toward a changed notion of what it means to practice contemplation in both philosophy and later Christian mysticism, but it is the idea of contemplation that is changed at the deepest level by the entanglement with vegetal life. Contemplation, as an activity convergent with Terran life, becomes emphatically vegetal. Yet that very plunge into wild growth also destabilizes contemplation. For, viewed from the perspective of a spectating contemplation, nature's *theoria* does indeed seem most "unnatural."

How is this tradition carried forward into Christian spiritual exercises, asceticism, and mysticism? It is this story that I will now be narrating before turning to Jeanne Guyon. The question at issue is to what extent accounts of contemplation are attentive to the vegetal attentiveness that sustains the one who contemplates—whether, that is, contemplation remains a spectating activity, with the contemplative eyeing "nature" from afar, or whether contemplation is a multispecies activity, with the contemplative recognizing themselves as already and irrevocably natural, part of *phusis*, and seeing other physical beings as their contemplating kin.

3

VEGETAL MYSTICISM

Growing up as a Roman Catholic, I was taught by the Sunday school instructor to consider contemplation somewhat *unnatural*: a rare and precious grace reserved for the devout and saintly. Thanks to my mother, however, I was also given a broader education in the concept. My mother, perhaps distrusting the Sunday school instructors, decided to give me stories of the saints to read for myself. I loved these books and soon began exploring the literature on my own. What I especially delighted in was how different the stories of saints' lives were, especially in their autobiographies, from what I was being taught about the spiritual life. Above all, I never received the impression that the experiences they had were rarefied. Rather, the loss of a sense of self described by mystics was also accompanied, in their writings, by a celebration of corporeality and creaturehood.

In medieval mysticism, the vegetal and mystical continue to form a close connection. We will be encountering references to cosmism and teachings regarding the lively matter of creation, but we will also be continuing to give attention to contemplation, ecstasy, and mystical theology. As Bernard McGinn has pointed out, when scholars focus too much on *what* mystics write and teach, there is "danger of losing connection with what most mystics themselves have claimed to be essential, that is, a special consciousness of the presence of God that by definition exceeds description and results in a transformation of the subject who receives it."[1] There is a relationship between how mystics describe the presence of God, on the one hand, and cosmism, or the contemplation of nature, on the other. In much medieval mysticism, the ability to be open to the world and experience shared participation in God with other creatures is prized, but so too is the ability to practice radical receptivity beyond representations. Affect is thus emphasized, yet prayer is without representations or concepts, "anoetic," in the tradition of Pseudo-Dionysius, whose work is given fresh attention in the period. There is in medieval mysticism both an attentiveness to creatures and "a real identification [with God], in which the *passive* aspect is strongly emphasized."[2] In other words, sensitivity and an ability to practice receptivity and continuous attentiveness are shared between negative theology and cosmism. Both of these themes, I will argue, are represented when mystics take to vegetal imagery in their writing.

There also seems to be a structural homology between the way mystics think about mystical union and the premodern notion of a vegetative or nutritive soul. This homology is remarkable for the way it differs from the hierarchical understanding of the vegetative soul in premodernity. Put differently, what in theology and philosophy is seen as the lowest form of existence—the purely sensitive life, devoid of self-awareness—becomes in many mystical texts the way of describing mystical union. Following Michael Marder, I take vegetal life to indicate resistance not only to species-thought but also to hierarchical thinking. Vegetal life is not plant specific but rather stands "for a tendency of living and thinking that promotes growth, decay and metamorphosis."[3]

VEGETAL MYSTICISM ᛘ 83

In the mystics we will be encountering in this chapter, vegetal life is articulated through that activity which, before thought, makes thought possible: "attentiveness to what is going on." Such attentiveness, which is how both plant intelligence and also mystical states are pictured, is easy but also effortful, signaling a shift to a different mode of attention. "Humans tend to pay attention to nature when the elements do not cooperate with us, upsetting our plan," comments Marder, noting that plants practice "another kind of attention, one that is not oriented toward death."[4] The preponderance of plants in medieval mysticism will be shown to be significant but not if it is taken to indicate species envy or misanthropy. Rather, the preponderance of plants will be connected to practices of recognizing the "plant in us."

With this chapter, I want to begin moving deeper into the vegetal world of mystics and, through readings of its contemporary voices, begin to articulate a "vegetal mysticism." The literature on nature in medieval mysticism is vast, and here I have focused only on a few of the figures and themes that relate to contemporary philosophies of vegetal life. Hildegard of Bingen, with her concept of *viriditas*, "greenness," looms large in the scholarship. After introducing *viriditas* and situating it in Hildegard's work, I turn to Marder's study of Hildegard. Here we find a detailed reflection on the way medieval women's mysticism "vegetalizes" thought, and I engage with this idea at some length. We also find a tentative connection drawn between Hildegard's ecstasies and vegetal life, a connection I begin to develop by pointing to Hildegard's letters and her descriptions of ecstasy. From Hildegard I pass onto Gertrude the Great of Helfta and the recent reading, by Liz Herbert McAvoy and others, of grafting metaphors and their role in Gertrude's account of ecstatic experiences. I am interested in the way Gertrude's mysticism overlays the erotic imagery of mystical union with an alternative, gender-queer hermeneutic of fecund desire inspired by plant life. With these readings forming the main part of the chapter, I then turn to Marguerite of Porete, condemned and executed for heresy in 1310. Unlike Hildegard and Gertrude, Marguerite has not figured in any discussion of the vegetal in mysticism; moreover, her relative silence on ecstasy and her critique of contemplation would seem to position her mysticism in a category apart. Nonetheless, I see Marguerite's practice of self-annihilation and her emphasis on embodiment instructive. Drawing the Marguerite scholar Amy Hollywood into conversation with Marder, I narrate a structural homology between self-annihilation and plant-thinking insofar as both insist on engaging "in a dialogue with that which is on the edges of or beyond reason." Hollywood's interpretation of Marguerite shows mysticism as a practice that confronts readers, today, with that which they "don't want to relinquish."[5] From a rather different angle, Marder engages medieval mysticism from the perspective of plant intelligence, inscribing mystical self-annihilation in a vegetalizing of thought that challenges Western metaphysics to relinquish the ties still binding it to anthropocentrism. With mystical self-annihilation entwined with the vegetalizing of thought, Marder situates plant intelligence in the midst of practical contemplation.

Following this chapter, an alternative perspective is then offered in a brief interlude on Franciscan spirituality. I engage with Franciscan spirituality through a meditation on Giovanni Bellini's fifteenth-century painting *St. Francis in Ecstasy*. Playing with the visual rhymes between the posture of Francis and the painting's arboreal and mineral subjects, I draw art-historical readings of Bellini into conversation with a historical reflection on the meaning of ecstasy in medieval theology.

VIRIDITAS

By far the most significant example of vegetal mysticism occurs in the work of Hildegard of Bingen (c. 1098–1179). A contemporary of Bernard of Clairvaux and, like him, inspired by the imagery of the Biblical Song, Hildegard also anticipates the flowering of horticultural imagery in later women's mysticism, which we will also be discussing in this chapter. Hildegard, abbess of the convent at Disibodenberg, into which she was entered as a young girl, became known to her contemporaries as the "Sibyl of the Rhine." This epithet and her subsequent veneration were due to her ecstasies and mystical visions, which began at the age of three, but Hildegard was also a student of medicine and natural philosophy (in addition to composing music and poetry). Hildegard's visionary texts present a vivid cosmology of creaturely relation, and her approach has been characterized as "creation-centered mysticism."[6]

Hildegard's concept of *viriditas*, "greenness," has received particular attention given the remarkable way that Hildegard develops it in her medicine, mysticism, and poetry. Hildegard follows earlier theologians, notably Gregory the Great, in using *viriditas* to describe the coming of Christ. For Gregory, *viriditas* was necessary because of the "dryness" and aridity of spiritual life before its redemption.[7] Hildegard interprets *viriditas* in a similar way, linking it to the incarnation and Mary's womb. According to the famous words of Hildegard to Bernard, "through the sweet power of green vigor (*viriditas*) [the Father] sent the Word to the Virgin's womb where it took flesh like the honey in the honeycomb."[8] In one of her many song sequences, Mary is hailed by Hildegard as "the greenest branch (*viridissima virga*)," a play on the similarity between the Latin for virgin, *virgo*, and branch, *virga*.⁹ Similarly, in Hildegard's poetry *viriditas* is linked to *virginitas*, "virginity." The Church, too (always personified, in Christianity, as female), is joined frequently to *viriditas*.

For Liz Herbert McAvoy, the fact that *viriditas* is so often "cast within a feminine system of configurations" is significant.¹⁰ She situates it in the context of the nuns under Hildegard's supervision, consecrated virgins often addressed by Hildegard in her written work and the intended performers of her music. What intrigues McAvoy is Hildegard's choice to link *viriditas* to virginal femininity. With Barbara Newman and others, McAvoy agrees that *viriditas* is an ontological rather than strictly gender-coded concept for Hildegard, who never personifies *viriditas* as a woman but rather identifies *viriditas* with the activity of the Holy Spirit: "O greenness (*viriditas*) of God's finger / with which God built a vineyard / that shines in heaven / as an established pillar."¹¹ Here, *viriditas* is equated with nothing less than God's creative activity; indeed, *viriditas* in Hildegard's work is present in *all* creation, including minerals. An alternative perspective is provided by Sarah Ritchey in *Holy Matter: Changing Perceptions of the Material World in Late Medieval Christianity*. Ritchey shows how a rare daring is evident in Hildegard's willingness to inscribe (as she often does) female virginity as well as *viriditas* in the divine. Yet what makes it daring is the extent to which the imagery seems to rethink femininity, as well as the Holy Spirit. She writes: "By attributing to virginity the fecund characteristics of fruits and flowers, [Hildegard] naturalized the virgin birth as a process now to be expected, ordinary. Hildegard's natural theology of virginity endowed consecrated virgins with a formidable role. Their labor reestablished the world as a paradise garden, renewed its former greenness, its *viriditas*."¹² The way I read it, following Ritchey, the interweaving of *viriditas* with *virginitas*, greenness with virginity, is not a feminization of the divine so much as it is the latter's vegetalizing, for it is not female gender stereotypes that are elevated in Hildegard's mysticism. Rather, for Hildegard the activity of the Holy Spirit is reimagined in ways that insist on growth beyond the horizon of mammalian motherhood. Consecrated virgins do not bear children; if they participate in God's creative activity, it is not in a way determined by their reproductive organs. *Viriditas* points toward a gender-queer fecundity; it indicates that vegetal life is not defined by norms of sexual reproduction. Rather, life is constituted by a process of growth that includes sexual reproduction but ultimately precedes those norms and subverts them. And this is precisely the kind of subversion Hildegard appears to impute to Mary, the virgin above all to the medieval Christian imagination: "Unfolding your leaves, [Mary] blossomed / in another way / than Adam brought forth / the whole human race . . . O branch, God foresaw / your blossoming / on the first day of his creation."[13] The crucial significance of the virginal in Hildegard's work is that it evokes the power of growth by exposing the reader's assumptions about what constitutes fecundity. The nun's abstention from sexual reproduction in order (paradoxically) to flourish and create provides an opening, a point of contact, with the reproductive plasticity of vegetal life. Hildegard's *viriditas* parallels the gender-queer grafting practices in Gertrude's writing; as the activity of the Holy Spirit, it joins humans to God not in isolation from the rest of creation but through relating to matter's vibrant becoming: "The Holy Spirit is a life-giving life, / moving all things: / it is the root of the whole creation . . . arousing and resurrecting / all."[14] In this way, Hildegard may be seen to provide a recapitulation but also a metamorphosis of the Neoplatonic and early Christian mystical view according to which God is known in and as vegetal growth.

It is thus not surprising that Hildegard should pay attention to gardens, both tangible and imagined. Hildegard was a cloistered nun who spent many hours in gardens, whether to work or take refreshment. She studied the medicinal properties of plants and wrote an important work of medieval medicine.[15] The spiritual significance of gardens is interpreted by her chiefly in relation to the mysticism of the biblical Song of Songs. The appearance of *viriditas* in her text is often redolent of the Song and its garden. In *Columba aspexit*, originally performed by her nuns, a multilayered allegory centers on a priest, St. Maximin, celebrating the Eucharist. Drawing on the precedence set by Ecclesiasticus (the Book of Sirach) 50:8–9, where the high priest Simon is described as a "green shoot of Lebanon on a summer day," Hildegard weaves into her allegory of Maximin the vegetal metaphors of the Song. Here, Maximin is a *gemma*—a word meaning both "gemstone" and "bud"—in the "garden of the king," a garden possessing "the sweetest greenness (*suavissima viriditate*)."[16] *Suavissima* is an adjective more commonly used to describe erotic delight, as in the Song, where "love" (in the Latin Vulgate translation familiar to Hildegard) is named *suavis*. The process in which the Song's eroticism comes to light is thus through *viriditas*. The liturgy of celebrating mass was something Hildegard would have associated strongly with celibate, that is "virginal," men. The erotic nature of the garden is thus affirmed, but its definition is challenged. Instead of modeling erotic delight on lovers' heterosexual union, delight is inscribed in *viriditas*, vegetal life. As McAvoy puts it, the garden becomes "a place of *process* where abundance is the result of action and intra-action—which is by implication, immanent, ubiquitous, cyclical and perpetual; it blooms; it gives; it supplies; it oozes splendid aromas; it imbues the occupant with joy; it counters the intrusion of sin."[17] What Hildegard achieves is a relocation of Eden from eschatological elsewhere to immanent now. The paradisiacal garden is manifested in the letting-be of life to grow and thrive. Perhaps the most significant part of Hildegard's mysticism is thus the remarkable extent to which her understanding of *viriditas* mirrors plant life. Considered as a power, *viriditas* is immanent growth, indicating an activity of metamorphosis.

VIA VEGETATIVA

The significance of Hildegard's *viriditas* is also discussed by Michael Marder in *Green Mass: The Ecological Theology of Hildegard of Bingen*. In the next few sections, I will engage with Marder's suggestions—tentative but ripe with possibility—regarding the convergence between Hildegard's mysticism and the challenges raised by scientific studies of plant intelligence. In this way, I implicitly call into question the assumption that the mystic's vegetal world is primarily a matter of metaphor, or rather, I propose that what we find is a convergence between metaphor and way of life. "Mysticism is always a process and a way of life," Bernard McGinn reflects, arguing that the texts of mystics express these ways of life.[18] This is an insight that is borne out with especial clarity in Marder's reading of Hildegard. Hildegard, Marder argues, is difficult to read without noting "the Plotinian underpinnings of [her] analogies," for, like Plotinus, she relates contemplation to vegetal life.[19] But Hildegard also seems to take Plotinian analogies further. Hildegard, as Marder puts it, "vegetalizes" theology by comparing the Holy Spirit to *viriditas* but *also* when she performs the gesture of self-annihilation.

Hildegard often disowned authorship. "The words which I speak are not my own nor those of a human being," she writes in an oft-quoted letter to Wibert of Gembloux, in which Hildegard presents her spiritual autobiography: "What I say comes from the vision which I received from above."[20] Such statements were a common enough trope, not least in women's mysticism, but Marder wonders whether they might not reveal something significant about what he calls "plant-thinking": "Her words are not really hers. . . . A mediator, if not the medium where the luminous message travels, Hildegard situates herself in the middling position she shares with plants and with the incarnate Word."[21]

When Marder describes Hildegard's mysticism as offering a "middling position she shares with plants," this statement is based on both Hildegard's theology (according to which *viriditas* is Mediator-Spirit) and on the philosophy Marder develops in dialogue with plant science. In *Plant-Thinking: A Philosophy of Vegetal Life*, Marder attempts to answer the question: "Who," or "what," does the thinking among plants? He responds by pointing to the problems in assuming there is an isolatable subject who does the thinking. Rather, where plants are concerned it is better to speak of an "it thinks." But the latter can also be misunderstood, as if it were a matter of identifying some vast impersonal mind. The way trees are able to communicate with one another in a forest has sometimes been compared to a human brain, with trees acting like neurons and mycorrizal networks of fungi acting as the nervous system, allowing signals to pass smoothly between individual root systems. However, even this model does not do justice to the decentralized ways of plant intelligence. As Merlin Sheldrake has shown recently, modeling forests on human brains imposes a hierarchy that elevates plants above fungi and obscures the radically collaborative way in which forests "think."[22] In epistemological terms, plant-intelligence is not plant-centric, if by the latter we imagine plants coordinating to form a gigantic organism. Rather, Marder writes, where plant-thinking is concerned, "the spacings and connections, communication lines and gaps between the participants . . . prevail over what is delimited within them."[23] The vegetal "it thinks" is not analogous to the human brain, because the brain is centralized; if there is an analogy here, it is one in which the brain "is a neurological elaboration on the decentered vegetal *it thinks*."[24] This is why Marder argues that plants are mediums: not only because they mediate between humans and the sun, providing us with essential nutrients, but because their thinking is medial, operating not in but as the in-between. An interesting parallel thus emerges, for Marder, between the role of the mystic and the role of plants. The mystic too, as Hildegard expresses it, speaks in ways that disavow personal identity. For Marder, what is needed is not a plant-centric philosophy but one that can think *with plants*, that is, in the metamorphosing in-between. This is what Marder thinks Hildegard offers in her mysticism.

At first, Marder develops this account by focusing on Hildegard's vegetal allegories. As he indicates, the way Hildegard tells the story of theology shapes the latter differently "when graced by leaves and flowers, roots and branches." Marder focuses on the habits of language in Hildegard's prose and verse. Hildegard is well known for her vegetal metaphors but also for her allegorizing style. Marder draws a connection between the two: "Apparently ornamental, [the poetic forms] let language flourish and blossom without forcing it to bear fruit." One example introduced early on by Marder in *Green Mass* and elaborated in subsequent chapters is Hildegard's description of Mary as a "leafy branch." "When Hildegard calls Mary 'a leafy branch (*frondens virga*),'" writes Marder, "she is playing on the verge, with the verge shaped as a virgin (*virgo*) and a branch (*virga*)." In the place of a "virginal theology," Marder reads *viriditas* as a "verginal theology," where "the entire temporal order, the body, flowering flesh, femininity, and virginity are so many unavoidable digressions, diversions, detours on the itinerary of the divine missive that make it what it finally must become without the end transparently visible from the beginning." The gendered language of the body in medieval women's mysticism is often seen as a tacit resistance to male ideals of embodiment based on power and force. What Marder shows is that feminist accounts of mysticism may also double as queerly vegetal accounts. In this fashion, the mystic's insistence on plants makes clear not only the human but the androcentric bias of the subjectivity that construes God—and nature—as remote, abstract objects of contemplation. In *Green Mass*, Marder also lingers with the question of divine love, which he compares explicitly to vegetal life: "Plant-knowing is the wisdom of love, because, almost always, it knows the world by kissing."[25] "Kissing" is the gesture of human erotics, but it is also a way of understanding how plants *know*. Kissing means interactions with the elements in a nonviolent way that knows through touching and in which lack is not figured in terms of voids needing to be filled. Then kissing also signifies the mystical union, since the language appears in the Song of Songs 1:1: "let him kiss me with the kisses of his mouth," a phrase that inspires many lines in Hildegard's writings.

Marder also, however, points to a convergence between Hildegard's spiritual practice—her role as medium for the Holy Spirit—and what he calls plant-thinking. In her remarkable letter to Wibert, which I mentioned earlier, Hildegard responds to a request for descriptions of her ecstasies. By the twelfth century, "ecstasy" was a common way of referring to the state subsequent to contemplation, although it could also be used synonymously with contemplation. Typically, ecstasy was described as a liberation from the senses; the word itself means "to stand apart," signifying an experience of being alienated from oneself. Hildegard repeats this view, arguing that when she is in ecstasy she does not see by virtue of her bodily senses. In the same letter, however, Hildegard also insists that she is not in fact unconscious or indeed removed from her body during her ecstasies: "I never experience the unconsciousness of ecstasy, but *I see all as if awake*, whether by day or night," she writes. Instead of experiencing mystical union as a release from the body, Hildegard experiences a different way of being embodied, a different way of being "awake." Her eyes are open, her senses are alive, indeed, she insists that she *does* see and hear; the difference is that in ecstasy the senses are as one: "I simultaneously see, hear, and understand."[26] To Marder, Hildegard's insistence on embodiment (albeit a transformed one) speaks directly to her concept of *viriditas*. If, as Hildegard argues, the Holy Spirit is *viriditas*, then experiencing the presence of God cannot take place outside the senses; at the same time, the fact that *viriditas* moves the body at a deep level not ordinarily accessed by awareness means that being attentive to it likely will feel like an out-of-body experience. For Marder, this paradox is brought to light through a reconsideration of mysticism as a *via vegetativa*, a "path of vegetation."[27] According to mystical theology, God is reached through a "path of negation," a *via negativa*, in which the senses, language, thought, and the sense of self are abandoned, as we see in Hildegard's letter to Wibert. Yet Hildegard in fact speaks of the experience of senses *transformed* rather than transcended. For Marder, one way of reading the role of negation in mysticism is thus not as an erasure of corporeality but rather as an extended shift in awareness, from human to vegetal mindfulness. What Hildegard describes in her account of ecstasy—in which she claims to be awake and perceptive yet no longer able to discern or process sense perception—is of a piece with Marder's understanding of plant-thinking, according to which plants sense the world without the mediation of concepts. Rather, plant-thinking is for Marder itself the middle; it is the medium that is the condition for the possibility of thought. Hildegard's description of ecstasy also intersects with one description of plant intelligence, according to which, as I showed earlier, Daniel Chamovitz suggests that plants have "anoetic consciousness." Plants sense the world and respond to external and internal stimuli, yet they do not "see" in pictures or "think" in concepts.[28] If, as Marder asserts, Hildegard's mysticism is a vegetalizing of theology, then the way of negation, the *via negativa*, is also a *via vegetativa*, a path toward—rather than away from—the growth that is life.

In summary, Marder's *Green Mass* resonates with Liz Herbert McAvoy's and Sarah Ritchey's readings of Hildegard, which see in *viriditas* a way of reclaiming the idea of mystical passivity through a radical reframing of corporeality as vegetal life. The critical insight borne out by these readings of Hildegard is that, for the life of the mystic, union with God is difficult to separate from an experience of being attuned, more deeply than before, to the body. Here, what happens in ecstasy is not the abandonment of the body in favor of God but rather an experience of recognizing God in radical corporeality. Hildegard presents a sensory experience of ecstasy, and one that insists on sensory knowledge, albeit of a kind that seems to kick back against the conventional idea of what it means to be "awake" to the world. In the same way, intelligence is today claimed for plants but in ways that reject, utterly, the conventional identification of intelligence with brain-led consciousness. It is not surprising, then, that Hildegard's vegetal imagery, her concept of *viriditas*, should also be associated with her mysticism. Rather, vegetal life seems to inscribe itself in ecstasy.

GRAFTING MYSTICAL UNION

Over the course of the thirteenth century, several women monastics connected to Bernard's Cistercian order (an offshoot of the Benedictines) developed the mystical garden in fascinating ways. They were aided by Bernard's influential sermons and other popular allegories exploring theology through the lens of garden hermeneutics. Of special interest is the garden imagery found in the writings of the Benedictine Gertrude the Great of Helfta (1256–1302), recently the subject of an important study by Liz Herbert McAvoy, Patricia Skinner, and Theresa Tyers.[29] Where previous scholars have focused on the relationship of garden imagery to human sexuality, McAvoy, Skinner, and Tyers's work pays attention to the way garden imagery also relates to the ways of plants. In the third book of her *Herald of God's Loving-Kindness*, Gertrude uses imagery drawn from grafting to articulate her experience of ecstasy.[30] Together with similar themes found in the work of her Helfta sisters, the metaphor is taken "to far greater heights than any previous or contemporary writers, reworking it ultimately to become a 'language' of some authority with which to speak of the divine."[31] In the medieval period, grafting came into fashion as a popular pastime, being widely written about in gardening manuals. It also began to appear in medieval romances as a metaphor for sexual intercourse. Yet grafting, according to a long-established theological view, was also viewed as morally ambiguous; it was thought that grafting was "unnatural," since it caused fruit to be borne by two plants not able to propagate by sexual means.³² As McAvoy, Skinner, and Tyers show, what is striking about the Helfta nuns in this context is their willingness to use such a fraught metaphor when describing how God related to humans. The ease with which Gertrude draws on the language of grafting reflects "the expansion of grafting's purpose from utility to delectation." Grafting also has a long biblical history, with Paul referring to early Christians as scions grafted into Jewish rootstock and Jewish "converts" as being grafted "back into" the tree of faith (Romans 11:11–31). The grafts of the Helfta sister Gertrude, however, are different. Here, Christ is scion, as well as rootstock, roles he exchanges with the mystic. The coming-together that is mystical grafting does not depend on hierarchical power-over but rather on "interchangeable" power relationships.³³

The authors point to the erotic imagery of Gertrude's mystical gardens, which at first appear to reinforce a gender binary but quickly reveal a more fluid configuration. Bernard is the main point of comparison: For Bernard (whose mystical garden would have been well known to the Helfta sisters), mystical union is modeled on heterosexual, human intercourse. At first, it seems that Gertrude conforms to this image and reinforces it: She sees herself as a Bride awaiting Christ in a fragrant paradise.³⁴ However, Gertrude also overlays this heterosexual imagery with a vision of union based on a type of asexual plant reproduction: grafting. Gertrude pictures herself as a plant, with Christ grafted onto her female "rootstock." Gertrude also acts as a scion, grafting herself onto Christ's wounded side, "[beholding] her soul ... in the likeness of a tree fixing its roots in the wound side of Jesus Christ."³⁵ The result is ecstasy expressed in a "range of sexualized and often gender-queer 'grafting' practices" where the female coding of Bernard's mystical garden undergoes metamorphosis. It is an image that disturbs the idea of mystical erotics modeled on heterosexual intercourse. At the same time, Gertrude retains the heterosexual coupling that is the basis for the Song: Bride and Bridegroom are united. What shifts is the manner of union: The penetration in question is reciprocal, received both by Gertrude and by Christ. Gertrude is "combining both hermeneutic sets," the sets of heterosexual coupling and plant reproduction, "into a hybridized linguistic agent."[36] The mystical language thus is itself a kind of graft, taking on the qualities of the grafting it describes. As Gertrude imagines herself grafted to Christ and Christ grafted to her, the language of mystical union merges with that of vegetal life.

The ineffable union between human and God is communicated here through a reflection on grafting practices. We encountered the idea of a spiritual grafting in the previous chapter, when we looked at how contemporary commentators interpret the spiritual practice of tree-sitting. However, the example of Gertrude draws directly on grafting practices when picturing mystical union, inscribing it into her most intimate accounts of ecstasy. In this way, Gertrude's texts suggest a geography that is "simultaneously material and spiritual," in which an originally allegorical garden is rethought through contemporary horticultural practices.[37]

McAvoy develops an interpretation of mystical grafting into a more systematic form of feminist theology in *The Enclosed Garden and the Medieval Religious Imaginary*, discussing in detail the way the Helfta mystics' use of grafting imagery destabilizes the power dynamics encoded in medieval biblical and theological understandings of the metaphor. In addition to secular horticulture, the main theological backdrop is Romans 11:11–31, where Paul threatens the Gentiles with being "grafted" into the Christian faith unless they convert and where God is described as having the power to graft persons back into divine rootstock.

As McAvoy points out, although grafting in the ancient world was widely used, it was seen nonetheless as morally ambiguous and "contrary to nature"—a term also used to describe illegitimate sexual practices. Paul's choice of metaphor can be seen to be based as much on the idea of coercion as on intercourse. Despite the flourishing of grafting as a practice, its ambiguous status was recognized by many medieval theologians, both Christian and Jewish, and is reflected in Moses Maimonides's association of grafting to pagan fertility rites; according to this view, which was repeated also by Thomas Aquinas, grafting resembled transgressive coitus producing "unnatural" offspring. The same idea of unnatural union is discernible, for McAvoy, in the Helfta mystics' reimagining of the erotic imagery associated with mystical union. For McAvoy it thus becomes important to recognize that the associations with a perceived "unnatural" behavior were not being avoided by Gertrude. Rather, "the women of Helfta . . . fearlessly take the metaphor of grafting to far greater heights than any previous or contemporary writers, exploiting its 'unnatural' connotations to express their understanding of the supranatural qualities of the divine and how these may, indeed, be 'grafted' onto the human."[38] Because of God's supernatural qualities, union with God is imagined in ways that, indeed, run contrary to "nature." But instead of picturing the contranatural in otherworldly terms, the Helfta mystics draw a structural homology between the supernatural divine and vegetal nonhuman. McAvoy blends the emergent, secular understanding of grafting as pleasurable pastime and lovers' union with the ambiguities inherent in the theological sense of grafting as both spiritual *and* as "against nature." Her understanding of mystical grafting proposes that the Helfta mystics recast rather than reject the idea of grafting as unnatural: The mystics need to unite to God in unnatural ways because God is supernatural, yet by casting the supernatural in terms of the vegetal, the otherworldly associations of divine supernaturalism are also held in doubt. As McGinn also points out in relation to Gertrude's work more broadly, she retains a "sense of belonging to heaven while still on earth . . . all things, the power and virtue of her soul and body, as well as the divine attributes and all creation, are called upon to offer jubilation to God."[39]

In this regard, the main attribute of grafting is radical openness to the other. However, this openness also signals radical reciprocity, since what grafting indicates is not a one-sided power relationship but an activity of co-becoming and symbiosis, of species "intra-action" rather than species interaction. Hence the interpretation, by McAvoy, Skinner, and Tyers, of these grafting practices as gender queer. Moreover, like the philosophies of interrelation, mystic grafting takes place in between parts of plants, which merge into a new plant with the ability to bear fruit. In this sense, the Helfta mystics' grafting imagery becomes a way of thinking philosophy beyond species hierarchies.

The foregrounding of plant life in McAvoy's reading of mystical grafting entails a new way of reading plant imagery in medieval mysticism. The world of plants, and especially of gardens, can be, as she puts it, "necrophiliac," emphasizing escapist fantasies of a return to paradisiacal existence after death. She sees such necrophiliac interpretations subverted in the mystical garden of medieval women, in particular when it comes to the grafting imagery of Gertrude. What happens in Gertrude's mystical gardens offers "opportunities for ideologically resistant, female-coded counter-narratives based on . . . flourishing and vegetal becoming identified by . . . Marder."[40] Indeed, as Marder writes in *Grafts*: "Grafting foregrounds the plasticity and receptivity of vegetal life, its constitutive capacity for symbiosis and metamorphosis, its openness to the other at the expense of fixed identities (even the identity ensconced in genetics) revealed, by their vitality, as illusory." Gertrude's idea of grafting resists identifying mystical union with species thought. Marder, as we have already intimated briefly, argued that grafting is not exclusive to plants. Although plants are able to reproduce through grafting, "the very fact that grafts can refer to animal or human tissues as well as to plant parts testifies to the word's and the practice's quiet rebellion against the strictures of identity." For McAvoy, when Gertrude recasts mystical union as grafting, her gender-queer interpretation of the practice points toward a similar, quiet rebellion against the strictures of identity. Grafting "discloses the vegetal character of corporeality" as such.[41] For McAvoy, when the Helfta mystics redraw mystical union as grafting, they are also demonstrating the way vegetal being is shared between species. Grafting as life's capacity for symbiosis and metamorphosis is situated at the point where, in mysticism, the human soul fuses with God as giver of life. God does not negate life, and the overlap between God and vegetal life is striking.

CONTESTED PRACTICES: CONCEDING TO NATURE WHAT IT SEEKS AND DESIRES

I will now be drawing on these vegetal readings of medieval mysticism and begin to develop a theme that has already appeared in Marder's work: the relationship between spiritual practices and vegetal life. Although vegetal life is not a prominent theme in her mysticism, the tradition of the *via negativa* with which Marder plays when creating the pun *via vegetativa* is significant to Marguerite of Porete (b. 1250). Marguerite, a French-speaking mystic, was accused of heresy and burned at the stake in Paris in 1310. I am interested, first, in the practice that Marguerite recommended, a practice she called self-annihilation before God, and the relationship between this practice and what she writes regarding nature. I will then suggest how her remarks on nature can be put into conversation with Marder's understanding of vegetal life.

Marguerite is thought to have belonged to the Beguines, a popular female spiritual movement with origins in twelfth-century Belgium. The Beguines, many of whom were accused of heresy (in some contexts, the word "Beguine" was synonymous with "heretic"), consisted of women who had taken informal vows to remain celibate but were not under the obligations of a monastic rule. In part, their persecution was motivated by misogyny and the fear of women's independence; in part, it was also driven by a widespread theological worry regarding mysticism. As Bernard McGinn points out, the medieval period was one of "unprecedented debate over the orthodoxy of certain forms of mysticism." The combination of negative theology with cosmism was seen as particularly contentious. Especially in Northern Europe and the Low Countries, but also in France, negative theology developed into an affective piety centered around the wordless, ecstatic enjoyment of God in this life, that is, in the body. Perhaps for this reason, nature became significant for those writers who emphasized negative theology. At any rate, even though "pantheism" did not yet exist as a term of abuse (being coined only in the late seventeenth century), McGinn argues that Beguine mysticism is distinct for leaning toward pantheist ideas in all but name.[42]

Marguerite was harangued for writing that "the soul annihilated in love of the Creator, without blame of conscience or remorse, can and ought to concede to nature whatever it seeks and desires," which, as one commentator puts it, "manifestly rings of heresy."[43] In Marguerite's only (known) text and the subject of her condemnation, *The Mirror of Simple Souls* (c. 1300), nature indeed plays a central albeit easily overlooked role. Originally composed in French, the *Mirror* is written as a dialogue, with Love instructing Soul and leading her to union with God through the annihilation of the individual will and its absorption in God. Along the way, Marguerite personifies Nature as a temptress, "subtle," full of lies and deception, all of which must be overcome by progressing through good works, meditation, contemplation, and finally the perfect annihilation—in God—of reason, will, and finally desire. At face value, then, Marguerite appears to deny nature. Yet the *Mirror* explains that it is possible to unite with God in this life, that is, in the body. Her book, as she presents it, is not a description of the afterlife but of lay practice, directed at readers she describes as "simple," meaning ordinary. In an exchange between Love and Divine Righteousness, the two explain to Soul that the spiritual way is not that of denying the body. "Why should . . . souls feel guilty about taking what is necessary if necessity asks for it?" Love and Divine Righteousness continue: "We receive the service of the four elements as Nature has need of without reproach to Reason. . . . These elements were graciously made by God as other things."[44] Moreover, although God is described by Marguerite as simple thought, divine simplicity is glossed in creaturely terms: God is "one simple Being of *overflowing fruition*."[45] In the *Mirror*, overcoming nature entails rejecting not creation as such but whatever it is that impedes a person from enjoying creation as God's work. In other words, Marguerite recapitulates the monastic ideal according to which union with God is presented as, paradoxically, both natural *and* contranatural but in which ultimately God is pictured in vegetal terms.

Despite its apparent independence from nature, and even from contemplation (in Marguerite's work, a lesser stage of spiritual practice), mystical self-annihilation thus bears a fascinating relationship to nature, as Amy Hollywood hints in *Acute Melancholia and Other Essays*. In the way Hollywood reads Marguerite, a mystic annihilates their self not by escaping nature or denying it but by letting-go to their "natural" rhythms and inclinations, without needing to experience the body as an obstacle. In this way, "[the mystic] can give to nature anything it wants and all that it wants will be licit."[46] Self-annihilation, in this sense, is the key to recognizing natural movements. But the vital role of self-annihilation in women's mysticism is frequently read differently: Over the past century, it has often been studied as an example of extreme world renunciation. In contrast to these readings, Hollywood suggests a model that, although it does not refer to vegetal life, nonetheless crosses paths with Marder's plant-thinking. Insofar as the vegetal is apparent in mysticism, it is not only in imagery pertaining to plants but also in practices pertaining to the loss of self in ecstasy and the transformations that issue from this loss.

However, what Marguerite means by "nature" does depend, in a crucial sense, on the context of the reader, as Hollywood has showed in her study *The Soul as Virgin Wife*. Marguerite leaves the "nature" of nature undeveloped or, better, purposefully ambiguous so as not to give false encouragement to the reader who is only a beginner on the path of prayer. "In renouncing the reason and the will," Hollywood writes, "the soul overcomes her only ties to the fleshly or bodily aspect of human nature and is no longer touched by their demands (except, the soul cautions, as they are necessary to maintain life)." That "except" is vital but seems to give to nature a vanishingly small role. Here, the "natural" body is liberated, but at the expense of reason, will, and desire—all the things that characterize a human experience.[47] Yet precisely for this reason, are they not also indicative of something *different* to the assumptions commonly held about what it means to be human? This question arises in Hollywood's *Acute Melancholia.* In a thought-provoking chapter on Marguerite, Hollywood begins by comparing Marguerite's mysticism to the act of critical reading. Observing that in critical reading a bracketing of personal inclinations similar to that enjoined by Marguerite is advised, Hollywood wonders whether self-annihilation has not often been misunderstood. "We often presume that to read religiously is to read *uncritically*," she reflects, "yet for Marguerite, the insight gained through the annihilation of reason, will, and desire gives rise to a powerful critique of reason itself." For Hollywood, this critique is powerful because it questions the assumption at the core of critical reading: the necessity of a reading grounded in rational reflection. For Hollywood, what is at stake in the *Mirror*'s call to liberate the body from reason is mindfulness rather than skepticism; it is a reminder that reason is fallible and that needful counterperspectives can be gained by considering alternative viewpoints. At this moment, Hollywood shifts in her approach to the *Mirror* from considering it as a literary text to viewing it, briefly, as a practical manual, asking: "What would it mean for me to read in the way Marguerite's text demands, to annihilate myself before the power of divine Love? ... Most importantly, how can I allow—and when might I claim successfully to have allowed—alternative conceptions of rationality, or conceptions of criticism not grounded in rationality, to challenge my own assumptions about critical reading? ... What is challenged by Marguerite that I don't want to relinquish?" To Hollywood, what a truly "critical" reading of Marguerite reveals is not consensus on the meaning of the *Mirror* but a willingness "to try to hear what I cannot assimilate."⁴⁸ What the *Mirror*'s unassimilable content might be, however, Hollywood leaves open. That it is divine *Love* is not held in doubt. But what is divine Love, for Marguerite?

A MIRROR FOR METAMORPHOSING LIFE

The problem with divine Love in the *Mirror* is that it claims the desire of Soul *after its annihilation of desire*. Not only will and reason but also desire is to be annihilated, for Marguerite—but how is it possible to experience love without desire? The question, of course, is not unique to Marguerite, and the idea of desire without lack (the prerequisite for human desire) is a commonplace paradox in Christian mysticism. Instead of looking to historical debates, however, I propose that Hollywood's question might be addressed through an entwinement with the readings of vegetal-mystical ecstatic erotics we have seen so far. Despite a marked difference to McAvoy, Marder, and others, Hollywood draws attention to the overlap between God, mystic, and *nature* in mystical self-annihilation. Like Marder, Hollywood views self-annihilation not as a rejection of the world but as an attunement to corporeality. Furthermore, both Marder and Hollywood are interested in rethinking *thought* from a perspective that does not privilege the activities usually looked to as its standards: will, rational deliberation, and indeed desire (as I will examine shortly). Second, the vegetalizing of thought, which Marder ascribes to Hildegard's spiritual practice, gains a denser outline in Hollywood's study of Marguerite. To be clear, Hollywood does not use the term "vegetal" in her reading of Marguerite or mystical self-annihilation more broadly. However, her reading of Marguerite—which positions Marguerite's work as an attempt to redeem the body not only from the rationale associating corporeality with sin, guilt, and shame but also from human reason—suggests an approach to corporeality driven by what can best be described as a recognition of the "plant in us." Yet for Marder the plant in us is not species specific, and the recognition of our constitution by vegetal life ends not in a new, existential determination but rather in a confrontation with metamorphosis and the destruction of certainty. In this sense, Hollywood's questioning and her own refusal to determine an answer to the question evoked for her by the *Mirror* is instructive and can help us deepen what Marder means by mysticism's vegetalization of thought. Though Hollywood does not engage with vegetal language when she discusses the *Mirror*, her understanding of nature in relation to God recapitulates the descriptions of gardens, plants, and *viriditas* that interest McAvoy, Marder, and others: Here, a vegetal growth that precedes organismic and species-specific determination is what is at stake. Finally, Hollywood's reading of the *Mirror* through self-questioning, doubt, and aporia indicates a process of metamorphosis that demonstrates, in practical terms, what it might mean to listen better to the "plant in us."

Reading with Hollywood, for whom Marguerite's God is discovered in or as—rather than beyond—nature, one might thus graft Marguerite's mysticism to Gertrude's grafts and Hildegard's *viriditas*, noting the extent to which Marguerite's description of self-annihilation, although relatively bereft of vegetal metaphors, mirrors what Marder calls mysticism's *via vegetativa*, its "path of vegetation." What is distinctive of Marder's concept is its play on *negativa*, the mystical "negations" often characterized by commentators as highly abstract: According to this view, apophatic theology abstracts the mind from nature to lead it to God. Hollywood's reading, although it develops along different lines to those of Marder and McAvoy, shares a commitment to challenging the idea that mysticism always leads away from nature. Hollywood's reading suggests that, for some mystics, an inverse relationship was true, with mystical self-annihilation constituting not an abstraction from nature but a destruction of the abstractions impeding easeful enjoyment of corporeality. It is also important to note, in this context, how Hollywood also asserts that Marguerite's accusers were not wrong in identifying this idea in the *Mirror*, even though their violent reaction to Marguerite's idea—leading to her execution—must be rejected as horrific. Rather, in a gesture not dissimilar to that of McAvoy reading Gertrude and Hildegard, Hollywood associates Marguerite positively with heresy. The similarity of the *Mirror* to heresy casts into clearer relief Marguerite's connection to the historical movements I discussed in the previous chapters, as well as some of the issues at stake in the burning of Marguerite. Those issues, of course, far exceed what I have been able to sketch here, and Hollywood also provides a much more detailed study of the theological, political, and literary complexities surrounding the *Mirror*. Yet the natural quality of self-annihilation is important and a question that deserves more attention than it has so far received. Mystical self-annihilation is a practice that declares the path to God to lie within, liberating a person from the mediation of priests and institutions, yet the emphasis on interiority is in part an illusion, since what is annihilated above all is the self, that is, interiority, and what is recovered is corporeality. In Marguerite's *Mirror*, this idea takes on explicitly political forms when she argues that priests are not necessary and that spiritual perfection is possible for all, even for the "simplest" of souls—if not especially for the simple.

We also find in Hollywood's reading of divine Love traces of the gender-queer vegetal sexuality encountered among recent interpretations of Gertrude and Hildegard. While Hollywood does not make any allusions to the vegetal, McAvoy and Marder do elaborate the relationship between God and vegetal life when it comes to desire. In the mysticism of Gertrude and Hildegard, desire is signaled by vegetal growth constituting the image of mystical eroticism. This vegetal life prefiguring mystical-erotic union invariably questions the assumptions brought to the concept of "desire." In McAvoy's reading of Gertrude, we find that sexual union is imagined as a grafting practice, while her interpretation of Hildegard stresses the gender-queer qualities of vegetal reproduction. Marder, for his part, focuses on the figuring of divine love in the Song's garden as vegetal "kissing." In either case, thinking desire with plants helps expose the degree to which concepts of desire are modeled, narrowly, on heterosexual but also more broadly animal pleasure. The fact that vegetal life is constitutive of animal life then becomes significant. As Jacob Erickson remarks in "Irreverent Theology: On the Queer Ecology of Creation," "if animal sexuality . . . is far more complex than is often assumed, what does that mean for theological reflection, ecological relationships, or human life and responsibility for nonhuman life?"[49] Divine love becomes a figuration of vegetal desire. Divine love means desiring in the manner of the "plant in us." My interest following these readings is in how they both recapitulate but also transform traditional definitions of divine love in which desire is proposed in nonhuman terms and in how such concepts might be lived through attentiveness to the metamorphic plasticity of life.

By engaging with these vegetal interpretations of medieval women's mysticism, I have situated ecstasy in the midst of life, in mystics' attentiveness to the "plant in us." The matter that now emerges concerns the practicing of such attentiveness and how mystics taught attentiveness. I will be addressing this question by lingering at length with a particular mystic and her texts of spiritual direction. While the ideas I have been considering are invaluable for allowing a vegetal interpretation of mysticism to take root, they have been concerned mostly with drawing connections between ideas, images, and descriptions of experience: The question of *what* practices mystics are referring to in their accounts remains to be answered. It goes without saying that those practices are as varied as the mystics who experienced them and are particular to context and individual inclinations. Yet certain key elements have already come to light, most important among them interior peace (in the previous chapter) and, in this chapter, self-annihilation. But what *is* self-annihilation? How is it practiced? And what might a closer look at the practice reveal about the entwinement I am proposing here, between mystical and vegetal being? I will be turning to the early modern women mystics striving to articulate a way of experiencing God without the aid of clerical guidance, a notion that resonates strongly with the tradition represented in writers like Marguerite. The tentative lines I have drawn between self-annihilation and vegetal being are partly elaborated in the work of Jeanne Guyon, who attempts to analyze the anatomy of ecstasy in nonorganismic ways that take its guidance from the elements—even though her imagery is often drawn from animal life too. It is in the highly systematized mysticism of the early modern period that I will find the most fruitful ground for vegetal mysticism.

Interlude

FRANCIS IN ECSTASY

Between Marguerite and Guyon several centuries of development in Western Christian mysticism unfold. While this book is philosophical-theological, rather than historical, even the selective vignettes I offer here would be incomplete without some mention of medieval Franciscan spirituality. Much has been written regarding Francis of Assisi's love for creatures, especially after Pope John Paul II and then Pope Francis placed Franciscan spirituality at the center of the ecological conversion of the Roman Catholic Church.[1] The literature on Franciscan nature mysticism, however, has focused mostly on how Francis interacted with creatures. What I will be reflecting on here is different and pertains to the connection between mystical practice and what is shared between species, drawing attention to the activities associated, in this book, with vegetal life: attentiveness, sensory perception, and metamorphosis. It will also be somewhat more imaginative, in the literal sense: I will be moving from text to visual art, considering ways in which vegetal mysticism may be seen to come to light in Renaissance painting.

According to Catholic tradition, Francis was fasting and praying in the mountain of Verna when he saw a seraph (a type of angel) nailed to a cross, who then granted Francis the stigmata, or five wounds of Christ. In the centuries that followed, it became increasingly common to depict the ecstasy of Francis as an outdoor event and to emphasize the rocky wilderness where Francis received his stigmata. In fact, landscape painting in Italy owes a debt to the iconographic tradition surrounding Francis's ecstasy, and later medieval and early Renaissance painters certainly came to view landscape painting as a religious expression. One of the more stunning examples of landscape painting inspired by Francis' story is the painting by Giovanni Bellini known as *St. Francis in Ecstasy* or alternatively as *St. Francis in the Desert* (c. 1475–1480), now held in the Frick Collection in New York. The reason for its double attribution relates to its emphasis on landscape and creatures. Unlike conventional portrayals of Francis's stigmatization, Bellini's painting contains astonishingly few references to the wounds piercing the hands of the saint: While there are faint red marks staining Francis's palms, there are no markings on his feet or on his chest. There is also no hint of the seraph usually pictured together with Francis at the moment when he receives the stigmata. Instead, a tree occupies the place where the viewer might expect the seraph to appear. Francis himself stands in the midst of a rocky landscape on the outskirts of a city. The place is painted in vivid detail. In the immediate foreground is a grotto; at the grotto's opening is a makeshift oratory, overgrown with ivy. Francis stands with his back to the oratory, face tilted upward and arms outstretched, looking toward the sky and out over the valley below, as sunlight pools on the surface of the rock behind him. A few paces away stands Francis's donkey, looking in the same direction as the saint. That is the whole scene: There is very little to suggest an extraordinary event.[2]

Still more striking is the fact that, on Bellini's canvas, Francis is not the only creature looking up in rapture at the sun, which

FIGURE I.1. Giovanni Bellini, *St. Francis in the Desert* (or *St. Francis in Ecstasy*), c. 1480, oil on panel.
Source: Frick Collection, New York.

shines not on Francis alone but on several parts of the ecology of which he is a part. There is the donkey, whose head is facing a similar direction as Francis's, but there are also the stone walls of the city in the background and the rock of the grotto, all of them basking in the sun's glow. Then there is the tree in the upper-left-hand corner, its boughs bending in toward the center of the canvas, creating a visual rhyme with the backward-arching posture of Francis. This bending curve is seen also in the illuminated part of the rock we see above Francis, again suggesting an anticipation of Francis's bodily posture. In fact, compared to the landscape, Francis appears to stand somewhat out of the light, with the mountainside and crevice plants receiving the majority of the sun's glow.

I am drawn to the visual rhyme between Francis's posture and the shape of the tree and the view of the rock. Francis's posture is receptive, but he is not kneeling; rather, his body is open and opening to the elements, which seem to draw him outward. The fact that the posture is repeated in the tree and the rock is significant. Rather than paint the landscape as a vivid backdrop to Francis's ecstasy, Bellini has painted the ecstatic Francis as but one in a crowd of creaturely ecstasies.

How to interpret this rhyme? Today, "ecstasy is a word that speaks of extremes," writes Peter Kwasniewski, yet in medieval theology it *also* spoke of the common experience of creatures, with an "'ecstasy of nature' no less than an ecstasy of grace" informing theological reflection on mystical union.[3] Looking at Bellini, I see intimations of an old tradition, stretching back to the Psalms, in which creatures are described as praising God. I also see traces of the Neoplatonic notion of nature contemplating, and of contemplation, in turn, as vegetal life—an idea we encountered in the previous chapter. Indeed, Kwasniewski detects traces of both Jewish and Greek traditions in medieval mysticism, including Franciscan mysticism. Among medieval theologians, it was widely believed that "*exstasis* [was] not held to be an extraordinary phenomenon at the remotest edge of possibility, irrelevant to common life." Kwasniewski notes the presence of this idea in Franciscan thought. Bonaventure (c. 1221–1274) saw ecstasy as "the normal culmination of the life of charity," "common to earth and heaven," pointing to the example of Francis.[4] Bonaventure imagines Francis living in a state of perpetual contemplation, constantly receptive to God; he also emphasizes Francis's famed friendship with creatures of all kinds. Roger of Provence, one of the earliest Franciscan mystics, writes in his *Meditations*, "even now as you withdraw yourself from God, all other creatures approach him and draw near to him. Do they not condemn you?"[5] In Franciscan spirituality, creatures of all kinds were thought to evidence the spiritual life, as Roger suggests. While humans withdrew from God, other creatures drew near to God effortlessly.

Kevin Corrigan points to a fact little noted by scholars, that in Greek *ekstasis*, "'standing aside' or 'outside' of one's normal nature or position does not simply connote extraordinary or preternatural experience, but the ordinary experience of existing in a world of change." The word "ecstasy," whose etymology relates to the physical phenomenon of growth by "displacement," is thus not confined to the mind: "ecstasy also points to the path of organic . . . development." However, "creatures too can be properly ecstatic toward other creatures." As Corrigan remarks, for Christian mystics, mystical union is shaped at the onset by a "profound paradox," since the Good experienced through contemplation is also the common experience of creatures. As a result, what is perceived in mystical union is a closeness with God but also with the world, "that ineffable generative power from which everything comes. . . . Mystical union is the most concrete experience." For Corrigan, this explains the otherwise puzzling way in which Christian mystics tended to view mystical union as an experience "shared" (or "participated") with creatures: "What each individual self is most fully is also paradoxically that which contributes most to the whole and which is, therefore, in a sense most shared."[6] The Western Christian mystical tradition, writes Kwasniewski, retains the idea that "the ecstasy of love takes place at all levels of being: it is the yearning of the cosmos, of all creatures, for their Maker."[7]

Returning to Bellini's painting, it is this movement of "organic development," "in a sense most shared" that, when I look at

Bellini's painting, creates connections between the visual depiction of Francis and vegetal life. Moreover, it encourages, in my reading, the roots of contemplation in *ekstasis* to entangle with the vegetal roots of nature in *phusis*. In both cases, growth appears through change but also through receptivity. What continues to draw my eye when it comes to Bellini's painting is thus not so much the preponderance of creatures other than humans as the way in which those creatures are drawn. In the painting known both as *St. Francis in Ecstasy* and *St. Francis in the Desert* a human in ecstasy is made to appear as sharing in the attitude of a tree and a rock. Rather than depict Francis's ecstasy as abnormal or extraordinary in relation to the creatures around him, Bellini chooses (for whatever reason, wittingly or unwittingly) to paint ecstasy across species. The tree and the rock, with their apparent stillness and passivity, exemplify the ecstasy depicted. According to this reading, Bellini's Francis would suggest a humanization of vegetal life (*vegetal life is ecstatic!*) but, equally, a vegetalization of ecstasy (*ecstasy is all vegetal!*). Such a reading is of course speculative. At the same time, art historians have come to similar conclusions regarding the theological implications of the painting. As Anthony Janson has shown, one plausible interpretation of *St. Francis in Ecstasy* is that Bellini has combined references to the stigmatization with visual cues belonging to another famous instance of ecstasy in the life of Francis, the moment when, looking in rapture at the sky, Francis composes the Hymn of the Sun. This poem begins with a greeting to God, followed by an enumeration of creaturely life, from the Sun to the Moon and the Earth, to Death: "Most High, all-powerful, good Lord . . . Praised be You, my Lord, with all your creatures, especially Sir Brother Sun, Who is the day and through whom You give us light . . . Praised be You, my Lord, through Sister Moon and the stars . . . Praised be You my Lord through our

Sister, Mother Earth . . . Praised be You, my Lord through Sister Death."[8] The link between Bellini's painting and the Hymn of the Sun has been resisted on the grounds that Francis's attitude in the pictures is "receptive" rather than "creative," yet an attitude of wonder and openness corresponds very well with the Hymn's sentiment. "Even if one does not agree that Francis is bellowing out a song," remarks Janson, "there is compelling reason to accept that he is looking in a state of inspiration to the sun, and that is the manifest relation between Bellini's and the saint's attitude toward nature."[9] It is this connection between the activity of the mystic and the activities that make life possible that I want to think with in the remaining two chapters.

4

LET NATURE BE AROUSED!

When I began practicing mystical prayer, I was in my late twenties. I remember joking to myself how lucky I was not to be a consecrated virgin. Unlike so many of the historical mystics I read about, I would be able to see if Georges Bataille had been right and experience for myself whether intense mystical states ultimately were indistinct from orgasm.[1] While the experiences I had subsequently were certainly *erotic*, they were not *sexual*, however. The language of enjoyment, delight, and arousal, so prominent in Western Christian mysticism, was both confirmed and defamiliarized. What I experienced was arousal, yet not arousal of my sexual organs. Rather, it was an arousal of my senses, of something deep and unconscious slowly erupting into conscious awareness. I was able to feel myself *feel*. It was this experience that initially made me think of contemplative, mystical states as vegetative. Feeling what it was to feel, I was made aware of myself as a sensitive creature, as participating in the sensitive life of other creatures.

The forms of mysticism that have appeared in this book entwine with vegetal being in a variety of ways that shatter the mystic's sense not only of self but also of human identity. We find significant metaphors of vegetal being in descriptions of contemplation, mystical union, and ecstasy, pointing toward a mystical rethinking of the vegetative soul. Contemplative life, in turn, we find indicative of both vegetative and divine life. The reality of vegetal life, however, also worries a tendency to idealize the passivity of the plant. As such, vegetal mysticism does not replace divine life with plant life by idealizing plants as other, remote or abstract. Rather, by insisting that God can be experienced in this life, it moves *both plants and humans* but also divinity toward common movements. Seen from the vantage of mystic allegory, the vegetal is circumscribed neither by the plant species nor by Spirit. The meanings of vegetal life, here, emerge from the blurring of boundaries separating specific life forms, boundaries that, in the narrative I am presenting, become different in mystical union, even as they preserve the differences between entities: Mystical union, on this understanding, is above all a practice of letting-be, abandonment, and rest. To see mystical union as constituted by a crossing of life forms through their mutual letting-be provides room for vegetal mysticism: It indicates the lack of separation between supernatural and natural in the spiritual life.

Many descriptions of contemplation, mystical union, and ecstasy describe the dissolution of the self in God as a suspension of nature. But the examples we have seen in previous chapters suggest that what is at stake, rather, is a critique of nature: an abandonment, for the human mystics, of "nature" not in the sense of corporeality but in the sense of an abstract idea of nature. A more nuanced sense of the vegetal can then take shape as a result of our reading of mystics in early and medieval Christianity. For many mystical thinkers, the vegetal is a way of representing God but also the mystic's body. The human soul experiences union with God as a vegetal process disruptive to the sense of human self-identity. Yet the already-vegetal nature of the human body, the extent to which it is capable of fecundity in ways that are not restricted to sexual reproduction but are compared to grafting and growth, reveals mystical union to be as much an earthing as an advancement of the "human." If contemplation is thought to be the highest state for a human being, it is also, through its analogy with vegetal life, pictured as the lowest state. The vegetal is not discovered beyond or after the human. Rather, the vegetal is discovered as the ground, the *humus*, of humans, thus offering the vegetal as a name for God, the ground of being.

Michael Marder's vegetal hermeneutic likewise insists on mysticism as an unselfing that nonetheless leads to an experience of God in this life. The negation of self in mysticism takes on a concretely vegetal meaning in the mystic's abandoning of subjectivity from awareness and the attempt to speak as medium, through a disowning of subjectivity and organismic autonomy, and an—uncertain—embrace of anti-individualism. Ecstasy, therefore, is decentralized and anarchic, lacking an organizing structure; in this way negation is what attunes the mystic to the vegetal being that makes possible the mystic's ecstasy. The path of negating the self through mysticism, the *via negativa*, intersects with the path of vegetation, the *via vegetativa*. With Marder's *via vegetativa*, we recognize that while mystics' plant imagery disrupts expectations regarding the union of human soul and God, it is negative mysticism that evokes vegetal life. At the same time, the fact that negative mysticism is articulated around a language of world renunciation obscures these entwinements and indicates the extent to which mysticism, despite its celebration in recent ecological theology, has been interpreted through the lens of a more rigidly defined dualism of negation *versus* corporeality. The vegetal structures that shape spiritual exercises have been pushed to one side in favor of the vegetal imagery drawn on by mystics. As a consequence, the part of mysticism arguably most important to those claiming to practice contemplative union with God is forgotten.

For this reason, in what follows I will be taking a closer look at mysticism by drawing on a wider array of studies that have tried to understand the significance of it as a spiritual practice of everyday affect. Early modernity is a period that has been shown to represent both the largest departure from premodern understandings of vegetal life and an exceptional array of countercurrents. I will be concerned with a current in early modern Catholic mysticism that runs counter to a prevailing orthodoxy regarding the meaning of vegetal life. By drawing on recent studies of the role played by nature and the natural in mysticism among women in seventeenth-century France, I will be indicating the relevance of the themes we have already discussed, but for a larger debate. Here I will be providing an inventory of typical practices associated with contemplative prayer; in the following chapter, I will be suggesting ways in which this inventory can weave into contemporary accounts of recognizing the "plant in us." I will be considering the work of the French Catholic Jeanne Guyon (1648–1717), struggling to defend what she called the "natural activity" of "annihilation" (*anéantissement*) in a theological and political environment that was growing increasingly hostile to mysticism at large and women's expression of it in particular. In the recent attention given to Guyon and her contemporaries, a reassessment of the spiritual practices at stake points to themes with strong bearing on our current question. My aim is to cultivate the graft of mystical and vegetal we have seen in previous chapters. Within the practices of Guyon's mysticism we may be able to discern the outlines of an art of living closer in time to the present day than those of Hildegard of Bingen or Francis of Assisi.

The contemplative method that I sketch, together with Guyon but also her earlier contemporary, Jane de Chantal (1572–1641), is rooted in the sensitive life and the cultivation of sensory perception through the arousal of affections. The self is lost not by escaping the body but by dissolving the perceived boundaries between object and subject. In Guyon's work we see an ontology of divine immanence in which God is experienced at the moment when the distance separating subject from object—a distance enforced by language—is abandoned in favor of radical mixture across boundaries. It is in this mystical mixture, where even the idea of God separated from creatures is abandoned, that we will find vegetal being.

LET NATURE BE AROUSED!

The entwining of mystical with vegetal being we have seen so far has concerned itself with the relationship between the *via negativa*, "way of negations," and cosmism, or the contemplation of nature. We ended the previous chapter with Marguerite of Porete and the controversies that surrounded her mysticism. I chose to conclude with Marguerite because there is a close theological and spiritual relationship between Marguerite and Jeanne Guyon. The Guyon scholar Marie-Florine Bruneau situates Guyon in the tradition of negative theology with roots in Beguine spirituality, and she shows that Guyon was familiar with this tradition, observing that "within the framework of the female mystical tradition, Madame Guyon most especially resembles the French Beguine Marguerite."[2] Despite the distance in time separating Marguerite from Guyon, I have thus chosen the connection between these two mystics as my starting point. (I will be returning to Guyon's more immediate influences later on in this chapter.) As Bruneau points out, many of the accusations leveled against Marguerite were also leveled against other mystics, such as Meister Eckhart and, later, in the early modern period, Teresa of Ávila, John of the Cross, and the young Ignatius of Loyola. What is striking about Guyon's case is that, like Marguerite, she formulated a "critique of the church of their time . . . arguing that the institution itself had little to do with salvation."[3] Bruneau goes on: "Like other mystics, [Marguerite and Guyon] implicitly invalidate the role of the hierarchy in spiritual matters; unlike most mystics, they sometimes did it quite explicitly."[4] This helps put the vociferousness of the attacks against Guyon in context; it also helps explain why certain theological questions were debated in the polemic against Guyon. Much could be said here, but, for the sake of my narrative, I will focus only on the question of "nature" and its relationship to the *via negativa*, or negative theology.

Guyon entered the history of Western Christian mysticism at a point when tensions between magisterium and lay spiritual practice in the Roman Catholic Church were exceptionally high. In part as a response to the Reformation and the European wars of religion, Catholic authorities intensified their persecution of certain forms of mysticism. Practices that emphasized the *via negativa* were seen as threatening and labeled as "Quietism."[5] The heresy of Quietism takes its name after repose or stillness (*quietas*, in Latin), but the debates were concerned more with nature than with repose. Interior peace was widely accepted as the aim of Christian mystical prayer.[6] But in the seventeenth century, a tension had emerged between Catholics who held that tranquility was possible in this life by natural means and those who did not. Alternatively, wordless prayer was seen as an advanced practice that ought not to be taught to the laity or to beginners. Accusations brought against Quietism in Spain, and subsequently in France, surrounded a particular claim made by mystics regarding contemplation as a natural state. The papal condemnation of the Spanish Miguel Molinos's 1675 *Spiritual Guide* (which became a template for the polemic subsequently brought against Guyon) stated: "[Molinos believes that] when the free will has been handed over to God . . . there is no longer any reason to worry about temptations. No resistance should be offered to them, except in a negative way without any effort. *And if nature is aroused, you should let it be aroused, because it is nature.*"[7] Following Molinos's trial in Rome, Guyon's *Short and Easy Method* was placed on the papal Index of Prohibited Books in 1689. It is from these accusations against Molinos that Jacques-Bénigne Bossuet, Guyon's principal accuser and the mouthpiece of French seventeenth-century antimysticism, describes Guyon as one who "forbids, as unfaithfulness, all real resistance to the most abominable temptations."[8] Bossuet wrote: "She would have it believed, that in a certain state of perfection, whereunto she speedily raises souls, there is no concupiscence, that [mystics] cannot sin . . . and [that they] enjoy the same peace that the blessed do in heaven."[9]

During the final decades of the seventeenth century, the Inquisition argued that priests were using mysticism to seduce young women into committing immoral acts, and Quietism became linked to a number of abuse scandals, principally involving vulnerable adolescents and their male confessors.[10] Meanwhile, women (both monastic and lay) were defending and developing contemplative prayer, quite independently of clerical guidance.[11] At stake for these women (but also some men, as we shall come to) was another widespread and old Christian tradition, the "enjoyment of God" (*fruitio Dei*), according to which the body was seen not as a hindrance but rather a path to God.[12] Guyon and others were advocates of the mystical tradition of negation, the *via negativa*. Words, speech, images, and discursive thought were seen as hindrances to the immediate experience of God in the present moment. Guyon proposed a specific practice for negating speech and representation: Through the arousing of the affections, reason, will, and even desire were laid aside. The aim was to become sensitive and receptive. Affections were seen by mystics like Guyon as distinct from emotion or feeling: a presubjective, even preconscious experience, rooted in the body and created by God as good and natural. As one historian puts it, "you gave up trying to make acts or to elicit emotions in your prayer; you remained simply attentive to God's presence": "This process, recommended in so many 'short methods' of interior prayer . . . led to the wide diffusion of mysticism in the seventeenth century."[13]

This leads us back to Guyon's strong critique of institutions. What worried theologians like Bossuet was not only the emphasis on nature in Guyon's mysticism but the possible ramifications of mysticism for the religious and social order. Following the wars of religion, hierarchy had become increasingly significant as a way for the Catholic Church to ensure continued control over the spiritual life of its members, especially its laity. In Guyon's most famous book, *A Short and Easy Method of Prayer*, first published in 1685, contemplative prayer is described as natural not only in the sense of being bodily but in the sense of dissolving hierarchies: "Princes, kings, clergy, priests, lawyers, soldiers, children, craftsmen, workers, women, and the sick" are all capable of experiencing contemplative prayer. Not only that, contemplative prayer "can be done at any time," since it "does not depend on any particular walk of life."[14] Guyon concludes her *Short and Easy Method* with a challenge to dominant clerical methods for teaching spiritual prayer. This position clashed noticeably with the more reserved approach to mysticism represented in popular manuals such as Ignatius of Loyola's *Spiritual Exercises* (1548). *Spiritual Exercises* is complex and requires the mastery of visualization techniques; crucially, *Spiritual Exercises* requires a spiritual director. It is presented as a preparation rather than an instruction for contemplation, with Ignatius choosing to maintain silence on contemplation itself.[15] By contrast, Guyon presents not only a method for contemplative prayer but one that lacked the requirement for a spiritual director: This was do-it-yourself mysticism for the seventeenth century. As a result, her teachings were embraced by the laity and especially by women, for whom Guyon provided a means of bypassing clerical authority in an era that offered more restricted spiritual education to women than in previous centuries.[16] If the emphasis on wordless prayer (*via negativa*) was perceived as dangerous to the social and religious order, the idea of prayer as natural reinforced the perceived threat. This political aspect of Guyon's mysticism is significant and inseparable from a denial of nature, as well as a denial of women's bodies.

Let nature be aroused, because it is nature! One theme that emerges when engaging with Guyon's mysticism today is the possibility of rethinking the terms that fueled its persecution, especially the idea of nature's "arousal." The commentators with whom I enter into dialogue in this chapter suggest as much, although they emphasize different aspects of the mysticism and offer varied commentary. The spread of different perspectives shows the importance of this form of mysticism, and especially of Guyon's work, for the question of *arousing nature*, which is one of the ways I will be figuring—with the help of Guyon—what it means to recognize the "plant in us." In the next chapter, I will find Guyon's use of "nature" to be close to the vegetal, as understood in contemporary philosophy. Nature in Guyon's writing, it will be shown, signifies spontaneous activity but also receptivity, and above all sensitivity. In other words, I will be continuing to think with Michael Marder's idea that spontaneity, involuntary activity, and passive effort provide an overlooked connection between vegetal life and mystical practices, continuing the line of thought that emerged in my engagement with Amy Hollywood's reading of Marguerite. In order to do so, however, it is useful first to consider the context of Guyon's mysticism more closely.

VEGETAL MODERNITY: LIVELY MATTER AND TRANSCORPOREALITY IN EARLY MODERN MYSTICISM

Throughout the medieval period, plants had been viewed as simple and low in the "scale of nature" (*scala naturae*), but vegetal life had also been seen as proper also to humans, corresponding to the nutritive life of animals as well as plants. As Fabrizio Bigotti has shown, during the early modern period and with the rise of mind-matter dualism this understanding shifted dramatically. What had once been viewed as part of human nature, albeit a (mostly) reviled part, was now viewed, increasingly, as wholly separate from what made humans human. According to René Descartes, the body acted according to mechanistic laws, while the spirit alone was free. Cartesian anthropology presented the human as a potentially infinite will bounded by matter lacking in agency. As a result, any interest, in this period, for the anthropological ramifications of vegetal life would represent "an approach that runs counter to but parallels the dualist accounts of mind and body in Descartes and his epigones."[17]

Among such counter-Cartesian approaches, the seventeenth and eighteenth centuries produced a steady stream of philosophers, poets, and writers who challenged the dominant view of a dualist, plant-less, anthropology in different ways. Elaine P. Miller, Natania Meeker, Antónia Szabari, and others have studied vegetal imagery as resistance in Western thought during the Enlightenment and beyond. Speculative fiction, poetry, and art play with the idea of recognizing what Marder calls "the plant in us" in ways that oscillate between seeing plants "soliciting our interest and refusing to ratify our concerns," as Meeker and Szabari write. Meeker and Szabari trace a pre-Romantic "materialist fascination" with the plant. They argue that this pre-Romantic fascination, in contrast to later, nineteenth-century responses, do not express fear of "the enmeshment of human and vegetal life as a response to Darwinian theories of evolution and common descent." Rather, in the period leading up to the nineteenth century, some intellectual currents were concerned with themes anticipating the contemporary interest in "lively matter or transcorporeality." While Meeker and Szabari do not address Western Christian mysticism of the period, other historians have pointed to similar themes in Guyon and her context, and in what follows I would like to view the latter from the perspective of what Meeker and Szabari call an emergent "*vegetal* modernity" unfolding in the seventeenth century.[18]

Guyon will be seen to adhere to what Bo Karen Lee has characterized as a low anthropology that speaks to the kind of "fascinating animacy" described by Meeker and Szabari.[19] Guyon attributes to the passivity of vegetal life (both in her own body and in other creatures) the activity of contemplating God. In the late seventeenth century, when Guyon was writing, such notions ran counter to the dualistic anthropology of Descartes but also to the idealization of vegetal life as divinely indifferent that would develop in the Romantic period. For Guyon, the aim of comparing contemplation to vegetal activities was not to idealize the spiritual life as remote and indifferent but to recognize it as properly creaturely. Like other nonconforming mystics of the period, Guyon "held a kind of materialist pantheism which identified God with the created world and so placed the spirit of life and cause of motion within terrestrial and celestial bodies themselves." "Materialist pantheism" is implicit in spiritual practices that teach mystical union in this life, meaning that all that was needed in order to experience God was for mystics to look "at the world around them . . . because all of nature is full of God."[20] What emerges from Guyon's work is not only a fascination with vegetal life as divine but also with divinity as lively matter—ideas that clash with scientific but also religious orthodoxies. Historians of Guyon's work have shown that her mysticism indeed emerged from "an epistemological current that existed concurrently with Cartesian and then Enlightenment rationalism but was at odds with it."[21] A recent approach has been to consider Guyon as a figure confronting as much as heralding modernity. This approach, which has been led by Marie-Louise Gondal, has shown Guyon's importance to feminist scholars as an example of resilience in the face of Cartesian rationalism and the different "selves"—patriarchal, self-possessed, and colonial—that are reinforced during this period as a result of the scientific revolution, urbanization, and the enslavement of indigenous peoples.[22] In this context, Guyon's mysticism is read rhetorically, as a way of reclaiming agency by disclaiming male-coded narratives of virility, ego, and power. I will be following in the wake of the latter approach but, engaging with the work of Michel de Certeau, will be concerned more with Guyon's practices than with the question of gender. By lingering with what Guyon writes regarding nature, I find that Guyon's mysticism disrupts gender binaries even as it provided Guyon and especially women in her period with a means of resisting patriarchal strategies.[23]

Above all, I will be interested in how Guyon connects what she calls contemplation to images of vegetal life. Guyon never calls contemplation vegetal: The word she prefers is "natural." Yet when Guyon describes nature it is to emphasize precisely those types of activities traditionally associated, in premodern anthropology, with the vegetable soul: nutritive capacity, growth, and spontaneous metamorphosis. One historian who has studied the anthropology that emerges from Guyon's emphasis on the nutritive and "passive" aspects of human nature is Charly Coleman. Coleman begins from a general consideration of what he calls the culture of dispossession in seventeenth-century France. During the reign of Louis XIV, self-interest was axiomatic: "The new orthodoxy stressed the need for souls to relate to themselves and to the objects surrounding them in possessive terms."[24] The desire for personal salvation was seen as a good thing, since it reinforced a perception of the body's natural sinfulness, anchoring the inner life in a hope beyond the body. By contrast, Guyon's mysticism represented the opposite tendency: what Coleman calls "anti-individualism." Guyon's anti-individualism, according to Coleman, was a "radical form of spirituality" focused on selfless behavior but also on celebrating nature in different ways.[25]

Coleman is particularly observant when it comes to the sense Guyon gives to nature. "Nature" for Guyon is not fallen but good and oriented toward God. To experience God, however, a person needed to reorient their natural inclinations. In the process described by Guyon, the components of self-interest (reason, will, and desire) needed to be abandoned, but according to

Cartesian anthropology, these were the same components that elevated human beings above other animals. In practice, this meant that Guyon's mysticism gave an enormous significance to what, under the new scientific and religious orthodoxy, was seen as inhuman: the purely sensitive life, devoid of reason and will.

Although Guyon herself did not advance an anthropology from these ideas, Coleman points out Guyon's relationship to later philosophers who did think of human beings against the Cartesian grain. Significant for the subject of this chapter, Coleman traces a line of influence from Guyon's mysticism to the radical materialism of the eighteenth century. This connects both to Meeker and Szabari's idea of a "vegetal modernity" and to Guyon's mysticism. In *Radical Botany*, Meeker and Szabari point out the relationship between, on the one hand, the seventeenth-century fascination with plants and, on the other, materialist traditions that have used plants to reflect on philosophical and political ideas. Coleman, for his part, sees materialist traditions in France influenced by a line of mystical thinking descended from Guyon. Coleman also focuses on the link between materialist traditions and critique of social and political ideals. François Fénelon (1651–1715), one of the most influential French theologians of the late seventeenth century, defended Guyon's mysticism and her thinking, showing its coherence from a historical and theological point of view. More importantly, Fénelon shared central ideas with Guyon. Coleman argues that Fénelon "emphasizes immanence over transcendence to such an extent that it could overtake the existential space occupied by the individual soul," leading to an unexpected affinity between "mysticism and Spinozism" in a literature not otherwise marked by Spinozist sympathies.[26] This theology of divine immanence was linked to politics. Fénelon's popular novel, *Telemachus* (1699), translates mystical terms into political ideas, attacking as self-interest the driving forces of empire and luxury and proposing selfless love as an antidote to egotistical consumerism. More significantly still, Fénelon shared Guyon's perspective on natural spontaneity and passivity. As Ryan Hanley has argued recently, the Quietist controversy involved debates about more than prayer: An entire spiritual economy of social relations was at stake. To Fénelon's nemesis, Bossuet, self-interest was thought to cement a just society because, although negative when inspired by greed, self-interest also propelled a person to secure their personal salvation and individual betterment, a situation that benefited the whole of society. Fénelon was of a different opinion, however. For Fénelon, self-interest rendered a society unjust not only because it encouraged accruement of personal property and thus inequality but because it presented the natural state of individuals and of the world as insufficient, lacking, and inherently sinful. In other words, Fénelon wanted to prove "the existence of [a] natural, free and nonvicious love."[27] In order to prove this existence he argued, just like Guyon, that the inclination toward God was natural and that it manifested itself in spontaneous, "passive" movements irreducible to reason, will, and understanding.

This brief reflection on some aspects of early modern mysticism in Europe and France indicates how Guyon's mysticism may be read as contributing to an emergent vegetal modernity in the seventeenth century. The similarities between her ideas and the traditional understanding of a vegetable soul provide an opportunity to draw connections. According to the practice implied by the critique of self-interest, "a stable, cohesive, and self-governing subject" is held in doubt.[28] In Guyon's mysticism, vegetal modernity becomes discernible also in the context of dissent and nonconformism. It is important to open a window toward this context, if only to show an example of the ways in which the arousal of nature, in mysticism, has acted as a nexus for the spiritual, political, and philosophical. With this context in place, let us now turn to the life and work of Guyon.

JEANNE GUYON'S MYSTICISM OF NUTRITIVE SELF-ANNIHILATION

The daughter of impoverished aristocratic parents, Guyon, née Jeanne-Marie Bouvier (1648–1717), was married at sixteen to secure the family fortune.[29] While still an adolescent and struggling to endure an unhappy marriage (her husband was eighteen years her senior, and his family was abusive), she set out to learn contemplative prayer. Through encounters with various teachers and private study, Guyon eventually developed the method of wordless prayer for which she was later imprisoned. Guyon gave birth to five children, three of whom survived to adulthood. Widowed at twenty-eight, Guyon chose to use her financial independence to pursue her own path. Trouble began when Guyon refused to accept the offer of becoming prioress (and thus principal funder) of an institution dedicated to the forced conversion of Protestant girls and women newly converted to Catholicism. Initially drawn to missionary work, Guyon quickly became disillusioned by the coercive methods used by the nuns in charge at the house in Gex, Savoy. A priest, one Father Lacombe, was approached by the bishop of Geneva to attempt to persuade Guyon, but Lacombe also refused, apparently impressed with Guyon. Guyon left Gex and wrote her first book, *Spiritual Torrents*, in 1682, in response to the experience. In the book, she argues for a different approach to conversion than that which she had witnessed at Gex. She presents, in this book, her method for perceiving the presence of God through a simple practice of wordless prayer.

In retaliation, the bishop of Geneva began spreading rumors of witchcraft and counterfeit. It was these rumors that lay at the bottom of her later incarceration. During a stay in Grenoble, in 1684–1685, Guyon composed her most famous book, *A Short and Easy Method of Prayer*, published in 1685, and the manuscript of a spiritual commentary on the entire Bible. Rumors continued to circulate, however, and the bishop of Grenoble expelled Guyon, who left for Marseille. Here, Guyon became acquainted with François Malaval, a French mystic soon to be condemned for Quietism. Returning to Paris and her family, Guyon was joined by Lacombe, who was promptly imprisoned in the Bastille, accused of Quietism. A month later, in November 1687, a pastoral letter was published condemning Guyon and her *Short and Easy Method*; the same year, a portion of her Bible commentary, on the Song of Songs, was published in Lyon. Guyon was placed under house arrest in 1688, accused of receiving instruction from Lacombe. Guyon, however, insisted that her teachings were her own. This resulted in further interrogations. A deal was suggested whereby Guyon's release was promised on the condition that she marry her daughter to the archbishop of Paris's nephew: Guyon refused.

Meanwhile, Guyon's work was finding receptive ears at court, and Madame de Maintenon (the secret wife of Louis XIV) organized for her release, causing the archbishop's public humiliation. Guyon now had access to court life, where she became the adopted leader of a society devoted to mystical ideas, gained a disciple in Fénelon, and was invited to share her teaching with a new religious house for women at Saint-Cyr. But the grace was short-lived. It seems that some of the young women taught by Guyon understood her teachings well—perhaps all too well—"as license for following their own intuitions and disobeying the rules of the [religious] house."³⁰ Madame de Maintenon suddenly withdrew her support from Guyon in 1693, perhaps fearing the archbishop's revenge, and raised the alarm of Quietism. Fénelon suggested to Maintenon that his old mentor Jacques-Bénigne Bossuet examine Guyon, but this choice turned out disastrous for both Fénelon and Guyon. During her imprisonment 1695–1698, Fénelon and Bossuet engaged in venomous polemic, which resulted in the pamphlet I quoted earlier: a ruthless ad hominem attack on Fénelon in which Guyon was also vilified at length. Guyon was then sent to the Bastille, where she was imprisoned from 1698 to 1703.³¹ During this period, Guyon endured eighty interrogations yet proved remarkably resilient to the methods of her examiners. As Bruneau points out, Guyon does not seem to have internalized the accusations brought against her, and she refused to sign any document against her conscience.

Finally released without further charges in 1703, Guyon spent her remaining years in the countryside home of her son. Here Guyon received a steady stream of visitors, many of them Protestant, and wrote an account of her harassment, *The Prison Narratives*, which was circulated privately among friends. When Guyon died in 1715 she left behind, in addition to the books already mentioned, her *Autobiography* and *Justifications*, dozens of poems, and hundreds of letters of spiritual direction. Her work gained a large audience, though much of it outside France.³² Through translations into English and Guyon's inclusion in John Wesley's hugely popular *A Christian Library* (1750), her method of contemplation reached an exceptionally wide readership among Methodists, Quakers, and other nonconformist Christians, especially in North America.³³ Lived experience "for all people" rather than conversion became important to Guyon, who thus anticipated ecumenical approaches to Christian practice.[34]

Guyon's mysticism makes for an interesting partner to the figures and currents I have been considering in earlier chapters. While it shares similarities with the vegetal mysticism I have been proposing, Guyon's work is distinct for the way it is situated amid intersecting histories of laicization and the critique of institutions. By reading slowly through Guyon's spiritual exercises—with their emphasis on nature but also their resistance to hierarchy—we may be able to grasp the ethics at stake in the philosophies of vegetal life I have been introducing, where these themes also appear. This will lead us by steps to reconsider what it might mean to practice contemplation in the way suggested both by mystics and philosophers like Michael Marder. As I read her, Guyon developed a mysticism that combines the themes I have been discussing in this book into a spiritual practice of attentiveness that "vegetalizes" thought. The principal imagery with which Guyon deals in her mysticism is based on the type of activity Marder defines as vegetal, by which is meant a spontaneous activity that lacks conceptual organization yet remains intentional, such as one finds in plants but also in humans: The activities of membranes, tissues, and skin are, according to this view, all examples of vegetal being. This sense of the vegetal is one way in which I will be approaching the use of "nature" and "natural" in Guyon's mysticism, which is concerned with questioning the idea that contemplation requires special learning. In Guyon's famous words, "nothing is easier than experiencing God and tasting him . . . the only way to look for him is as easy and natural as breathing the air and is no more than that."[35]

Guyon's emphasis on nature is closely related to an interpretation of the *via negativa* we encountered in the work of

Marguerite and earlier mystics. Marguerite's mysticism is famous for insisting on the practice of self-annihilation. According to Guyon, too, contemplation required the complete annihilation (*anéantisement*) of the sense of self, including will, reason, and desire, even the desire for salvation. Self-annihilation in Guyon's work has been interpreted as pathological or violently masochistic. While her language may trouble the contemporary reader, the practice she describes is distinct from self-harm. For Guyon, self-annihilation is the opposite of self-interest or self-love (*amour propre*).[36] As a result, any practice of inflicting deliberate violence on nature is rejected in no uncertain terms by Guyon. A person should live simply and selflessly but should not mortify the flesh unduly. Austerities are criticized in part because Guyon sees them as privileged activities reserved for the able-bodied, meaning that "not everyone is capable of outward austerities."[37] Austerities are also criticized because Guyon views the body as essentially good. Contemplative prayer is practiced by exciting the affections, not by rising above them. The words Guyon uses to describe the inner life, "heart" (*coeur*) and "depth" (*fond*), are similarly embodied or made physical. They indicate a sense of sensation or "affect" rather than psyche—"a spontaneity of our being, not subject to logical, rational, and discursive methods."[38] When describing prayer, Guyon accordingly chooses images of spontaneous behavior in human bodies, such as breathing, eating, and nursing, but also images of nonhuman life and of the elements: She is intensely preoccupied, in *Spiritual Torrents*, with the way rivers flow toward the sea, using this as an analogy for contemplation. Her poetry, too, is replete with comparisons between the practice of contemplation, for an adult human, and the natural activities and movements she observes around her. A mother of three children, she often returns to the instinctive activities of a nursing infant, using the analogy of breastfeeding repeatedly and in striking ways. A nursing child will begin by making efforts to stimulate the flow of milk, "but when the milk comes in abundance, he is content to drink it with no more movement" and will continue in this way, even though it scarcely seems possible "that he is getting nourishment . . . gently in peace without moving."[39] In contemplation, one need not do nothing; one need simply know when nothing more needs to be done in order for there to be satisfaction, that is, when to let go in order to let things be. Like other mystics accused of Quietism, Guyon is interested in the idea of letting-be and letting-go. Her contemporary, Molinos, writes: "To be attentive to God, to reach for [God] . . . are true acts" yet are "almost imperceptible in the great tranquility with which the soul produces them."[40]

Guyon's instructions for how to practice contemplation often contrasts contemplation with meditation.[41] Whereas meditation is the result of going within the self and defending it from outside influence (by picturing the self as a fortress or mansion), contemplation is the result of the opposite movement. In contemplation the self is disarmed, meditation relinquished, and God recognized in the "outside" from which meditation would separate the practitioner. Another way in which Guyon typically describes this is in terms of a distinction between involuntary and voluntary effort. Whereas meditation is the result of willing to move toward a specific goal, contemplation is the result of allowing oneself to be moved, an experience described as a passive activity or simply as passivity, although Guyon insists it is a combination of both activity and passivity. Finally, Guyon was interested in the elements and how they move. Guyon compares contemplation to the way air receives the sun's energy and is warmed by it, or (developing the Augustinian image of contemplation as a yielding to gravity) to a stone falling into the sea "descending . . . at an incredible speed without noticing this plunging."[42] The variation in imagery is offset, though, by a remarkable consistency in the accounts of contemplation. From Guyon's mysticism there emerges an image of spiritual exercises not as a reinforcement of *human* nature but rather as a fresh intimacy with the kinds of activities practiced by many species.

When Guyon describes an activity as "natural" she has in mind the combination of receptivity and spontaneity that is distinctive of vegetal life. Despite the lack of plant imagery in her writing, Guyon offers perspectives on what Marder calls mysticism's vegetalizing of thought. Guyon gives an arresting image of the human-divine relationship through practices aimed at centering attention on the obscure and barely noticeable passive activities that constitute life, something particularly evident in her manual, *Short and Easy Method*. In the next chapter I will be grafting Guyon's handbook to philosophies of the vegetal, in particular the work of Emanuele Coccia and Luce Irigaray, and think about the way in which such grafting can help us conceive of the vegetal as an ethical as well as philosophical concern.

DEMOCRATIZING MYSTICISM: CARMELITE SPIRITUALITY, FRANCIS DE SALES, AND JANE DE CHANTAL

What I am reading here as Guyon's vegetal mysticism is a remarkable example in Catholic religion of the period. Yet Guyon also participates in a wider current of thought. In part, that current can be described in relation to a history of religious dissent and nonconformism. It also connects Guyon to a current of early modern, female monastic spirituality. The type of mysticism prized in Guyon's practice has an interesting backstory that helps place its distinct emphasis on nature in a larger context. With roots in the negative theology of the medieval period, Guyon's practices share much in common with the teachings of the Discalced Carmelites, who arrived in France in 1604. The Discalced Carmelites were a Spanish order that emerged from the spiritual reforms of Teresa of Ávila and John of the Cross. The spirituality of the Discalced Carmelites is distinctive for its emphasis on contemplative practice but also on what Lytta Basset, in an insightful article, calls the "democratization of mysticism." In the Gospels, Christ encourages his listeners to observe birds, lilies, and children. Discalced Carmelite sisters interpreted this to mean that mystical union could be achieved by cultivating spontaneity and other "natural" forms of behavior. Rather than modeling mystical experience on union with the divine or on an amorous encounter with God, the example of creatures and especially of *infants* was favored by the Carmelite sisters. If mysticism taught that the aim was to let go of intellect, the Carmelites saw the infant as already free from the constraints of intellect: "For them, it is only to *receive*, whether they know they are receiving or not."[43] Discalced Carmelite sisters developed the idea of a distinct kind of cosmism, one focused not on the grandeur of creation but on its "small" and "simple" aspects—words that appear often in Guyon's vocabulary, as do infants as models for spiritual perfection.[44]

The Discalced Carmelites were popular in France: By 1644 there were forty-four Carmels in the country. Among the French spiritual reformers most influenced by Carmelite spirituality, two would become significant to Guyon's thought: Francis de Sales (1567–1622) and Jane de Chantal (1572–1641). In Sales's *Treatise on the Love of God* (1616), a book that Guyon admired and studied as a young girl, metaphors of nature abound and are very similar to those used by Carmelites. Here, infants but also animals and especially plants appear as models for contemplation. The soul, writes Sales, should imitate the attitude of the sunflower, which "moves not its corolla only but the whole plant" when following "the Sun of Righteousness throughout His course."[45] *Love of God* is strewn with similar references, all describing an attitude of receptivity and spontaneity, most of them inspired by Hebrew and Greek scripture. Sales also develops the Carmelite "democratization of mysticism" in new ways. The work of Sales is pragmatic, often aimed at lay persons, and accessible to a wide readership. Making mysticism accessible *is* one of the main aims of Sales, who, together with Chantal, helped found a new order, the Sisters of the Visitation of Mary (*Visitandines*) in 1610, a congregation for women unable to enter the Discalced Carmelites or other existing women's orders. According to her autobiography, the young Guyon wanted desperately to join the Sisters of the Visitation, and the influence of Chantal's work is plain to see in Guyon's whole approach to prayer.[46] Chantal's work, principally letters but also several volumes of informal discourses delivered to her religious sisters, gives a remarkable account of mystical prayer as a practice that is not opposed to natural activities but rather flourishes by means of them.

We find in Chantal's mysticism a distinct teaching regarding *arousal*, a word that also appears in polemic against Quietism, although Chantal's work predated the Quietist controversies, and she escaped condemnation. According to Chantal, contemplative prayer is the result of addressing God as divine Love without the use of formal prayers but simply by "arousing the affections."[47] As in Guyon's work, the word "affections," for Chantal, designates something distinct from emotion, relating instead to what today might be called "affect" or "sensation": a prereflexive response that precedes subjective emotion.[48] While Chantal does not describe the affections in terms of corporeality, she often uses, like Guyon, the imagery of the "heart" (*coeur*), which carries the meaning not of a purely psychic experience but of a deeper spontaneity. It is clear that, for Chantal, the arousing of affections is supposed to involve the body in profound ways. After some time, explains Chantal, one will experience a brief but overwhelming "flow" of affection such that speech but also thought becomes extremely difficult. Chantal is at times quite detailed regarding the physiology of the experience: One's throat will become constricted, tears will well up, and so forth. In this state it is important "not [to] force our brains to make considerations" but to "stop a little . . . [while] enjoying them [i.e., the affections]" and finally "arouse the affection again when it flows away." Chantal argues that "self-annihilation," the same practice that is developed by Guyon, begins with these moments of "enjoyment." Cultivated over time at each successive "ebb," they are intensified and prolonged and then expanded into an everyday disposition: "Outside prayer, we ought to be such as we should wish to be during it."[49] In practice, Chantal's sisters were completely lacking in "the heroic and visible exploits abounding in other religious orders,"[50] at least where spiritual discipline was concerned. Advises Chantal: "You must never go and say to these Fathers in religion to whom we sometimes speak, 'I do nothing in prayer'; for those who are led by that way of loving simplicity do nothing by activity, but they do a great deal by possession."[51] In Chantal's mysticism, as in that of Guyon, there is a rigorous defense of "doing nothing," insofar as the "idleness" defended is identified with the body's natural state. At the bottom of her mysticism is an idea that sin is not inherent to the body. Sin is not caused by the body, nor is nature inherently fallen. Finally,

Chantal argues that such practice is possible because, in a certain respect, everyone is already performing it spontaneously. As Chantal writes: "For you have all these virtues [required for enjoying God] really and in substance, but you have neither the consciousness nor the feelings of them."[52] What contemplative prayer offered, for Chantal, was not a path to a disembodied event but a practice of bodily cultivation; contemplative prayer was a way of becoming sensitive to God's presence.

Like the contemplative practices of the Discalced Carmelites, Chantal's methods emphasize an alternative view of mystical experience, taking as its model the natural activity of affect. By contrast to the label sometimes given to it by historians in earlier decades, the mysticism that most influenced Guyon does not amount to an "abstract" spirituality.[53] Rather, as Wendy Wright and Joseph Power note, Chantal's mysticism displays a striking "lack of indifference" to corporeality, something that sets her apart even from Sales, whose work is less focused on descriptions of affect. This "lack of indifference" may be understood in terms of the doctrine of "spiritual indifference," offering us the opportunity to modify our understanding of this established concept often connected to mortification and the denial of the senses through fasting and other forms of bodily and sensory deprivation. Chantal uses the language of "indifference," but she does not put emphasis on mortification and warns against its overuse. When Chantal addresses her nuns, mortification means not the destruction of the body but rather the loss of self, "all its seekings and interests."[54] What stands in the way of God is not the body but a sense of subjectivity that impedes the arousal of the affections. As a result, praying to God requires not austerity but gentleness. "Our vocation is a humble, gentle spirit, supporting and considerate of all," exhorts Chantal when addressing one superior's delight in austerities: "Please . . . be most gentle in spirit, word and action, and . . . treat your own body and those of your Sisters better than you have been doing."[55]

We see in Chantal's readiness to draw connections between corporeal life and religious experiences, between the concrete and the apparently abstract, hints of the ability to "vegetalize" thought that I have been discussing in this book. As Wright and Power note, Chantal's letters "show her as willing to deal realistically with the natural process of grief, as able to admit a great deal of her own . . . experience into the articulated process of abandonment [to God], as aware of the importance of relationship in her life, as willing to live with ambiguity and as capable of admitting the poignant human need for explanation that arise at times of inexplicable loss."[56] In this sense, Chantal may be seen to affirm but also subvert early modern gender stereotypes, "[seeking] something more complex than autonomy as it is defined for men, a fuller not a lesser ability to encompass relationships to others." For an early modern woman in Catholic France, one way to develop this way of life in relative freedom was in community with other women. Indeed, the Visitation order, which Chantal cofounded, was not, like other female orders, an offshoot of a male community but founded exclusively for women: "Chantal's primary experience, the environment in which she attained spiritual growth and the community to which she was primarily called to minister, was female." However, Chantal's methods, while in many ways so similar to Guyon's, are also limited by their monastic audience, narrowing the idea of widened, "natural" accessibility on which the order was founded. Guyon thus played a crucial role in laicizing Chantal's methods, by situating them in contexts that were not intended primarily for nuns or for women alone. Nonetheless, this original, "especially feminine" context for the mysticism that chiefly inspired Guyon is significant.[57]

While there is nothing essentially feminine about Chantal's methods, which were enjoyed by a mixed audience of readers, gender plays an important role in their formation and initial dissemination.

The enjoyment of God, when looked at from the perspective of the French spiritual reformers and especially Chantal, bears a close relationship to the acceptance, recognition, and, moreover, arousal of corporeality. More than a close relationship, however, we may speak of an identity. For it is in the practice of arousal that mystical prayer is said to consist: According to Chantal, contemplative prayer is an affective state, an immediacy of affect that momentarily suspends rational thought and, if not self-identity, then certainly reflexivity. The whole practice as outlined by Chantal is about being open to *being moved*; without affect, there is no mystical prayer. Likewise, neither God nor divine love is encountered elsewhere but in the body's ordinary life, as Chantal writes when advising against extreme austerities: "Your minds and bodies will be wrecked if you stubbornly refuse to accept humbly what we are saying."[58] Thus the emphasis on corporeality that emerges from the French spiritual reformers that immediately precede Guyon and inspired her rethinks the culture of renunciation insofar as the latter distances contemplation from corporeality. Rather, the language of renunciation is repurposed so as to refer principally to the renunciation of self-interest. Moreover, this practice is seen to be entwined, as in the case of Guyon, with questions of gender, social norms, and life according to nature. In the work of Guyon, these concepts come together in a practice of resilience. But before we now look at Guyon's practice in more detail, it is helpful first to engage with it from the perspective of philosophy and feminist thought.

LOW ANTHROPOLOGY

The practice of becoming sensitive is the experience from which Guyon's mysticism takes its bearings. This means that the practice of becoming sensitive shapes also the form and expression of mysticism. As Michel de Certeau remarked in his classic study of early modern mysticism, *The Mystic Fable*, mystics focus on the "'almost nothing' of sensations, of meetings or daily tasks," in which the senses become a source of secret power, rather than a prison containing the spirit.[59] It is not difficult to see how questions regarding the possibility of women's freedom, in this period, might take on a wholly different form. The mystic, as Guyon, Chantal, and others show us, is someone who takes the first steps toward freedom despite and within finitude. Finitude is not broken; rather, its thrall over the person is deactivated by a practice of quiet resistance that gives attention to what is ignored: the imperceptible agency revealed in affect.

Affectivity as the site of mysticism echoes throughout de Certeau's *Mystic Fable*, shaping it in different ways. For de Certeau, early modern mysticism "does not, like the Cartesian *cogito*, initiate a field for clear and distinct propositions to which a truth value might be assigned. Far from making up a field of its own, it brings about a general metaphorization of language in the name of something that does not arise from language and that leaves its mark there."[60] While de Certeau has been criticized for overemphasizing the role of interiority in early modern mysticism and for exaggerating the degree to which it anticipates the discipline of psychology, de Certeau in fact defines mystical interiority in terms that question a psychological reading of mysticism.[61] De Certeau argued that in the late sixteenth and early seventeenth centuries spiritual exercises became the subject of a distinct discourse, which its French advocates called *la mystique*, "mystics." One feature of mystics, for de Certeau, was the way in which it seemed both to exaggerate the theme of interiority while at the same time rethinking interiority in terms of apperception and affect. In this type of mysticism, "Something stirs within the everyday." De Certeau was fascinated by the "pathos of the detail," by which "little by little, common everyday life begins to seethe with a disturbing familiarity—a frequentation of the Other." De Certeau's *Mystic Fable* ends with mysticism as the process of awakening an "uncanny memory, prior to meaning," that resides in the body and takes hold of the latter before speech, initiating "a new rhythm of existence—some would say a new 'breath,' a new way of walking a different 'style' of life."[62] Without going further into the detail of the arguments in *Mystic Fable*, de Certeau's work on mystics was also the basis for a comprehensive critique of practice from the perspective of the everyday, in which he sought to show how "[the ordinary] introduces itself into our techniques—in the way in which the sea flows back into pockets and crevices in beaches—and how it can reorganize the place from which discourse is produced." In *The Practice of Everyday Life*, de Certeau pictured the ordinary not as a lack of technique but as "tactics" of opposition affording resistance to what he called the "strategies" imposed by systems and institutions. "Strategies" are defined as a "Cartesian attitude . . . it is an effort to delimit one's own place in a world bewitched by the indivisible powers of the Other," an attitude de Certeau associated with modern science, politics, and military strategy. By contrast, tactics were seen by de Certeau as precisely embracing the other: "The space of a tactic is the space of the other." Like "mystics," "tactics" in de Certeau's description are open to the Other. Again, tactics shares with mystics an orientation to the moment; tactics are "limited by the possibilities of the moment"; they are also "determined by the *absence of power* just as a strategy is organized by the postulation of power."[63] De Certeau thus wanted to draw attention to the "intellectual creativity" of the ordinary, everyday, and quotidian, shifting the emphasis away from the "Cartesian" attitudes that had previously been the focus of historians.

Inspired by de Certeau, the Guyon scholar Marie-Florine Bruneau argues that Guyon's mysticism in particular may be seen to participate in tactics: on the one hand, a general tactic used by women throughout Western history in order to oppose attempts to control women's bodies and, on the other hand, a nondiscursive tactic that overlaps with women's resistance but is also distinct from it. As she explains in *Women Mystics Confront the Modern World*, "the mystical experience would be a particularly deep experience of daily practices that would allow the subject to oppose pernicious and vicious instances of dominant power while transcending, without resolving them, deep contradictions that would otherwise tear the subject apart."[64] In addressing de Certeau's concept of "tactics" as a "deep experience of daily practices," Bruneau is especially interested in the way it relates to the history of women's resistance. Questioning de Certeau's claim that corporeality and the emphasis on the everyday comes to the fore *only* with early modern "mystics," Bruneau draws on feminist studies of medieval women's mysticism to show that Guyon's emphasis on corporeality continues an old tradition, with forerunners including, among others, Marguerite of Porete. For Bruneau, Guyon's mysticism thus intersects with much older "tactics" of resistance.

Bruneau's interpretation of Guyon via de Certeau prepares, in my reading, for the entwining of Guyon's mysticism with contemporary philosophies of vegetal life. Furthermore, the fact that she articulates Guyon's tactic in a wider historical tradition of women mystics makes her work more relevant to my reading. So far in this book, we have seen contemporary philosophies of vegetal life turning to Neoplatonism and Byzantine and medieval mysticism but not early modern mysticism. Yet, one can find in Bruneau's development of de Certeau plenty of overlap with the critiques raised by the mystical-vegetal readings of Michael Marder and others. Bruneau's understanding of the way the everyday, in Guyon's mysticism, resists dominant power and of the importance of self-annihilation and attuning to corporeality when attempting that resistance is germane to the stories I am entwining. Bruneau adopts, like the philosophies of vegetal life, a rethinking of what it means to *think*, beginning not from reason but from responsiveness. Again, like the philosophies of vegetal life, Bruneau affirms that this opening of thought is not its dismantling, or not precisely: "Guyon or the mystics were [not] negating the usefulness of reason, but rather . . . they were delimiting its power and acknowledging it as but one of the possibilities of the psyche, and a limited one at that; another reality, for them, lay beyond words and duality." She continues: "The inner freedom created by [Guyon's] mental practice allowed her full resistance."[65]

Bruneau's ideas find ample confirmation from Guyon, who writes of the narrow view of those who dismiss the methods of contemplative prayer, suggesting that they might "live less in the intellect and more in the affections, and if it be manifest that they are gradually substituting the one for the other, it is a sign that a spiritual work is being carried on within them."[66] The critique of intellect and recognition of the affections as a way of living is significant in both discourses, the discourse of mysticism and the discourse of vegetal life. If philosophies of vegetal life seek in sensitivity and responsiveness the condition for any experience of subjectivity, then mystics discover in contemplative prayer the same experience as expressed in the life of the affections. At the same time, there is in Guyon's description of the affections something still more *vegetal* than what is conveyed by Bruneau's description of Guyon's practice located in a "psychic possibility" and "mental exercise." The practice of contemplative prayer as taught by Guyon demands precisely a reexamination of mental exercise and its place; in fact, it disavows mental reflection as fundamental to the experience of God, arguing that the experience of God is natural in the sense of being spontaneous. Here I would return to de Certeau, with whom Bruneau also engages. While Bruneau's reading offers profound insights regarding Guyon's place in a longer tradition of women mystics attending to corporeality, the mysticism of Guyon requires something closer to Certeau's notion of mysticism sketched in bodily rhythms and "breath," a still more sensual approach to mysticism. As Bo Karen Lee has clarified in a recent study, Guyon's mysticism is above all one of delight and pleasure in this life. She places Guyon in a tradition of mystical theology according to which "one of the greatest tasks of theology was to facilitate the enjoyment of God; likewise, it was imperative that theologians cultivate [their] own delight in God." Lee continues: For Guyon, "knowledge without intimate enjoyment of the object of knowledge is . . . no knowledge at all." This is because knowledge ultimately is not, for Guyon, abstracted from the body and liberated to a mental space but embodied and situated in deep experiences of daily life. The human is thus "lowered" insofar as it is not seen as more important than other creatures in relation to its ability to relate to God, resulting in what Lee describes as a "low anthropology."[67]

According to Lee, Guyon's "low anthropology" refers to her deliberate devaluation of those aspects of human behavior that traditionally are thought to elevate humans above other creatures: intellect, reason, will. Yet Guyon is also perceptive when it comes to human agency; one of her claims (as Bruneau rightly points out) is that mysticism allowed her to resist, actively, clerical authority. This is one of the reasons why Guyon's mysticism, in which the human is not elevated, evidently remains at the same time a practice and way of *human* life. Rather than escape the human, Lee argues, Guyon's mysticism seeks to decenter an "agenda," specific to her time and place but found in many contexts, that accompanied human interests.[68] While Guyon addresses human readers, she wants those readers to consider their common ground with creatures other than human. Guyon understands the state of union with God as already existing in life, at the point where life is at its most receptive and open. Union with God, in this sense, is thus comparable to vegetal life or, more accurately, converges with vegetal life. Being open and receptive is something plants, for instance, know better than humans, since this is their "natural" way of being, while for humans, it requires a demanding spiritual exercise of cultivating attentiveness. The mystic's attentiveness, in this sense, must contain or gesture toward a kinship with the vegetal.

SOMETHING LESSER THAN THE MEANEST INSECT

Several passages in Guyon's work attest to a particular awareness of the vegetal and a deliberate, sometimes remarkably direct, attempt to draw connections between mystical states and vegetal life for the reader. The most obvious, and undoubtedly the most disturbing to her interrogators, would have been the following passage from *Spiritual Torrents*: "Men would condemn such a [mystical] state, saying it makes us something less than the meanest insect; *and so it does*, not by obstinacy and firmness of purpose, but by powerlessness to interfere with ourselves."[69] The way to God, the possibility of experiencing God in this life, does not lie beyond life but is immanent to life. More than this, however, the path to God lies in a vegetal anthropology. In Guyon's imagery, it plunges the human beneath the "meanest insect," that is, to the state of the plant life popularly understood, during the early modern period, to occupy the lower end of the Great Chain of Being. Subsequently, "firmness of purpose" cannot generate this possibility, since it is not created by humans. Rather, the possibility for experiencing God is what *creates* humans, sustains them by an imperceptible activity unfathomable to the will yet constituting it at every moment. At bottom, for Guyon, every part of life—not only plants—is limited by what she calls "powerlessness to interfere with ourselves."

The same theme reappears in Guyon's poetry. Guyon wrote many poems, later set to music and popularized with illustrations. All of them relate to the idea of the spiritual life as spontaneous and natural. Creaturely life features prominently, and pastoral tropes appear frequently in Guyon's lyrics. The poem that conveys her theological views most clearly is "Scenes Favorable to Meditation," apparently a reflection on her experience of persecution. It begins by declaring the "Wilds horrid and dark with o'ershadowing trees, / Rocks that ivy and briers unfold, / Scenes nature with dread and astonishment sees," before claiming these "horrid wilds" her sanctuary: "But I with a pleasure untold; // Though awfully silent, and shaggy, and ruse, / I am charm'd with the peace ye afford; / Your shades are a temple where none will intrude, / The abode of my lover and Lord." Addressing the trees of the forest, Guyon recognizes them as the home of her divine lover. It is humans, not wolves, she continues, that constitute her true enemy: "Here I and the beasts of the desert agree, / Mankind are the wolves that I fear; / They grudge me my natural right to be free, / But nobody questions it here." Even though forests are considered gloomy at night, Guyon writes, they do not judge; in this way, they grant Guyon freedom. Reflecting on what her freedom consists in, she remarks: "I am nourished without knowing how I am fed / I have nothing, and yet I abound."[70] Natural freedom, for Guyon, is experienced, first, through the act of being left alone: "Nobody questions me here." It is also experienced, however, in the recognition of dependency that letting-be facilitates: "I am nourished without knowing how I am fed." As in the low anthropology of *Spiritual Torrents*, Guyon circles back to vegetal life. Meeting the divine lover is to meet vegetal life not only in the trees surrounding the persecuted Guyon but in her body: *I am nourished*.

The practice of contemplative prayer as the "meanest" life opens the door toward the human-divine relationship but also to a vegetalizing of human freedom: Guyon feels herself with God when she feels her participation in vegetal life. I say vegetal life rather than plant life, because Guyon is not tying natural freedom, here, to species envy. The trope of vegetality that I am finding in Guyon, the outlines of which are intimated by de Certeau and Bruneau's work, becomes, in my reading, the basis for what Bo Karen Lee calls Guyon's low anthropology. Guyon experiences union with God not insofar as she possesses the power to rise above nature but in her powerlessness to withstand nature. Yet she also insists that this powerlessness does not amount to resignation. Rather, the inability to exert power over oneself indicates the extent to which all selves are constituted by passive activities, radical openness, and vulnerability. One might also say that God is made weak in Guyon's mysticism, since God is above all figured through an experience of the vegetal, of "powerlessness to interfere with ourselves." The mystical God and the mystic's self are weakened, together, by vegetal life. Michael Marder describes vegetalization as analogous to a weakening of thought. It is a process of loosening the tight grip categories hold over things: "consenting... to let beings be, to save singularity from the clasp of generalizing abstraction, and perhaps to put thought in the service of finite life."[71] This perspective is quite different to the traditional way of equating freedom with the ability to control what is external to oneself, whether by physical means or indirectly by naming and systematizing. Listening to vegetal being worries these categories because of the way in which vegetal existence seems so thoroughly to reject the idea of exercising power-over as a criterion for freedom. In the same way, contemplation—and the mystical tradition of the *via negativa* that shapes it—dismantles the categories under which freedom has been understood. For Guyon, freedom is not mastery of nature but natural spontaneity. As we have already seen, in her *Short and Easy Method*, Guyon uses the analogy of a stone falling through air: "Unless some strong and vigorous force stops it, it moves in that direction with force." She continues: "It is the same with water and fire which, being left alone, move incessantly toward their depths."[72]

This idea of being left alone in order to move is particularly prominent in Guyon's *Commentary on the Song of Songs of Solomon*. Here she writes against "those who say [mystical] union can only happen in the next life." Guyon insists that mystical union, to the contrary, is embodied: "I hold for certain that it can happen in this one [i.e., this life] here." The insistence on *this life here* introduces her *Commentary on the Song of Songs*. In this commentary, Guyon sees the vegetal imagery of the Song as symbolic but also and at the same time as nonallegorical. Guyon follows Jewish and Christian tradition, reading the lovers' union in the garden of Solomon as a description of the human-divine relationship. Yet she does not tie this erotic imagery to the sexual eroticism of human sexuality. Rather, like the vegetal mysticism we encountered in the previous chapter, plants in the garden of the Song appear to inspire, instead, a breaking away from human sexuality as a model for mystical union. In Guyon's mystic garden, while the Bride and Bridegroom unite erotically, the sexual act modeling mystical union is gender-fluid: "Her Bridegroom is in her, as much as she is in her Bridegroom."[73]

The Song is a text characterized by plant imagery, and plant life is a direct model for the mystical life in Guyon's text. For instance, the vineyard of the Song is glossed as the interior state, and God is pictured as a flower planted in that vineyard. "I am the lily of the valleys that only grows in annihilated souls," God speaks in Guyon's commentary. In another place, God is an apple tree under which the mystic takes refuge; further on, God is described simply as earth: the land of eternal springtime where mystic souls arrive to rest. These images help shift the emphasis from specific plant life to vegetal life. At one point, the mystic is described as a person searching for God among creatures, unable to find God. Rather than *rejecting* creatures in order to find God, however, Guyon surprises the reader by suggesting that the Bride needs simply to let creatures be in order to experience her Beloved. Once the Bride has done so, she discovers that "her Beloved is everywhere and in everything, and that everything is himself, without her being able to distinguish anything from him who is in all places without being enclosed in any."[74] Thus the mystic *does* find God in creatures, albeit not in a specific creature. God is discovered, rather, as that without which there would be no creatures. The discovery of God "everywhere and in everything" is a discovery that, importantly, is not pushed into the afterlife or, alternatively, relegated to the disembodied life of the spirit. The discovery of God "everywhere and in everything" happens in life, as life. Life, however, is appreciated in its power of barely noticeable activity, figured preeminently in the vegetal; it is as the blurring of boundaries between identities and species ("without being able to distinguish anything from him who is in all places"), therefore, that brings God into relation, a relation that disrupts the opposition between subject and object, self and other, activity and passivity.

LIBERATING SPIRITUAL EXERCISES FROM SPECIESISM

Mystically, the practice of letting-be in Guyon's work points toward a decentering of anthropocentrism in ethics, and it asks: What happens to freedom in a more-than-human world? On the one hand, there is the need to be left alone, free of harassment. Being left alone, like the stone allowed to fall unimpeded to the ground in Guyon's simile, evokes a sense of liberation *from* and a reclaiming of agency. This is very clearly articulated in Guyon's politics and her own use of mysticism as a tactic of resistance to clerical control. On the other hand, freedom for Guyon does not signify autonomy in the sense of sovereignty and power-over. Rather, there is the need to leave others alone. Being left alone, like the vegetal life to which Guyon compares her mystical state, does not entail absence of agency but simply absence of power-over; it is the recognition of dependence and negotiation between entities and, within entities, between the entities of which they are composed. Beyond the politics of liberation, there is a deeper liberation of politics to life. Life, in Guyon's mysticism, does not invariably signify a specific form of life. Rather, life is a spontaneous activity of being nourished "without knowing how." The mystic reflects on plants in the Song of Songs but finds the plant within. Might not Guyon's mysticism indicate a practice of recognizing what Marder called the plant in us? If so, how might the practices in which Guyon's mysticism is rooted root vegetal life in ethics? What are the practices that might develop were we to take Guyon's handbooks seriously as the manuals of practice they were intended to be?

The potential of Guyon's mysticism for philosophies of vegetal life demands more careful study, which I will turn to in the following chapter. I will end by reflecting that Guyon practices mysticism by weakening it, that is to say, by loosening the grip of "God" and "self" over the mystic attempting to practice. Borrowing alternately from Marder and Bo Karen Lee in turn, I have called this weakening a vegetalizing of thought and a low anthropology. The vegetal is part of that weakening, as symbol for the mystic but also as symbiosis: It is by listening to the vegetal activities of their own bodies that mystics experience God, in "this [life] here."[75] The politics that emerge from this practice may be described, following Certeau and Bruneau, as a "tactics," to indicate their resistance to systems of authority ("strategies"). Tactics lead Guyon "beyond duality and the hierarchical discrimination of difference."[76] With Guyon, mysticism is everywhere and nowhere; imperceptible, as the practices she invites us to consider and the God whose presence she compares to gravity, oxygen, water, fire, seed, milk. It is in this imperceptibility that the entwining of mystical and vegetal being can happen.

5

THE PLANT IN US

The experiences that made me question the abyss so often assumed to exist between plants and humans took me by surprise, yet they did not feel extraordinary. For a full eighteen months before the weird feeling of becoming like a plant erupted into my everyday awareness, I had been practicing mystical prayer daily, often several times a day. My sense of what Michael Marder calls "the plant in us," in other words, grew gradually, through a process of habituation, repetition, and daily commitment. Later, as I researched what would become the material for this book, I understood that my experiences most likely were not coincidental: Mystics centuries before me described similar states, following similar practices, in ways that resonated remarkably with my initial idea of a "vegetative soul" coming to the fore during contemplation. Yet so much of what has been written, from an ecological perspective, about feeling attuned to Terran kin passes over *practices*. Similarly, much of what is written about Western Christian mystics, from an ecological perspective, tends to focus on mystical visions and theological ideas, to the exclusion of the practices that make the ideas possible.

This chapter will be thinking through what it might mean to recognize participation in vegetal life as human animals. My companion will continue to be the early modern mystic Jeanne Guyon. Guyon interests me for her remarkable attention to contemplative prayer. Guyon's strong critique of institutions meant that she was encouraged to devise methods that would be practicable without a spiritual director or liturgy; her writing, therefore, is focused on the practical aspects of the method she recommends. I will be addressing contemplation, one of the terms Guyon prefers for describing her method of prayer. We encountered contemplation already in chapters 1 and 2. Contemplation is central to Guyon's mysticism not only because it is, to her, the form of mystical prayer but because lively matter is viewed, by Guyon, as already contemplative, constituted by radical openness, vulnerability, and powerlessness. I will be drawing the work of several contemporary philosophers of the vegetal into dialogue with the method of contemplation Guyon presents in her influential handbook, *A Short and Easy Method of Prayer* (1685). While philosophies of the vegetal articulated among critics, historians, and philosophers today identify vegetal life with contemplation, Guyon's method of contemplation attempts to rethink it from the perspective of nutrition, growth, breath, and elemental cycling. In both, the need to rethink agency in terms of receptivity, openness, and vulnerability is paramount. Yet Guyon's mysticism, written as a manual reflecting years of experience (and struggles) practicing, is able to attend more carefully to the urgent questions posed by contemporary philosophies of the vegetal. What does it mean, not merely hypothetically or hopefully, but pragmatically and tactically, to speak of attuning to the plant in us?

Part of that answer has already been glimpsed in the previous chapter. Here, I will be deepening my reading by returning, first, to contemplation as it has appeared in some contemporary philosophies of vegetal life, especially the work of Luce Irigaray and Emanuele Coccia. Both Irigaray and Coccia, but perhaps especially Coccia, show fascinating parallels with Guyon's account of practicing contemplative prayer. Coccia's attempt to overhaul metaphysics and begin not from the organism but from the plant "contemplating" its environment provides a helpful way of articulating mysticism's tactics, tactics that resist systems of oppression through practices of quiet rebellion. I then address both from the perspective of critical plant studies and the "vegetable contemplation" of Gilles Deleuze.

RETHINKING PASSIVITY: PRACTICAL CONTEMPLATION IN CONTEMPORARY PHILOSOPHIES OF VEGETAL LIFE

For Jeanne Guyon's practice of contemplation, *passivity* is key. Passivity, however, emerges as both invitation and challenge. The passive points toward receptivity, sensibility, and dependence and thus toward entanglement. Yet it does not repudiate freedom; instead, it rethinks freedom in terms of letting-be. Guyon, together with the philosophies of vegetal life I am considering here, rejects the idea that freedom is *opposed* to passivity, asking instead whether passivity truly entails a negation of agency, and proposes that agency, in turn, needs to be rethought completely. A regard for contemplation is not a rejection of action in favor of passive inertia but a rejection of widespread disregard for the imperceptible activities that appear under the veil of passivity, preceding—and thus making possible—will, choice, and desire. It is the reorienting of thought from heroism to the imperceptible, the everyday, and the barely noticeable.

If passivity has this central role in Guyon's mysticism, the connection to *vegetal* life that we saw in previous chapters also relates in particular ways to contemplative practices. Marder's philosophy of vegetal life is drawn toward what he calls "practical contemplation," developed through his reading of the French feminist philosopher Irigaray. As I intimated earlier, Marder both thinks with and against Irigaray in his plant philosophy, and his understanding of practical contemplation emerges from rethinking, rather than replicating, Irigaray's work. In particular, Marder takes care to situate Irigaray's gendered account of vegetality. In *The Philosopher's Plant: An Intellectual Herbarium*, Marder briefly engages with Elaine P. Miller's *The Vegetative Soul: From Philosophy of Nature to Subjectivity in the Feminine*, a philosophical application of Irigaray's feminist criticism to the representation of plants in Western philosophy. In *Vegetative Soul*, Miller argues that the recovery of the plant is inseparable from "the possible configuration of a feminine subject that is neither atomistic nor confrontational."[1] She identifies a double maligning of plants and women in Western philosophy. In Irigaray's *Elemental Passions*, Irigaray evoked the woman's body itself as a flower, with the vegetal representing her sexuality. For Miller, this poetic text by Irigaray challenged but also reclaimed the association of woman and plant. While the male gaze initially seeks to render the woman a flower, that gaze also fails continually to grasp the fullness of the vegetal it has conjured and wishes to possess: "Why do you fear that this flower will be taken from you?" asks the woman-flower in *Elemental Passions*, adding: "Before you, there was the nurture of the plant."[2] Miller looks to feminist criticism's attempts to reclaim, instead of reject, vegetal "passivity." Given that women traditionally have been aligned symbolically with nature, changing how we speak about the latter "might have the possibility of restructuring or even creating feminine subjectivity in a way that would make a real difference to women." She clarifies: "Rather than simply pointing out the flaws of traditional philosophy's linkage of the feminine with the earth or nature, Irigaray focuses on the redemptive possibilities inherent in the very metaphors that have been used to reduce the feminine to the silent, concealed ground of Being, just as a 'plantlike' reading transforms its textual object in metamorphic growth."[3] When Marder engages with Miller in *Philosopher's Plant*, what he lingers on is the centrality given, in Miller's work, to representation and, especially, gendered representation. Marder argues that "Irigaray vigilantly guards against the reduction of plants (or of any other living beings for that matter) to symbols by moderating the theoretical impulse with practical contemplation and by letting them grow, leaving them be, freeing them from the noise of *logos*."[4] For Marder, the emphasis on language and representation might even invite a kind of inadvertent relativizing of the very vegetal, more-than-linguistic life at stake, as Miller argues that "nature" here should never be confused with the real thing. Miller comments that "'nature,' then, in the broader argument of this book, refers to that which is *symbolized* as nature (as opposed to culture), although by virtue of being called 'natural' it is sometimes presented as if it were essentially and inevitably figured in a particular way."[5] By contrast, Marder suggests that what is at stake, for Irigaray, is "practical contemplation." Marder argues that there is more to Irigaray's philosophy of vegetal life than a representation of feminine subjectivity. While he maintains a strong critique of Irigaray on the question of plants and gendered representation, he thinks Irigaray's practices offer an alternative view, one that foregrounds vegetal life, rather than sexual difference.

Marder turns to *attention*, which weaves in and out of Irigaray's writing on vegetal life: "Attention undisturbed by understanding clears the space for thinking *and* for life—for the wonder, with which philosophy begins, and for existence, which is not forced into the ready-made categories of cognition."[6] Irigaray's reflections on plants are the result of a decades-long practice of "taking refuge" in the vegetal world, as she explains in her dialogue with Michael Marder, *Through Vegetal Being*. Here, Irigaray recounts her exclusion from the academic world in the 1970s following the publication of her classic study *Speculum of the Other Woman* and discusses the importance of learning how to inhabit the world afresh after this change. Vegetality then became paramount, not only as something to look at (Irigaray recalls the significance of urban gardens) but as a kind of recognition: "A coexistence with vegetal beings—I could almost say: this vegetal existence—keeps me alive and secretly goes with my words." While contemplating a flower, "the combination of the sensible quality of the flower gathers me," writes Irigaray, "thanks to an attention they awaken at various levels, and imperceptible, I am brought from concentration to contemplation. If I take the time to live such a state, it can be converted into a sort of ecstasy, which results from a culmination of energy." Irigaray describes her experiences practicing Yoga, where breathwork is used in order to heighten awareness of sensory perceptions. She discovers exercises for attending to breath but also remarkable plant teachers. Irigaray writes: "Little by little, I discovered a universe that I was searching for in which breathing is crucial and life as such is respected and cultivated [and in which] some masters ... not to mention the Buddha himself—had asked trees for help, as I was doing."[7] In Marder's reading of Irigaray, thinking with plants is then more than developing an alternative, thought-provoking metaphor for speaking about women's bodies or even simply human bodies. Rather, it provides a means of attuning to life, since all life depends on the exchange of gases with the environment. The cultivation of sensory perception is what emerges from "asking the trees for help."

In *A New Culture of Energy: Beyond East and West*, Irigaray puts her experiences with Yoga into dialogue with themes from Christian spirituality. While maintaining that Western traditions have neglected the practice of attending to breath—and thus of attending to human dependence on vegetal life—she finds that the story of Mary furnishes appropriate "words or images" for someone wishing to practice attentiveness to breath in a cultural context distinct from that of Yoga.[8] Irigaray is drawn to the association of Mary to the Holy Spirit and thus to God but also to air. In the biblical story, Mary conceives Christ by the Holy Spirit, and Irigaray interprets this to mean that Mary had a special relationship to air. For Irigaray, Mary's "virginity" is thus not sexual (a notion that she rejects) but rather vegetal. She writes: "The virginity of Mary is interpreted as a capability to preserve the artlessness and the receptiveness of an autonomous breathing . . . in order that Mary could welcome the other as other, even in herself, without losing her maidenhood." While acknowledging that Mary's "maidenhood" has been interpreted differently and used to control women's bodies, Irigaray argues that another, *vegetal*, reading lies just under the surface. At stake is the literal meaning of *spiritus*: "The divine is linked with air, with breath. The one who is designated by the name of God in our tradition creates with his breath, and those who enjoy spiritual powers have a relationship with air, with wind, with the source and movement of life."[9] In Irigaray's work, new connections between vegetality and spiritual practices open up. Following on from Marder and Irigaray on "practical contemplation," the questions I will be asking are: How do vegetal life and practices of attention relate to each other? In what ways might our understanding of mystical passivity for a writer like Guyon change were we to see it from the perspective of practices such as breathwork? And conversely, how do contemporary philosophies of the vegetal alter when viewed through the lens of mystics, like Guyon, for whom prayer is compared to breath? It may be that what we find invites philosophy to be practiced not only through vegetal but also through mystical being.

Another philosopher of plant life who has been rethinking the apparent passivity of plants in ways that indicate contemplative practice, especially breathwork, is Emanuele Coccia. Although he does not respond directly to Irigaray, the parallels between the positions taken by Coccia and the trajectory represented by Irigaray's remarks on contemplation are helpful, not least because Coccia has a background in agronomics. *The Life of Plants: A Metaphysics of Mixture* is a philosophical text informed by plant science to a large extent. Against the traditional, philosophical understanding of plants as contemptible, Coccia suggests plants as contemplative. Plants are contemplative, argues Coccia, not because plants are like us: Plants are different. Plants "don't have senses, but they are far from being shut in on themselves: no other being adheres to the world that surrounds it more than plants do." In his reading of plants, Coccia thus adopts Daniel Chamovitz's suggestion to think of plant consciousness as "anoetic." We encountered Chamovitz's idea in an earlier chapter, and Chamovitz is also cited by Coccia, who argues that plants are conscious yet stresses the difference of their consciousness from human or animal consciousness. This allows Coccia to draw connections between vegetal consciousness and contemplation. He follows an apophatic or negative view of contemplation, equating it with openness to a God beyond human perception. He then freely interprets the direction of the mystical "beyond," situating it not in transcendent but in vegetal being. Vegetal consciousness thus takes the place of mystical communion with God, with God, in turn, contained in the word "environment." As Coccia explains: "Plant life is life as complete exposure, in absolute continuity and total communion with the environment." The plant is "the purest observer when it comes to contemplating the world in its totality."[10] Coccia's philosophy of plants, therefore, from the outset renders plant consciousness and plant life into spiritual matters, or rather, matters of spiritual practice. The attempt to think with plants becomes a question of attuning human consciousness to vegetal awareness. As Coccia's narrative develops, the species-specific image of plants at the beginning of the book, sketched by their radical alterity and difference from humans, for this reason unfolds into a recognition of the plant-like activities constituting also a human body. Like Marder, Coccia adopts the ancient Greek sense of vegetal activity as not "simply a distinct class of specific forms of life or a taxonomic unity separated from others, but rather a place shared by all living beings." But the accessibility of the plant that thus emerges does not mean the appropriation of vegetal life by human speculation. Rather, human reason, being itself constituted by vegetal life, realizes in the plant its own finitude and plasticity. What Coccia proposes is philosophy as plant-life—that is, philosophy both open to the life of plants and recapitulating plant-like openness in its own forms-of-life—a concept close to Irigaray: "Reason is a flower: reason is not and can never be an organ with well-defined and stable forms. . . . It is risk, invention, experimentation."[11]

To develop his idea of the vegetal as contemplative, Coccia places passive activities at the center of his account of life. "When there is life," writes Coccia, "the container is located in the contained (and is thus contained by it); and vice versa. The paradigms of this mutual overlap is what the ancients called 'breath' (*pneuma*)." When breathing, we penetrate the atmosphere, which also penetrates us: Activity is thus inseparable from passivity. Passivity constitutes life. Passivity also creates life: The atmosphere is the work of photosynthesis, elemental cycling, and the exchange of gases—in a word, of passivity. Plants "are the ones who *made* our world, even though the status of this making is quite different from that of any other activity of living beings." For this reason, Coccia argues that, rather than see plants as outliers on account of their passivity, they should be appreciated as paradigmatic. Plants are paradigmatic in their passivity not because they are more inert than animals (in fact, they are constantly metamorphosing as they grow) but because they evidence what passivity is able to accomplish: life. A world without plants is not a world that can be imagined by creatures whose capacity to imagine depends on vegetal life: "Plants have transformed the world into the reality of breath."[12] As in Irigaray's work, part of Coccia's rethinking of passivity is thus bound up with a cultivation of breath and breathing. Breath is shared with plants; breathing becomes a way of thinking with plants in their active passivity. Yet in Coccia's work, spiritual traditions of breathwork are not discussed directly. Coccia accomplishes this argument, instead, by slowly reshaping the theological associations of *spiritus* until they acquire vegetal meaning. The "life of the spirit," a concept Coccia introduces in his book, is not the activity of a disembodied soul but the passive activity of breathing and being breathed. One "contemplates" not by placing before one's eyes "an inert and immaterial image" but (echoing Plotinus) by growing, a passive activity. Growth is the "force that allows one to transform the world and a portion of its matter into a *singular life*."[13] If philosophy no less than theology has been guilty of defining the spiritual in anthropomorphic terms (Coccia writes of spirit as an "anthropomorphic shadow"), Coccia draws attention to the vegetality implied in spirit when we return to its etymology: "The world is the breath of the living." This world Coccia describes as one in which "action and contemplation can no longer be distinguished," owing to the lack of distance between subject and object in the process of breathing: "In this world, everything is in everything." At the same time, this world is not a complete fusion; rather, Coccia calls the world a "mixture," a cosmology of "interpenetration and reciprocal influence."[14] In this world, interaction, rather than action, generates life.

Despite his difference in approach from Irigaray and from a mystic like Guyon, Coccia seeks to rethink the passive in ways that share concerns with the writers I have been considering. Coccia finds the privileging of activity problematic, arguing that life is created passively, through a radical openness he calls contemplative, even as he insists that contemplation is itself a force: the force of growth. In a way, Coccia's argument is especially close to the one I am developing here, where the mystical and the vegetal reveal between themselves a symbolic closeness. Moreover, for Coccia, as for myself, symbols bend into symbiosis, and here Coccia's starting point among plants rather than mystics is helpful to linger with when considering the strange fruits that are emerging from the graft I am cultivating. For, in Coccia's *Life of Plants*, not only are plants seen afresh, but contemplation is also rethought as a vegetal process. In an earlier chapter, we saw how Marder made a similar observation, and Coccia's *Life of Plants* develops along related lines. For Coccia, what needs to be seen is that contemplation is normative not because everyone *should* practice spiritual exercises but because, at a deeper level, everyone *already is* living by virtue of vegetal contemplation: Everyone already is immersed in environments in such a way that "the opposition between motion and stillness no longer exists." The anthropomorphic language commonly attached to mysticism is transformed, and the sense of contemplation is opened: What results is a shift from human practice to practices of the living. At this point in my reading, however, I am especially interested in Coccia's gestures toward practices. What Coccia describes as the "cosmology of mixture" speaks to the classical language of mystical union, as we shall see. But if we stop at the level of imagery and metaphor, we risk overlooking what is at stake: life and the living. Following Irigaray, I want to ask how resistance to Western philosophy's anthropocentrism can be enlivened: Is there an ethics here, or is it merely a question of providing an alternative vision, a "better" cosmology? In this regard, I am drawn to Irigaray's recent accounts of practicing breathwork and to how she weaves these into a critique of metaphysics. I am wary of a certain presumption on the part of philosophy to provide maps that distance readers from the particularity of practice, as when Coccia looks forward to "the most radical form of speculative activity . . . indifferent to the places, forms, and ways in which it is practiced." Coccia urges us to look at practice free of ideological or disciplinary constraints. What is perhaps less clearly narrated is the situated nature of any practice, even when the practice in question is so ordinary as to become universal and thus "indifferent" to its conditions of appearance. I do not think Coccia is suggesting that philosophy can be practiced in a state of indifference to the world, seeing as how "it is impossible to liberate oneself from the environment in which one is immersed, and it is impossible to purify this environment of our presence." Coccia takes with profound seriousness the inseparability of practice from environments. The "indifference" he enjoins is an indifference to the agendas accompanying practice; for Coccia, plant philosophy is not an elite approach available only to the few. Yet despite this acknowledgment, there is a tendency to shy away from what, following Michel de Certeau and the Guyon scholar Marie-Florine

Bruneau, I have described as everyday tactics. I sense that Coccia's remarks, in his care to avoid tying the vegetal down too closely to this or that situated practice, inadvertently makes practicability appear secondary. Like other contemporary philosophers of vegetal life, Coccia is aware of the dangers of appropriating nonhuman experience. By insisting on the universal, vegetal, and common nature of practice, the human is effectively decentered in ways that resist the fixing of thought. He writes: "Philosophical thought is nowhere and everywhere. Like atmosphere."[15] By denying to philosophy a situated story of human practice, Coccia in a way is reminding that even where humans practice and cultivate awareness of their participation in the world's breath, this is but one perspective and not one that possesses inherent privilege.

At the same time, the passive activities that are vegetal life cannot be reduced to an ideal. They are here, among us, with us; they *are us*. In the same way that Coccia, Marder, and Irigaray argue for the close relationship between vegetal life and the form of philosophy, I want to propose that this relationship be understood as pragmatic. I am keen to avoid presenting the vegetal as an escape, for humans, from the situated forms of knowledge that compose readings of books like Coccia's *Life of Plants*. Rather, philosophies of vegetal life emerge and return to practices of breathing the world.

CULTIVATING SPONTANEOUS ATTENTIVENESS: GUYON'S *SHORT AND EASY METHOD*

How, then, does one begin to practice vegetal life? What would it look like, practicing what is already practiced passively by ourselves, without the "self" having any formal knowledge of the fact? How can that which is unconscious become the object of awareness, reflection, and conscious effort without exposing itself too much to the gaze of reason? If contemporary philosophies of vegetal life point toward contemplation when attempting to articulate such a practice, Guyon's practice of contemplative prayer gestures toward vegetal life in its striking analogies and comparisons. In Guyon's instructions for contemplation, metaphors are concretized in practices, where evocation of the vegetal is not simply ideal or symbolic. Rather, metaphors of the vegetal, used to picture the human-divine relationship, also incarnate into lived experiences. The establishing of new ways of life, of shifting perceptions and "a new rhythm of existence,"[16] is what is at stake in Guyon's practice of contemplation.

More concretely still, an older mystical tradition aids Guyon in her understanding of contemplation. In the first place, Guyon can be said to build on the Carmelite passive loving attention as articulated by John of the Cross and Teresa of Ávila. Passive loving attention, however, requires some parsing, since for John and Teresa it designates something different to mere gazing. Passive loving attention is in fact closer to attentiveness than to paying attention; it designates a state of being, unconscious activity, or comportment, rather than a specific action. It is defined as the ability to perceive others spontaneously without covetousness and the desire to possess, comprehend, or otherwise control what is different to oneself. It is also defined as something quite different to simply sitting in stillness. Attentiveness, in this tradition, is cultivated through receptivity and takes the form of a deliberate opening toward the other.[17] Contemplation is not a conscious or deliberate choice, something one decides to do one day while preferring not to on another. Contemplation is a *habit*, a form of activity that is practiced yet not consciously deliberated upon. Contemplation is involuntary and informs the direction taken by will, reason, and desire, which succeed contemplation. In other words, contemplation is a habit in the philosophical sense of habit as "second nature." At the same time, contemplation is also "first nature," since what it expresses is not a specialized activity (a skill comparable to mastering a musical instrument, for instance) but prereflexive responsiveness or sensitivity.[18] As I see it, this is why Guyon favors metaphors of vegetal life and why her understanding of contemplation bears a similarity to contemporary philosophies of vegetal life. In both cases, what lies before the writer is the elusive, cryptic, yet constantly vigilant doing that is life. In addition, Guyon's contemplation is tactical. Guyon's practice participates in laicization and resistance to clerical authority. Contemplation taught as practice, the technique that shapes Guyon's mysticism, is not only a way of tuning into corporeal affect but also a way to reclaim agency without conforming to a dominant discourse. *Silence* is at the heart of that tactic, for Guyon. Contemplation could—and was—practiced in a variety of circumstances, in the midst of domestic routines as well as persecution, imprisonment, and harassment, offering comfort but also means of resilience and empowerment. Guyon's persistent desire, in her work, is to offer practical ways for readers to cultivate modes of agency that would evade capture by systems of domination.

What Guyon calls contemplation is presented using different metaphors in her work, metamorphosing like the vegetal life it so often invokes. In *The Spiritual Torrents* (1683), her first major book, we find it referred to as "the passive way." For Guyon, the capacity to follow the passive way is given by God to those who turn to God, yet she also describes it as natural; Guyon compares the passive way to instinct. It is "not like something distinct, which [the soul] knows, sees, attempts, practices, but as that which is natural to it ... such as breathing."[19] In *Short and*

Easy Method, contemplation is described in more detail. Here the starting point is nature rather than conversion: "All who want to experience contemplative prayer can do so." The ability to contemplate is evident not only in those who turn to God but in everyone. Formal prayers are not necessary, nor is literacy a prerequisite. Meditation, that is, visualization, is also not necessary. Even so, Guyon stresses that it takes a certain kind of effort to contemplate. She emphasizes the need to make an initial effort and suggests two preliminary practices: "informal meditation" and "meditative reading" (she includes a version to be used when teaching those who cannot read). They are, however, quite different from what one might find under similar names in Ignatius of Loyola's *Spiritual Exercises*. In Guyon's "meditative reading," the aim is not to read at speed or to understand the text but to "savor" it (Guyon does not specify which text and suggests that any text that is meaningful to the practitioner is suitable). Similarly, during "informal meditation," the aim is not to think *about* a specific image or idea of God but rather to "place oneself in the presence of God," figured here as Divine Love. In both cases, the purpose is to become familiar with a different mode of relating, "exciting our will through our feelings, rather than by our understanding."[20] Practicing "informal meditation" in this way over time allows a person to relax spontaneously into the open and receptive state required for contemplation. At stake is the ability to listen to the "heart" and the "affections" without spoken words. Rather than speak of prayer as dialogue, a word indicating spoken exchange, Guyon prefers to compare prayer to breathing, tasting, savoring, digesting, and enjoyment. We saw already in the previous chapter the significance of these concepts and what they indicate. The "heart" is not a mental realm, nor does it signify what we mean, today, by emotion. Rather, the heart is prereflexive spontaneity, the deep responsiveness in a creature that is sensitivity and affectability. "Breathing," "digestion," and so forth are not only symbolic. This is because what Guyon describes as "heart" and "affection" cannot find expression outside the body and because the body is the site of opening toward God. Fabrice Blée comments that with Guyon's preliminary exercises in *Short and Easy Method*, Catholic contemplative prayer develops in directions that share features with Buddhist mindfulness practices, in which attentiveness to the body's rhythms, most notably breath, are cultivated. Guyon rethinks contemplation as embodiment when claiming that it begins with a centering in the here and now, in silence.[21]

However, these preliminary exercises do not constitute contemplation. Contemplation works as a form of passive activity once openness has become habitual and once a person no longer needs to set aside time for the practice. Guyon contrasts the "forcing" of spiritual exercises during retreats to the spontaneous and free practice that emerges when a person follows a "natural" course. Instead of forcing the movement of prayer using spoken word and rituals, one is to cultivate what Guyon calls "suppleness."[22] The spiritual life should not be dictated by dogma but by openness and the ability to be changed. The present moment is emphasized. This concept for Guyon is the "key to inner life" and represents the moment of spontaneous responsiveness to God: "The moment is an infallible declaration ... being inevitable and shared by all." Responding to the present moment is illustrated by more allusions to vegetality. In the same way that a baby knows when to stimulate flow and when to desist from too much movement, in the same way that a seed's sprouting cannot be rushed, in the same way that a river flows inexorably into the sea, so too, in prayer, the movement is natural. The point is not to do or to say nothing; the point is to know when to desist from forcing the movement. The example of the nursing infant is then expanded on. Guyon argues that some people are quiet because they have nothing to say, while others are quiet "from having too much to say." "We keep quiet," Guyon argues, "because of excess, not lack." An infant's action at the breast illustrates this, for Guyon. The breastfeeding infant will move their lips vigorously but stop once the flow has been stimulated. If they persist in their vigorous movements, the milk will spill over, and nourishment will be interrupted. Milk is then compared by Guyon to grace, and the infant's peaceful activity to contemplation. "You see that the soul is led here naturally," she comments, "without any discomfort, without thought, without artifice." Throughout, contemplation is compared to something "completely natural," and thus it "carries a seed of life and fertility."[23]

Contemplation "seeds" itself by becoming indistinguishable from ordinary life. Guyon writes that the feeling of God's presence should be continual. It is only in the beginning, when a person is new to the practice, that she advises seeking out a quiet part of the house in which to practice. But once the practice has become habitual, this search for solitude is no longer necessary. Avoidance ought not result in physical inertia or retreat from the world, nor in disdain of the quotidian tasks of daily life. Enjoying God in silence "is . . . an action, but an action . . . so tranquil, that it seems to the soul that it is not acting because it moves completely naturally." Silence, the characteristic of Guyon's method, appears here as a way of describing a quality of *any* action undertaken by the mystic. "Silence" does not quite convey what Guyon has in mind, nor does "tranquility." "Attentiveness" is more apposite, perhaps, since Guyon does not stipulate an absence of speech or action. As she writes in *Torrents*, it is possible to enjoy intimate communion with God while playing cards and chatting, as one of Guyon's acquaintances reported.[24]

Thus Bruneau notes that "this practice of silence by a woman must not be confused with the imposed silence traditionally demanded of women."[25] Rather, Guyon's practice of silent prayer was a subversion of the control imposed on women. Silence here indicates an ongoing yet indeterminate attentiveness that escapes the grasp of clerical and patriarchal authority even as it shapes every determinate action. While "formerly it was necessary to exercise virtue in order to perform virtuous works," now "the meanest action equally with the greatest" is performed with the same attentiveness. In other words, silence is very lively. Everyday domestic routines are not a hindrance to contemplative prayer, nor is family life or the "world" at large an impediment, despite Guyon's frequent condemnation of society's ills. In fact, Guyon argues that the desire to retreat from the world and to talk endlessly of spiritual concerns to the neglect of one's family, friends, and social responsibilities is "a horrible abuse."[26] It is taken as a sign that contemplation has not become fully natural if one is not able, both, to contemplate God as well as work, eat, have sex, socialize, weep, and laugh. Retreating from the world, in this context, is tantamount to declaring those in the world to be tragically enslaved, "naturally" fallen. It is with this pessimistic attitude to nature that Guyon's mysticism wrestles.

When contemplating, being attentive is key to continuous practice. Guyon looks to her own body's nutritive activities as models of contemplation but also to the movement of water, fire, and air and the growth of plants. Nature, in Guyon's mysticism, is not the mechanistic matter as envisaged by seventeenth-century philosophers like Descartes. To the contrary, as we saw in the previous chapter, Guyon's "nature" is much closer to Natania Meeker and Antonia Szabari's "vegetal modernity," with its materialist pantheism. To open mysticism toward nature, Guyon shares with vegetal modernity a similar idea of nature's passivity as *secretly* dynamic. Meanwhile, Emanuele Coccia's rethinking of passivity through vegetal life pointed him in the direction of contemplation as a way of describing an activity that is neither fully active nor purely passive. "Vegetal activity encrypts itself in its modes of appearance," observes Marder, "by representing itself in the guise of passivity, which is to say, by never presenting itself as such." What we have in vegetal being is not inertia, yet neither is it willed movement; rather, it is movement that is "driven from the outside," a form of life that is neither active nor passive, the idea of which "has become completely opaque to contemporary consciousness, out of touch with the ontology of vegetal existence."[27] These ideas cross paths with Guyon's understanding of contemplation as a natural activity, supple, dynamic, and vibrant yet almost imperceptible because of its apparent "passivity." For the mystic who contemplates, there is no true distinction between activity and passivity, effort and grace, action and devotion. Contemplation, for Guyon, is neither doing nor desisting. Rather, contemplation is the background rumble of creation and of corporeality. This is why an activity like breathing is used so often to describe contemplation. Breathing indicates ongoing and, moreover, nourishing activity yet an imperceptible one that is often overlooked or taken for granted. For this reason, the everyday becomes a touchpoint for Guyon's mysticism, as Michel de Certeau also saw. The imperceptibility of the everyday and of its sensations and details becomes a training ground for the contemplative wanting to find God in nature. The insignificance of the body's natural activities takes on a different meaning to the contemplative, as Guyon describes: "All the actions of life, such as breathing, are done naturally, without thought, rule, or measure; and they are done unconsciously by the person who does them. It is thus with [faith] . . . which continually develops, as the soul is more transformed."[28]

Returning to our earlier question regarding the significance yet equivocation of practice in Coccia's *Life of Plants*, I am wondering if contemporary philosophies of vegetal life can be articulated pragmatically together with Guyon, not in the sense of fixing their expression but in the sense of situating them in life, in *a* life. In particular, I wonder if Coccia's idea of philosophical thought being "like atmosphere" can be experimented with through Guyon's attentiveness to breathing, breath, and air, images that are metaphoric but also indicative, as we have seen, of tuning into corporeality: "Just as if a person could live on air, he would be full without feeling his plenitude, or knowing in what way he had been satisfied ... [the] soul here is in God, as in the air which is natural to it."[29]

SPIRITUS

I want to linger for a while with this image of God as atmosphere and of the mystic's breath mixing with the breath of the world. Breathing is an image but also an activity; it is the literal sense of *spiritus*, "breath," and it is one that gives no privileged place to humans but rather indicates a common co-creating of atmosphere between Terran life forms. Breathing is what vegetal life creates, and thus breathing creates many creatures, including human animals. Breathing is a potent image of natural activity in Guyon's mysticism, yet the practice of attending to breath is not given a special place. I would like to think more concretely with Guyon's method of contemplation, which we have already seen in terms of arousing the senses, also in terms of breathing and breath. I see it as one way in which to shift from contemplation told through metaphors of the vegetal to contemplation lived through vegetal life.

The way I read it, Guyon's contemplation finds a shared vocabulary but also method in the recent work of Irigaray. Irigaray's *New Culture of Energy* is particularly interesting. In this book, Irigaray is interested not only in plants but in the air they create. The book collects two shorter texts, one on Yoga and breathwork, the second on Mary and the breath of the Holy Spirit. The neglect of air in Western philosophy is a theme that has preoccupied Irigaray in earlier writings; in *New Culture of Energy*, she addresses the problem from the perspective of practices. Irigaray traces Western but also Eastern spiritual practices that have attempted to submit nature to rules and techniques. As a result, spirit has been elevated above nature: Spiritual freedom is what liberates human beings from the shackles of their bodies. Irigaray's reclaiming of air places breath at the center of spiritual life, recognizing the literal sense of *spiritus*. In other words, spirit, for Irigaray, is the breath of life and the living. Humans participate in spirit not to dominate nature but to become "cultivated living beings" among other living beings. Irigaray imagines "cultivation" not in the sense of human culture *versus* nonhuman nature but in the sense of humans as living beings worked over and tilled, "cultivated," by the habit of spiritual exercises. By reclaiming the literal sense of spirit as breath, Irigaray proposes breathing as one way of thinking about spiritual activity. To Irigaray—and this is where the resonance between Irigaray and Guyon can be heard—the spiritual is evident in a person's relationship to breath and breathing. Common to both Irigaray and Guyon is a sense that the way in which humans relate to nutritive activities indicates the extent to which there is spiritual freedom: Humans are not free until they are at ease with the nutritive activities through which they live and breathe and have their being. Rather than attain freedom by struggling against nature, humans become free when coexisting with other creatures. In many traditions, spiritual freedom is learned by attending to breath, and for Irigaray this can be done to advantage in a "predominantly vegetal environment." Plants are significant for Irigaray's practice because they help create the air at stake in breathwork, bringing human attentiveness to breath into direct contact with its source of oxygen. And, just as contemplation, for Guyon, is inseparable from nature, so too for Irigaray, breathing in a vegetal environment leads to contemplation. She writes: "All the sensory qualities of the flower awaken in me an attention that is situated at different levels that these qualities combine without my even knowing it. It is my whole being that, little by little, is gathered together in this way and, imperceptibly, passes from concentration to contemplation. If I take time to live this state, it is transformed into a culmination of energy that can lead to a form of ecstasy."[30] This is because breathing and contemplation, for Irigaray, are fundamentally the same activity. Every breath is a radical openness to the other, and contemplation is simply that openness attended to through a deliberate act. Irigaray understands this to be the state of *samādhi*, or deep mental absorption, as described by the *Yoga Sūtras* of Patañjali. But instead of aligning her thought with Patañjali's, she questions his emphasis on mind. She reflects that, in contemplation,

> all perceptions are . . . modified. I no longer look in order to comprehend and appropriate. And it is the same for the other sensory perceptions: I perceive in order to respect the difference between what, or who, I am and what, or who, the other is, in order to contemplate and praise a reality that is not mine, in order to marvel at the richness of life in accepting my not being the whole. Perception does not become, at best, an *ecstasis* through a mental appropriation that annihilates the object of my perception, instead

it becomes an increase of energy that can result in a kind of ecstatic instance because of the extra energy that another living being reveals and brings to me.[31]

Irigaray's understanding of contemplation emerges, like that of Coccia's, from an entwinement with vegetal life. Like Coccia, she insists on relinquishing a mind-matter duality, even when it comes to enlightenment: "The enlightenment that I am trying to evoke here is instead an illumination of the flesh. . . . It brings us back to our roots."[32] Rather than appealing to those roots in abstract terms, though, Irigaray seeks to live them in a practice of becoming aware of breath but also, as we see in this passage, sensory perception more broadly. As Marder writes, reflecting on Irigaray's work, "Like leaves, we breathe on the surface of our skin, not only through our lungs. Every one of these innumerably tiny breaths is a channel between the body and the elemental milieu wherein it is immersed. Seemingly effortless, the breathing of the skin and of the leaf, their minute attention to air, is nourished by the living energy of life."[33]

Irigaray's focus on breathwork should thus be supplemented with Marder's and Coccia's vegetal understanding of breathing as a specific expression of a vegetal attentiveness that is not, however, specific to the lung as an organ. Rather, what is at stake is attentiveness, its practice and cultivation, of which the activities of the lung are but one example. As I read it, this is where Jeanne Guyon's perspective and that of the mystical tradition she emerges from provides possibilities for fruitful grafting: For Guyon, like Marder, what is important about breathing is not the lung as organ but rather the lung as participant in a spontaneous, "passive," activity: nutritive, vegetal life. Another possibility is provided by *silence*, which, for Irigaray in particular, goes together with contemplation. She connects silence to plant life as well as contemplation. Without silence on the part of the one attending, nothing is heard. She writes: "Certainly nature is not absolutely silent, but what is heard there corresponds to the murmur of life itself—the sound of the wind, the buzzing of insects, and so on." In order to perceive the "murmur of life," there needs to be a certain stepping-back from talking over the other, be they human, animal, plant, or mineral. In ethical terms, it is a way of letting the other be and through that gesture allowing the other to live. Silence, therefore, is "in no way a privation of words, nor is it a reticent or even a hostile attitude."[34] For both Irigaray and Guyon, the silence of contemplation is a form of attentiveness that shapes speech, rather than the necessary absence of speech. In its way of letting the other be so that one might be left alone to exist, it receives the other in relation, opening the possibility to mutual nourishment and growth.

PRAYER: VEGETAL-SPIRITUAL BREATH

Irigaray's understanding of contemplation brings together philosophies of vegetal life with lived experiences of vegetal attentiveness, pointing toward a reclaiming of *spiritus* as breath and of the spiritual as breathing. Marder's vegetalizing of breath aligns with Irigaray's interest in breathing as a way of cultivating sensory perceptions. At stake is not breath as organismic activity but the attentiveness through which nutritive activities are constituted. Yet Irigaray's and Marder's starting point in Buddhist practices and Yoga implies a certain distance from Western spiritual traditions and to the mysticism I am considering here. According to Irigaray, the missing link is the cultivation of sensory perception, something that, she argues, has been lost in later centuries of Christian spirituality: "A culture of our sensory perceptions ought to have a crucial part in a tradition of incarnation, and it ought to lead us little by little to the perception of a sensible, incarnated transcendence."[35] Irigaray's reading of Mary, to which I pointed earlier, is interpreted as figurative, perhaps, more than pragmatic. Indeed, the role of breathing in Western Christian mysticism has often been seen as metaphorical. In her classic 1954 article, "Breath and Prayer in Ancient and Modern Times," Agnes Selo compares Christian to Buddhist and Hindu practices and observes that while breathing is a central image in Christian spirituality, "the Biblical (Jewish and Christian) standpoint recognizes breath *merely* as an analogy, a symbol, or metaphor for spiritual action—the effort of man toward God, the inpouring of grace from God to man." At the same time, Selo admits that the Desert Fathers appear to have recommended paying attention to the breath and that the Eastern approach "contains a substantial truth which . . . the saints of the early Church were quick to seize upon and utilize."[36] Interestingly, one of the mystics quoted by Selo is none other than Jane de Chantal, the teacher who so greatly inspired Guyon. Given what we have seen of Guyon's, but also Chantal's, practice of contemplative prayer, might a more literal, pragmatic reading of breath be possible, even likely? For Guyon, God is figured, metaphorically, as the air that is breathed in, and the ability to contemplate as the ability to breathe naturally. Yet the practice of contemplation, for Guyon, is learned by observing the nutritive activities of creatures. Commenting on Guyon's mysticism, Patricia Ward notes how an "emphasis on spontaneity and naturalness is a recurring theme."[37] Breathing, in this sense, is both a fitting metaphor and a suitable practice. For a mysticism emphasizing naturalness, regard for natural activities is central; the one who practices contemplation, Guyon writes, "no longer looks forward to deliverance from the body in order that it may be united to God."[38] Rather, they recognize that contemplation "is revealed to babes" and are content to learn from the example of the living, even infants.[39] Guyon's mysticism is vegetal in ways that are both metaphorical and literal, symbolic and symbiotic, syntheoric with Terran kin. It is rooted in root-life, in the unconscious, spontaneous, yet intentional activities without which Terran life as we know it could not exist. What Irigaray describes as a cultivation of sensory perceptions comes to resemble what Guyon—and so many before her—defends as contemplation: God does not condemn the senses but is enjoyed through their arousal. In other words, contemplation is an act of continual receptivity incarnated in those aspects of life that amount to the "nothing but" of affectability. As Michael Marder reminds us, reflecting on Irigaray, sensory perception is also where human life is most evidently vegetal. "Totally exposed to the atmosphere, which they replenish with oxygen," he writes, "plants breathe throughout their entire extension and, most of all, through the leaf. Inhaling with the skin, perceiving the world with our whole bodies, we grow a little plantlike."[40] What I am asking is: Could we not view Guyon's mysticism, and the tradition on which she builds, as emerging out of a practice, a determination, to "grow a little plantlike"?

The philosophies of vegetal life that I have lingered with in this chapter have turned to spirituality in decisive ways in order to develop the promise of a vegetal practice, a vegetal ethics. Seen from the perspective of Guyon's mysticism, spirituality is connected intimately to breathing and breath as organismic but also *vegetal* activities that indicate a creature's fundamental powerlessness to interfere with the activities of attentiveness that sustain them. In the mystic's contemplation, every natural activity is significant insofar as it expresses an already evident, radical exposure to the environment, to the other who is both God and *phusis*, or vegetal growth. Contemplation is the practice of recognizing consciously this unconscious yet ongoing activity of radical receptivity, for no reason other than to delight in it. Contemplation, therefore, takes on the name of enjoyment. This enjoyment, however, is not an enjoyment *of* something but is "without thought, without artifice."[41] Contemplation in itself, that is, as a habituated activity imperceptible to intellect, is not accessible to reflection and is only written of imperfectly: Words—that is to say not speech as such but the speech that would categorize experience—cannot convey contemplation. A mysticism invoking vegetal life gives rise to practices that are not so much articulated as disarticulated in the everyday sensations—the vegetal life of the human body—that elude capture by discourse: The significance of *silence* is another theme that links contemporary philosophies of vegetal life to Guyon. Nevertheless, and paradoxically, the simplicity of contemplation from the point of view of practice lends to mysticism a certain genre: the genre of method, of the "how" rather than the "what" of contemplation. And it is as a method that Guyon's mysticism strikes the reader. Unlike many other mystics in the Christian tradition (and here she differs rather markedly from figures like Hildegard of Bingen, at least in terms of genre and style), Guyon is not interested in ecstasies in the sense of extraordinary phenomena or visions. Guyon is interested in ecstasy as a continual state in which God is experienced "under the veil of a most common life."[42] A "most common life" is insignificant from the point of view of a culture that privileges exceptional and heroic acts. Yet, in the same way that the "most common life" incarnates a sharing of vital breath, it is divinely significant—if, as the mystics argue, God is that which is accessible to all alike. This is how the vegetal moves from metaphor to metamorphosis. The vegetal is intimated, often in profoundly embodied ways, in the mysticism of earlier figures, but it is with Guyon, her teachers, and her followers that we can speak of mysticism as a vegetal practice. I propose that Irigaray helps us see this movement and see the connection between spiritual practices and vegetal life. However, the previous chapter should also indicate the extent to which Guyon's methods are already steeped in a living tradition of cultivating sensory perceptions. What I want to ask now is: How can this entwining help us return to the questions with which we opened our story, questions posed by philosophies of vegetal life? In what ways might the entwining of vegetal and mystical being provide substance to an art of noticing entanglements between species?

CREATING AS CONTEMPLATING: TOWARD A CONTEMPLATIVE PLANT THEORY

As I showed at the end of chapter 1, critical plant studies provides many useful concepts for reading the entwinement between vegetal life and contemplative practices in Western Christian mysticism. Among these I pointed to Gilles Deleuze's notion of contemplation (*theoria*) as vegetal activity, a puzzling image that seems to anthropomorphize life in ways that run counter to the critique of subjectivity otherwise so prominent in Deleuze's philosophy. Discussing Deleuze in *Plant Theory*, Jeffrey Nealon remarks that Deleuze uses the concept of vegetable contemplation "somewhat *oddly*."[43] Nealon wonders whether the language of contemplation does not do injustice to Deleuze's understanding of vegetality as the process whereby "entities come into being and continue to transform." To attribute a power of contemplation to mechanical bodily processes, Nealon worries, is "precisely the sort of thing that will get you called a 'naive vitalist.'" The idea of vegetal life practicing a spiritual exercise seems naive. The ascription of a human-like agency to matter would indeed seem to fail at decentering human beings from Western metaphysics in the way attempted by vitalists like Henri Bergson. For this reason, Nealon argues that Deleuze's concept of vegetable contemplation should be read in relation to vegetal life rather than to spiritual exercises. Nealon argues that the key to Deleuze's vegetable contemplation is its emphasis on activities shared between species. "Ontologically," he writes, "life is not housed exclusively in living animal or human beings and their potential-saturated worlds; rather, life names a distributed, inorganic swarm of emergent singularities that has often gone by the name of 'vegetable soul.'" In Nealon's summary of Deleuze's philosophy, life is the activity that "connects everything to everything else, an ecological mesh that forms an intense territory for living."[44] Nealon's perceptive reading of Deleuze, however, overlooks the history of contemplative ecology in Western philosophy and, moreover, Western Christian mysticism, a history that contributes to vegetal modernity and, ultimately, to the thought of Deleuze himself. As I showed in chapter 2, the notion of vegetable or vegetal contemplation is not, as Nealon would suggest, a Deleuzian quirk.[45] The idea of "nature contemplating" is well known from Plotinus, whom Deleuze also cites in *Difference and Repetition* and later texts; moreover, Deleuze is not alone in drawing attention to Plotinus's *Ennead* 3.8.1. In chapter 1, I discussed the significance of Plotinus for Michael Marder and to Pierre Hadot, for whom the idea of nature contemplating and of nature as "vegetal growth" became a significant touchstone when theorizing philosophy as spiritual exercise and way of life. For Pierre Hadot, as for Marder, the connection to Western Christian mysticism was much more pronounced than in Deleuze's work. Deleuze writes: "By its existence alone, the lily of the field sings the glory of the heavens, the goddesses and gods—in other words, the elements that it contemplates in contracting.... Organisms awake to the sublime words of the third *Ennead*: all is contemplation!"[46] One way of reading this passage would be to conclude that Deleuze is using "contemplation" in a way that runs counter to tradition. As one commentator explains: "This contemplation, of course, is not the contemplation readily recognized by the tradition."[47] Nealon tackles Deleuze's "vegetable contemplation" in similar terms, as a subversive, antitheological rethinking of contemplation. Yet we also saw alternative approaches from theological readings of Deleuze. As Kristien Justaert remarks, although Deleuze's thought and "any aspect of Christian theology would seem absolutely irreconcilable ... both share a passion for (divine) life."[48] Many theologians have, in recent years, taken an interest in Deleuze's work, particularly its relationship to mysticism. Jacob Holsinger Sherman sees Deleuze's contemplation as subversive, but not of Western Christian mysticism; rather, Deleuze's contemplation subverts philosophical and theological portrayals of contemplation as extraordinary, miraculous, or supernatural.[49] Against the latter view, Deleuze appears to recapitulate premodern ideas of contemplation as ordinary, everyday, and natural. Another way of looking at Deleuze's arresting passage on vegetable contemplation in *Difference and Repetition*, where Matthew 6:28–30 is overlaid with *Ennead* 3.8.1, would be to argue that what Deleuze attempts is not so much an overturning of the Western contemplative heritage as a reorientation toward its hidden depths. Another way of putting this would be to say that plant theory cannot be articulated without also taking into account plant *theoria*, "theory" in its original meaning of "contemplation." What I mean to say is that something of the practice implicated in contemporary turns to the vegetal may be found much closer to *theory* than might be assumed at first glance. Here, it is worth remembering Marder's point about the ancient links between theory in the sense of *theoria*, "contemplation," and vegetal life. It will also be useful to bear in mind Hadot's and Deleuze's reflections on contemplation as vegetal activities. I sense that "plant theory" easily can become abstracted from life as long as the literal sense of theory as *theoria*—with its long history of being enmeshed with both practices of attentiveness and practices of attending to vegetal life—remain hidden from the story of what it means to attend to the doing of human bodies in the here and now.

Having now reached the final chapter and having seen some of the ways in which contemplative practices in Western Christian mysticism point toward the activities called "vegetal" and vegetal life toward descriptions of mystical states, I propose to sketch an alternative way of understanding contemplation, *theoria*. Through readings of historical mystics and contemporary philosophies of vegetal life, beginning in Neoplatonism and ending with Luce Irigaray, it is possible to see the outlines of a vegetal, contemplative vitalism. Plotinus's notion of nature contemplating becomes attractive to Deleuze, who is looking for ways of articulating a form of agency that acts without being determined or driven by a will: "Deleuze sees the concept of life as a kind of passive creation which escapes the traces of subjectivity remaining in agency."[50] Deleuze's vitalism needs to be understood as positioned against any privileging of agency, "to the point where agency remains only ever as fractured."[51] Instead, Deleuze's vitalism roots itself in matter's fundamental abandonment to itself.

The matter of life is not active, yet neither is it inert or fully passive. Rather, matter is active by being passive. Creation is not willed from within but is made possible through openness and radical receptivity. As Giorgio Agamben writes in his commentary on Deleuze's concept of vegetable contemplation: "*Theoria* and the contemplative life, which the philosophical tradition has identified as its highest goal for centuries, will have to be dislocated onto a new plane of immanence [so that] there will be little sense in distinguishing between organic life and animal life or even between biological life and contemplative life and between bare life and the life of the mind."[52] Just as contact with the contemplative life elevates vegetal life by anthropomorphizing it, so associating with vegetal life lowers contemplative life by vegetalizing it. The result is a different understanding of lively matter. Through a fundamental passivity that is yet boundless in its ability to create, there is agency. Agency does not happen heroically but imperceptibly. Contemplation, *theoria*, is the practice of becoming-aware of the imperceptible, and in this awareness it is possible to attune to the wild, unpredictable *phusis* that is the world of metamorphosis, growth, and decay.

Guyon's practice of contemplation, her notion of attentiveness as an activity as easy as breathing, in many ways is homologous to a Deleuzian contemplative vitalism. Above all, the example of Guyon points to the complex nature of the challenges posed by mysticism, challenges that parallel those thrown up by the vegetal in Western philosophy. Vegetal lives have been viewed negatively, suppressed, or simply ignored, as have those human activities—digestion, breathing, sensing—which reveal the plant in us. The vegetal, writes Catriona Sandilands in *Veer Ecology*, reminds of "what we have chosen to forget in dominant Western philosophical and scientific imaginations of our human selves as primarily rational, self-organizing, and independent beings over and above all others: a sense of our profound dependence on and location in the conditions of our growth and decay, including the other beings with whom we share these elements of liveliness."[53] Similarly, and in common with the vegetal life whose elusive, barely noticeable activity she invokes, Guyon's mysticism is a reminder of modes of being habitually forgotten by Western imaginations of human agency. Any philosophy that connects agency exclusively with autonomous, self-determined activity can make as little sense of Guyon's practice of stillness, attentiveness, and affectivity as it can of the idea of plant intelligence. Yet in neither case are we confronted with, on the one hand, a rejection of human agency or, on the other, an idealization of carefree inertia. The practice of contemplation, as Guyon understands it, is not so much about defending a laissez-faire approach as it is about rethinking a notion of selfhood defined in terms of power-over. Guyon is interested, instead, in associating selfhood with states that are powerless from the point of view of reason yet contain a cryptic liveliness. Similarly, among contemporary philosophers of the vegetal, Sandilands expresses a desire to show that "when people vegetate, they are not so much being *passive* as demonstrating those *activities* that are consistent with the vegetal undergrowth of the *psukhe*: growth, nutrition, reproduction, decay."[54] The task that now confronts us, then, is to imagine these "vegetating" activities in ways that, as Sandilands writes, "could indicate a practice through which people might come to feel the pulsing vibrations of our . . . common enactments of liveliness."[55] To indicate a practice of this magnitude but also imperceptibility—for what could be more fundamental yet less easy to perceive than that without which there would be no life on earth as we know it—is to engage in a labor that is distinct although not separated from that of outlining an ontology or a metaphysics. Indicating a practice of "common enactments of liveliness" is not about stating the fact of shared life so much as it is about becoming aware of the activities that already constitute life—and then understanding what tactics might allow for attuning to these continually. In Guyon's mysticism, it means a radical opening toward God in the "nothing more than" of a natural activity.[56]

However, while Guyon articulates this practice in religious terms, I would argue that it is not a confessional practice but an art—more specifically, an art of noticing. Guyon's spiritual exercises are concerned with preparing readers to notice God in the seemingly insignificant sensations of everyday affectivity. While this art aims at God, it also rethinks "God" in the process, from remote deity to creative, creating life. If Irigaray and Marder show some of the ways in which Christian spirituality harbors seeds of vegetal attentiveness in its notion of spirit as breath, it is possible to conclude that Guyon's notion of contemplation in "this life here" amounts to an intense experience of nutritive life. What I have sought to do, however, is not to define the mystic's God as vegetal life, even if such definitions at times suggest themselves from the texts. Rather, I have sought to think with vegetal life, as it appears in mystical texts, in order to rethink the practice from which the human-divine relationship emerges: the practice of contemplation. Contemplation is made strange through a graft with philosophies of vegetal life, even as it shows plant intelligence from an aspect intimated but not explicated in critical plant studies: contemplative activity. In this sense, plant theory is contemplative, if by contemplative we mean not an abstract gazing on nature but a letting-be of nutritive life, through a letting-go to the plant in us. In turn, Guyon's understanding of contemplation is vegetal and vegetalizing. De Certeau once remarked that the study of mysticism "makes a *nonreligious exegesis of religion possible*."[57] One way of interpreting the vegetal mysticism I have sketched in this book is as a nonreligious exegesis of religion. It gestures toward a theological reclaiming of condemned practices that resists, nonetheless, the reintegration of those practices in the history of orthodox texts and institutions. By thinking about mysticism through vegetal being, I have wanted to articulate the ways some forms of mysticism discombobulate and defamiliarize. The meaning of contemplation is re-cognized in the graft of mysticism with philosophies of vegetal life. In turn, the intimations of practical contemplation in contemporary philosophies of vegetal life are irreducible to literary tropes. Rather, they point toward the practices and activities that were at stake for mystics like Guyon. This is why I have argued that it is important to read the two together. Guyon insists that contemplation should not be confused with a denial of nature. Nature is contemplation, for Guyon; being already contemplative, natural activities teach the mystic how to pray.

Through a dialogue with contemporary philosophies of the vegetal, the graft we have cultivated in these chapters also shift ways of imagining contemplation in the history of Western Christian mysticism. What is evidenced in readings of historical mystics such as Hildegard of Bingen, the Helfta sisters, and Jeanne Guyon by Michel de Certeau, Amy Hollywood, Michael Marder, Douglas Christie, Liz Herbert McAvoy, and others is a vegetalizing of thought through descriptions of contemplation, ecstasy, and mystical union. These new readings of mysticism contribute to the vegetalizing of thought in the ways they reveal "the fluid similitudes and symphonic connections between psychic states and faculties, plant organs and phenomena, religious figure and biological processes."[58] Mysticism has this quality because of the way in which contemplative practices are described as putting the status of the human in doubt, fragmenting the sense of self-identity, and decentering awareness from intellection to affection and affectivity. Mysticism's relationship to the vegetal is not reducible to allegory and metaphor, nor can it be summarized in the significance of vegetal milieus: The preponderance of *plants* in mysticism, however significant this is as a topic for investigation, is not what is at stake for the graft I am cultivating here. Rather, as Marder points out, it is in a "rigorously non-allegorical" way that mystics turn to vegetal imagery, owing to the undeniable fact that vegetal life composes every human breath, making it impossible to regard the invocation of vegetal activities in mystical texts as merely literary tropes. Lurking behind this definition is the commitment to *contemplative practices* that we saw Marder draw attention to in the case of Irigaray's work. Plant-thinking, as Marder writes in his dialogue with Irigaray, is not simply thinking *about* plants; it is to "linger with plants, in thoughtful and physical proximity."[59] Moreover, it means attending to the plant-like activities that compose a human body and, in that act of conscious attention, discover the prevenient attentiveness of our bodies to the elements: the plant in us. Contemplation is not a human activity, nor is it the privilege of plants; rather, contemplation is what ecologies do but also what they are: Ecologies are contemplative. We arrive at an ecological understanding of contemplation but also at a "contemplative ecology" such as was introduced by Douglas Christie. A contemplative ecology would refuse to see the vegetating activities of life as insignificant, but it would also reject the idea of the vegetal as nothing but an object of attention. Ecologies are contemplating us as we contemplate them, and, as we struggle to cultivate habits of attentiveness, ecologies cultivate life by virtue of passive syntheses.

Epilogue
ECOLOGIES OF ECSTASY

*Symbols must not be arbitrary but must be found inscribed . . .
in the very nature of things.*
   —Simone Weil, *On Science, Necessity, and the Love of God*

In the history of Western Christian mysticism, the vegetal symbolism I have been narrating can be interpreted as symbiotic with the forms of spiritual practice it intimates. Another way of putting this is to say that vegetal life, rather than being merely an image chosen for what some humans do when they contemplate, may also be attuning human mindfulness to vegetal life. As I have suggested throughout this book, the structural homology between descriptions of vegetal, non-neural intelligence, on the one hand, and contemplative practices, on the other, is not arbitrary. While there is no knowing precisely why vegetal symbolism was chosen by historical authors like Isaac of Nineveh, Hildegard of Bingen, Gertrude of Helfta, or Jeanne Guyon, today it can be read as pointing to "what we share with other entities,"[1] a reminder that such sharing is inscribed in the very vegetal nature of things. How can a philosophy of vegetal life be practiced? What are the methods, the skills, that might make vibrant shared participation in common acts of liveliness?

At various places in this book I have hinted that what you are reading is also a spiritual manual or handbook of sorts, and I have claimed that a good portion of the impetus behind writing *Ecologies of Ecstasy* came from my experiences implementing the methods described within its pages. I dropped those hints neither to mystify nor boast but rather to demystify the "spiritual" in spiritual exercises, returning some forms of Western Christian mysticism to their Terran atmosphere. Nonetheless, I have been mostly silent regarding the details of my practice, and while I cannot speak to all of it here, the past chapters—especially the chapters on Guyon—provide enough context for me now to go into more depth on the pragmatics of what I have called "vegetal mysticism." Two provisos are in place, however. First, what I will relate is, needless to say, situated knowledge. I am a Scandinavian-born, university-educated woman philosopher and theologian from a mixed religious, ethnic, and cultural background. Arctic Pietism and remnants of Indigenous traditions on my mother's side vies, on my father's side, with continental Roman Catholicism. While I was raised Roman Catholic, my experience of Nordic Catholicism was of a tradition where many religious expressions mingled. This is perhaps why I was drawn to contemplative prayer, which, in contemporary Catholicism, has developed into a largely ecumenical practice. Second, and following on from this, even though I chose, somewhat unusually, to work from historical texts, my approach is undoubtedly contemporary, shaped by contemporary concerns. Above all, the vegetal life that I came to experience was something that interested me because of the way it resonated with ecological thought and the demands of the current epoch. In turn, my life story led me to develop an account of contemplation that deliberately foregrounds methods and themes in ways that, at times, are distinct from the historical texts that taught me how to practice contemplation.

That being said, historical texts initially were my only guide when it came to practical contemplation. Unlike many of my Catholic peers who were interested in contemplative prayer, I did not learn Centering Prayer or any other of the twentieth-century interpretations of the forms of mysticism I have written about in this book. I learned those only much later, years after I had established my own practice. When I began, I decided instead to follow the instructions of Jeanne Guyon as summarized in chapters 4 and 5. My reasons for choosing to work from Guyon's text should by now, hopefully, be clear to the reader. Guyon's open and inclusive practice had an irresistible appeal to me for intellectual reasons. In addition, there were personal motivations. Ever since I first read it, the clear, direct, and unadorned style of *A Short and Easy Method of Prayer* had been inviting me to experiment. I had felt drawn to this text rather than others because it focused so entirely on *practices*. Beliefs, theological ideas, and religious dogma . . . these were all irrelevant to Guyon. Indeed, she speaks of their negative influence.

Following Guyon's recommendation, I decided to dedicate a total of around half an hour a day to practicing. I began with Guyon's "meditative reading," meaning that I would recite a piece of text that I found meaningful, speaking the words slowly, with feeling. I moved between texts, building up a rotation of five to six pieces that I would recite and eventually learn by heart. Some pieces were from the Hebrew Book of Psalms; others were not religious at all but rather expressive of the desire to open myself to the Other, the Unknown, and to Love. Guyon does not stipulate the kinds of text to be used during informal meditation, and as a result I did not restrict my choice either. The point of meditative reading is to prepare the practitioner for informal colloquy or dialogue with God, "informal meditation," but I was not ready for that at the beginning. I tried, of course, but I found I was self-conscious and nervous. So I went back to meditative reading, occasionally drifting into spontaneous periods of informal meditation but mostly sticking to reciting texts, that is, continuing with a kind of formal prayer. For about nine months, that was all I did. I found I could not transition to informal meditation, try as I might. As a result, toward the end of this first period, I felt myself becoming more and not less self-absorbed, resenting the daily commitment and sometimes simply rattling off the memorized texts without giving the activity much attention. I then put the practice aside for a while, knowing I would return but sensing I needed to shift my perspective and priorities before doing so.

Six months went past, and then, one day, quite without knowing why, I felt a deep *tug* to start practicing again. I began, as before, with meditative reading but found that I could now transition to informal meditation with little effort. Soon I began having the experiences I have described at the beginning of this book, the experiences I compared to an awareness of my vegetative soul, or the plant in me, to borrow Michael Marder's expression. It took another four months or so for me to cultivate the experience. I cannot say exactly how it happened. There was no sudden, extraordinary ecstasy or dramatic event, nor was there any change to my outward habits. Rather, there was a slow shifting of perception and a growth in my ability to notice. The best way to describe it is not as a heightening of awareness but instead as a metabolizing of perception. It happened so slowly I had time to acclimatize myself, which was lucky, because I am not sure I would have been able to retain a grip on reality if the change had happened overnight: As it was, I was able to sustain this changed perception for very long periods, sometimes days at a time. Agnes Arber, the botanist, has described something similar when recounting the "ecstasy" of another contemporary of Guyon, the seventeenth-century mystic Jacob Boehme. In Arber's words, Boehme "never slackened his grasp upon finite reality, and when . . . he fell into an inward ecstasy, he tested it by going out into the green fields, where he became conscious that he was looking into the very being of herbs and grasses and that his revealing insights were harmonious with external nature."[2] I speak for neither Boehme nor Arber, but reading Arber's words, they resonated with my experiences. My "ecstasy," such as it was, began with a very distinct and unmistakable constriction of my vocal chords and an inability to speak or think clearly. Tears would flow, and a dull ache, reminiscent of growing pains, flooded my body. Simultaneously, my skin would grow more sensitive, or perhaps better, I became gradually more aware of the sensitivity of my skin to the elements; if I left the house and ventured outdoors, plants were particular catalysts for this sensation, which would arrive as soon as I assumed the specific, relaxed attitude that I had come to associate with the onset of informal meditation. I knew from my studies that what I was experiencing was "wordless" prayer or contemplation. The sign to look out for was the inability to speak and recite formal prayers, combined with a sensory "arousal" that was both painful and pleasurable. I found this to be true: If I tried to recite anything, the words fell flat and were a hindrance rather than, as before, an aid.

The notion of becoming vegetal was less easy to correlate to anything I read in the manuals, though. As I have already explained, it took me some time—in fact, several years—to develop a clear picture of the historical entwinement between mystical and vegetal in Western Christian mysticism. What set me on the right track was Mircea Eliade's classic study *Yoga: Immortality and Freedom*. Here I learned that a connection between mystical and vegetal states had been known for a long time in many Indigenous and non-Western traditions, especially in Buddhist and Hindu practices of meditation. Describing the historic manuals of Yoga, Eliade observed how they "apparently [assimilated] the yogin to a plant." "This homology," remarked Eliade, "would imply no pejorative judgment, even if it were adequate to the reality of the situation [since, to the writers in question, the] vegetable modality is not an impoverishment but, quite the contrary, an enrichment of life."[3] Becoming cognizant of perspectives from traditions outside Christian mysticism was encouraging and prompted me to persevere with my research into what, eventually, became *Ecologies of Ecstasy*. For some time, though, I hesitated as to whether I should frame my research in terms of a broader, comparative perspective that would enter into dialogue with the history of religions and anthropology. The literature on kinship with plants in Indigenous traditions is detailed and fascinating.[4] In the end I decided to develop a theoretical perspective rooted in Western Christian mysticism not because it proved better at answering my questions (in many ways, it proved less willing to do so) but simply because Guyon's method was the practice in which I had come to experience vegetal life. I wanted to understand the phenomenon more deeply within the lineage of her tradition—of negative theology and mystical cosmism—rather than through a comparative lens. One thing that I took with me from my comparative research, however, was a strong critique of anthropocentrism. Revisiting another classic, Eliade's *Shamanism: Archaic Techniques of Ecstasy*, I rediscovered Eliade's many interesting accounts of shapeshifting in mysticism and the integral role of human-animal and human-plant relations in trance, ecstasy, and spirit possession.[5]

For Eliade, as for others who have worked on ecstatic religion more recently, the phenomenon seems to be one in which the status of the human is held, continuously, in doubt.[6] Although I did not apply anthropological theory directly to my work, reading it certainly strengthened my resolve to keep looking, in the literature of Western Christian mysticism, for intimations of vegetal life in the tradition of Guyon.

I also became curious about the fate of vegetal life in Western Christian mysticism following the decades of theological controversy in which Guyon's work played such a major role. In this book, I have addressed the period 300–1700, typically taken to represent the classical period of Western Christian mysticism. Another narrative tendril that invited itself into my work, however, was the vegetal mysticism of the eighteenth, nineteenth, and twentieth centuries. Although there is a natural hiatus to the entwinement between mystical and vegetal in Western Christian mysticism as I have told it, this should not be taken to imply a definitive withering. Rather, the vegetal continues to play an important role in various Christian spiritualities of the modern period, including in Catholic mysticism, the main focus of this study. In the nineteenth century, for instance, contemplative practice once again began to be recognized favorably by church authorities. So much so that, a little over two centuries after her "arousal" of nature landed Guyon in prison, a not dissimilar celebration of naturalness was seen as reason to canonize Thérèse of Lisieux (1873–1897). A French Carmelite, Thérèse was influenced by the same Discalced spirituality that had inspired Guyon.[7] Thérèse criticized the emphasis on austerities and extraordinary, visionary experiences. Rather, and very much like Guyon, she taught a method rooted in natural activities, wordless prayer, and the arousal of the affections. In a remarkable choice of imagery that connects her vividly to the vegetal mysticism I have been narrating, Thérèse even adopted for herself the name "The Little Flower." In the bedside discourses recorded by her sisters, the ailing Thérèse (who passed away at the age of twenty-four, from tuberculosis) allegedly conversed with plants and generally expressed a particular kinship with the vegetal world. Her poetry returns often to vegetality in ways strongly reminiscent of Guyon but also recalling the "spiritual arborescence" of medieval mysticism that we saw in chapter 3.[8] In a poem, *"Abandon's* the delicious fruit of love," Thérèse plays with arboreal imagery to articulate the spontaneity she associated with contemplative prayer. Abandonment is a "fruit" imagined in arboreal terms. "There is on earth a Tree," begins this Emily Dickinson–esque lyric, "That bears a wondrous fruit; / That grows . . . O mystery!— / In Heaven is its root." Rather than picture a tree representing the mystic's ascent to heaven, however, Thérèse makes heaven a kind of earth and locates earth, instead, where heaven would typically be placed: on terra firma. Indeed, "On earth that fruit divine / Has given me content," she affirms, going onto identify the tree as "Love." The play with arboreal imagery then shifts into Thérèse's favored image: herself as a "little flower." She writes: "A *little* flowerlet I, / Half-open to the Sun."[9] Moving from this shape-shifting allegory into the familiar mystical vegetality of the Song of Songs, Thérèse's poem depicts an amorous encounter between the flower and the Sun, recapitulating more themes familiar from vegetal mysticism: the mystic as a plant, opening to the Sun of Righteousness, receiving "grace" figured in the sun's warmth.

Thérèse's plant mysticism is but one striking example among several nineteenth- and twentieth-century mystics preoccupied with vegetal imagery that I discovered while researching this book. Although she was apparently unfamiliar with Thérèse, Simone Weil (1909–1943), yet another French mystic, was fascinated with vegetal analogies. Like Thérèse and, before her, Guyon, Weil kicks back at the idea of contemplation as extraordinary or the result of special grace. Rather, contemplation is natural, as is grace, which, in Weil's mystical theology, flows like solar energy. "The plant does not have any control or choice in the matter of its own growth," she remarks in *Waiting for God*, before continuing: "As for us, we are like plants that have the one choice of being in or out of the light."[10] Weil was struck by the similarity that, she believed, pertained between a plant's attitude toward the sun and the mystic's relationship to God in prayer. The latter she called a "negative effort" and "passive activity," following a long tradition in Western Christian mysticism—as summarized in this book—of representing the human-divine relationship in vegetal terms.[11] In one essay, from which I quoted at the beginning of this epilogue, Weil reflects at length on the analogy. A person who wants to pray, Weil writes, should observe the example of plants and how they grow. "In the same way [as a plant grows]," writes Weil, "the only effort we can make toward the good is so to dispose our soul that it can receive grace, and it is grace which supplies the energy needed for this effort." For Weil, there is a convergence between the involuntary nature of attention during prayer and the involuntary nature of the vegetal life to which a person is attending. In other words, at this moment the one who prays is sharing in the world on its own terms, "looked at for itself and not as a background for day-dreams," as she puts it. At the heart of Weil's parable is the passive synthesis (to adapt the language of Gilles Deleuze) by means of which vegetal life is able to make use of sunlight and transmute it into green sap. All this is achieved by the plant without the plant deliberating or setting its mind to the matter, and it is this lack of deliberation and inveterate spontaneity that Weil thinks is of the utmost importance for contemplation, not only because contemplation is an attitude of receptivity but because, according to the Western Christian mystical tradition, contemplation is (or at any rate should be) nothing less than the receiving of an already-present God. Hence Weil does not see this parable as a mere simile, or, perhaps better put, she does not view simile as necessarily less than the divine truth to which it is supposed to point: "Symbols must not be arbitrary but must be found inscribed . . . in the very nature of things."[12]

While space has not permitted me to cultivate fully the graft between vegetal and mystical into the nineteenth century and beyond, I gesture toward it here to indicate the possible connections between *Ecologies of Ecstasy* and the modern history of Western Christian mysticism. It has also been necessary to forgo the fascinating topic of vegetal life in Western esotericism and the many new spiritual idioms that have developed in the centuries since Guyon. These are questions for further study, some of which I plan to address elsewhere and many of which are already the topic of study in the remarkable work of Aliya Say, which was conceived at around the same time as this book and shares, to my mind, many core observations regarding mystics and vegetal life.[13] The connections I draw between vegetal life and the experiences of mystics participate in emergent discourses, and it is my hope that this book will contribute to a deeper understanding of the genealogy underpinning these fresh hermeneutic currents, not only where mysticism is concerned but also as regards the practice of philosophy.

ACKNOWLEDGMENTS

How to thank those who will never read this book yet without whom I would have been the poorer in wisdom? Above all and first, the grove of Pōl'-cum ōl (*Umbellularia californica*) at the Redwoods Abbey, where the final form of this study became clear to me. *Ecologies of Ecstasy* is dedicated to the monastic community at Redwoods Abbey and to the memory of Sister Veronique, in gratitude for listening. I would also like to thank the following people for their generous invitations to present my work-in-progress over the past years: Thomas Arentzen, Jeffrey Bishop, James Bryson, Ann Jeanette Ekberg, Stephan van Erp, Cassandra Falke and Michael Heneise, Michaela Hulstyn, Esaias Järnegard, Line Kallmayer, Ludvig Lindelöf, Ariel Mayse and the Applied Colaboratory for Religion and Ecology (ACRE), Sam Mickey, Petra Carlsson Redell, Aliya Say, the folks at the Serpentine Galleries, Daniel Siedell and the International Congress for Infrathin Studies, Ola Sigurdson, Thomas Soyer and the Simone Weil DenkKollektiv, Henning Tegtmeyer, Paul Tyson, and Giles Waller. My approach to earth ethics originated in the classes co-taught together with Hjördis Becker-Lindenthal at Cambridge's Faculty of Divinity, and I am grateful to Hjördis and to our students. Since the seeds of this book go back a long way, there are many from my time at Cambridge who have helped shape my thinking on mysticism, philosophy, and vegetal life, but above all Catherine Pickstock, Jacob Sherman, and Robert Macfarlane. The University of Oslo and the ECODISTURB Research Group provided the time and resources needed to complete this project. I extend a special thanks to the ECODISTURB project leader, Marius Timmann Mjaaland, and to Gunnar Gjermundsen. Partial and early versions of the text were published as "A Natural History of Contemplation: Contemplative Ecology Beyond Species Thought," *Journal of Contemplative Studies* 3 (2025), and "Practicing Passivity: Through Mystical and Vegetal Being," in *The Routledge Handbook of Eco-Phenomenology*, ed. Michael Heinese et al (2025). Final revisions to the manuscript were made among new colleagues at the Institute for Literature, History of Ideas, and Religion at the University of Gothenburg, and I could not have asked for a better birthplace to *Ecologies of Ecstasy*.

I am grateful, as well, to Wendy Lochner of Columbia University Press and her amazing team, especially for Wendy's ideas—and those of the anonymous readers—regarding the need to include some personal reflections on contemplative practice. Several people have directly affected my practice, but none more so than my daughter, Freja, and my husband, Simon Jackson, who has supported me lovingly at each juncture even when what I was doing seemed fruitless. I would also like to thank Jo'el Adifon, Douglas Christie, Kia Alice Groom, Johannes Gårdbäck, Hayley Huston, Alexander Moore, Elizabeth Powell, and Vijnananath, for talking shop about contemplation and sharing skills. Lastly, I want to thank the babies, toddlers, and children of my friends, particularly my godson Aubrey, "like a green shoot of Lebanon."

Thank you to the rights holders for use of the following image and quotations in my work:

Giovanni Bellini, *Saint Francis in the Desert*, c. 1480, copyright © 2025 Niday Picture Library, Alamy Stock Photo. Used by permission. All rights reserved worldwide.

Scripture quotations are from the New Revised Standard Version Bible, copyright © 1989 National Council of the Churches of Christ in the United States of America. Used by permission. All rights reserved worldwide.

Excerpt and English translation from Gilles Deleuze, *Difference and Repetition*, translated by Paul Patton, translation copyright © 1994 The Athlone Press Limited, renewed © 1994 by Columbia University Press. Used by permission.

Excerpt and English translation from WAITING FOR GOD by Simone Weil, translated by Emma Craufurd, translation copyright © 1951, renewed © 1979 by G. P. Putnam's Sons. Used by permission of G. P. Putnam's Sons, an imprint of Penguin Publishing Group, a division of Penguin Random House LLC. All rights reserved.

Excerpt and English translation from Thérèse of Lisieux, *Collected Poems*, translated by Alan Bancroft, translation copyright © 2001 Gracewing Ltd. Used by permission. All rights reserved worldwide.

NOTES

PREFACE

1. Michael Marder, *Plant-Thinking: A Philosophy of Vegetal Life* (Columbia University Press, 2013).
2. Jeffrey Nealon, *Plant Theory: Biopower and Vegetable Life* (Stanford University Press, 2016), 107.
3. On the arts of noticing, see especially Anna Tsing, Heather Swanson, Elaine Gan, and Nils Bubandt, eds., *Arts of Living on a Damaged Planet* (University of Minnesota Press, 2017), 10–13.

1. SPIRITUAL EXERCISES ACROSS SPECIES

1. Agnes M. F. Selo, "Breath and Prayer in Ancient and Modern Times," *Life of the Spirit* 9, no. 98 (1954): 53–62.
2. Emanuele Coccia, *The Life of Plants: A Metaphysics of Mixture*, trans. Dylan Montanari (Polity, 2019), 6.
3. Luce Irigaray and Michael Marder, *Through Vegetal Being: Two Philosophical Perspectives* (Columbia University Press, 2016), 47.
4. For the expression "cosmism," see Louis Cognet, *Post-Reformation Spirituality*, trans. P. Hepburne Scott (Hawthorne, 1959), 55. The literature on Christian nature mysticism is vast. For a good overview of the theological foundations and source texts, see Olivier Clément, *The Roots of Christian Mysticism: Text and Commentary*, trans. Theodore Berkeley and Jeremy Hummerstone (New City, 1995), 213–29 ("The Glory of God Hidden in His Creatures"); Douglas Christie,

"Creation and Revelation," in *The Oxford Handbook of Mystical Theology*, ed. Edward Howells and Mark McIntosh (Oxford University Press, 2020), 529–48.
5. Patricia Miller, *In the Eye of the Animal: Zoological Imagination in Ancient Christianity* (University of Pennsylvania Press, 2018).
6. William Gorrie, *Illustrations of Scripture from Botanical Science* (1854). This is still the most comprehensive and detailed discussion of vegetal life as depicted and employed metaphorically in Hebrew and Greek scripture.
7. Thomas Arentzen, Virginia Burrus, and Glenn Peers, *Byzantine Tree Life: Christianity and the Arboreal Imagination* (Palgrave Macmillan, 2021), 9.
8. Arentzen, Burrus, and Peers, *Byzantine Tree Life*, 109.
9. Sara Ritchey, "Spiritual Arborescence: Trees in the Medieval Christian Imagination," *Spiritus* 8 (2008): 64–82.
10. Naïs Virenque, "Dendrites' and Preachers' Trees: A Literary and Iconographic Study of Mnemonic Images," in *Spiritual Vegetation: Vegetal Nature in Religious Contexts Across Medieval and Early Modern Europe*, ed. Guita Lamsechi and Beatrice Trînca (Brill, 2022), 27–48.
11. *Acta Sanctorum*, ed. J. Bollandus and G. Henschenius (Paris-Rome, 1863–1940), 3 February, 668 (*Vita Edigna von Puch*). My thanks to Emily McMillan for introducing me to Edigna's story. The linden tree attributed to Edigna can be visited in the parish church of Puch, modern-day Fürstenfeldbruck, Germany.
12. Ritchey, "Spiritual Arborescence," 65.
13. Anne Winston-Allen, "Gardens of Heavenly and Earthly Delight: Medieval Gardens of the Imagination," *Neuphilologische Mitteilungen* 99, no. 1 (1998): 83. See also F. J. Griffiths, *The Garden of Delights: Reform and Renaissance for Women in the Twelfth Century* (University of Pennsylvania Press, 2011).
14. B. Beck, "Jardin monastique, jardin mystique: Ordonnance et signification des jardins monastiques médiévaux," *Revue d'Histoire de la Pharmacie* 48, no. 327 (2000): 377–94.
15. Bernard of Clairvaux, *On the Song of Songs*, trans. Irene M. Edmonds and Kilian J. Walsh (Cistercian Publications, 1979); see also M. B. Bruun, *A Companion to Bernard of Clairvaux* (Brill, 2011), 249–78.

16. Ariel Evan Mayse, "Gardens of the Spirit: Land, Text, and Ecological Hermeneutics in Jewish Mystical Sources," *Dibur Literary Journal* 11 (2022): 60–61.
17. Mallory A. Ruymann, "Nuns as Gardeners: Using and Making Enclosed Gardens," *Athanor* 35 (2017): 41–47.
18. Grace Jantzen, *Becoming Divine: Toward a Feminist Philosophy of Religion* (Manchester University Press, 1998), 156–70. See also Grace Jantzen, "Feminists, Philosophers, and Mystics," *Hypatia* 9, no. 4 (1994): 186–206; Grace Jantzen, *Power, Gender, and Christian Mysticism* (Cambridge University Press).
19. Elaine P. Miller, *The Vegetative Soul: From Philosophy of Nature to Subjectivity in the Feminine* (State University of New York, 2002), 189, 188.
20. Barbara Newman, Review of Liz Herbert McAvoy, *The Enclosed Garden and the Medieval Religious Imaginary*, *Speculum* 97, no. 4 (2022): 1226–27. On nature and its representation, see Barbara Newman, *God and the Goddesses: Vision, Poetry, and Belief in the Middle Ages* (Pennsylvania University Press, 2005).
21. Irigaray and Marder, *Through Vegetal Being*, 115.
22. Irigaray and Marder, *Through Vegetal Being*, 80.
23. Liz Herbert McAvoy, *The Enclosed Garden and the Medieval Religious Imaginary* (D. S. Brewer, 2021), 117, 137, 128; emphasis in the original.
24. Richard of St. Victor, *The Twelve Patriarchs, The Mystical Ark*, ed. and trans. Grover Zinn (Paulist, 1979), 136.
25. Francis de Sales, *Of the Love of God*, trans. H. L. Sidney Lear (1888), 281.
26. Jeanne Guyon, *Spiritual Torrents*, trans. A. W. Marston (H. R. Allenson, 1909), 135.
27. Richard Knox, *Enthusiasm: A Chapter in the History of Religion, with Special Reference to the XVII and XVIII Centuries* (Oxford University Press, 1950), albeit outdated, is still a good history of the relationship between heresy and mystical theology in the West. See also Columba Stewart, *"Working the Earth of the Heart": The Messalian Controversy in History, Texts, and Language to A.D. 431* (Oxford University Press, 1991); Barbara Newman, *From Virile Woman to WomanChrist* (University of Pennsylvania Press, 1995), 172–81; Alastair Hamilton, *Heresy and Mysticism in Sixteenth-Century Spain: The Alumbrados* (University of

Toronto Press, 1992); Bernard McGinn, *The Crisis of Mysticism: Quietism in Seventeenth-Century Spain, Italy, and France* (Crossroad, 2021).
28. McGinn, *Crisis of Mysticism*.
29. The historical debates concerned the difference between "acquired" and "infused" contemplation in writers like John of the Cross. Many contemporary theologians now consider the "heresy" of Quietism to be based on an erroneous interpretation of contemplation, and the controversy is laid aside today "in favor of a broad description of the experience of contemplation." See Ernest Larkin, "The Carmelite Tradition and Centering Prayer/Meditation," in *Carmelite Prayer: A Tradition for the 21st Century*, ed. Keith Egan (Paulist, 2003), 202–22, 221n3.
30. Thomas Merton, *Mystics and Zen Masters* (Delta, 1967), 91–113.
31. Douglas E. Christie, *The Blue Sapphire of the Mind: Notes for a Contemplative Ecology* (Oxford University Press, 2013); Bruce Foltz, *The Noetics of Nature: Environmental Philosophy and the Holy Beauty of the Visible* (Fordham University Press, 2014); Jacob Holsinger Sherman, "Beyond the Greening of Faith: Contemplative Practice in the Anthropocene," *Toronto Journal of Theology* 38 no. 2 (2022): 214–27; see also Hjördis Becker-Lindenthal and Simone Kotva, "Practicing for Death in the Anthropocene: Reading Christian Asceticism After the End of the Human," *Environmental Humanities* 15, no. 2 (2023): 105–23.
32. Christie, *Blue Sapphire*, 7.
33. Andrew Prevot, *The Mysticism of Ordinary Life: Theology, Philosophy, and Feminism* (Oxford University Press, 2023).
34. Barbara Lanzetta, *Radical Wisdom: A Feminist Mystical Theology* (Fortress, 2005), 96. See also Mary Potter Engel et al., "Roundtable Discussion: Mysticism and Feminist Spirituality," *Journal of Feminist Studies in Religion* 24, no. 2 (2008): 143–87.
35. Kent L. Brintnall, "Erotic Ruination: Embracing the 'Savage Spirituality' of Barebacking," in *Negative Ecstasies: Georges Bataille and the Study of Religion*, ed. Jeremy Biles and Kent Brintnall (Fordham University Press, 2015), 66–67.
36. An Yountae, *The Decolonial Abyss: Mysticism and Cosmopolitics from the Ruins* (Fordham University Press, 2016), 11–13.
37. Kevin Corrigan, "Ecstasy and Ecstasy in Some Early Pagan and Christian Mystical Writings," in *Greek and Medieval Studies in Honor of Leo*

1. SPIRITUAL EXERCISES ACROSS SPECIES ◌ 215

Sweeney, S.J., ed. William J. Carroll and John J. Furlong (Peter Lang, 1994), 27–38.

38. Catherine Keller, *Cloud of the Impossible: Negative Theology and Planetary Entanglement* (Columbia University Press, 2015), 232.
39. J. W. Perkinson, *Political Spirituality in an Age of Eco-Apocalypse: Communication and Struggle Across Species, Cultures, and Religions* (Palgrave Macmillan, 2015), 121.
40. Sallie McFague, *The Body of God: An Ecological Theology* (Fortress, 1992), 49–52. See also Simone Kotva, *Effort and Grace: On the Spiritual Exercise of Philosophy* (Bloomsbury, 2020), 174–80.
41. E.g., Laurel Kearns and Catherine Keller, eds., *Ecospirit: Religions and Philosophies for the Earth* (Fordham University Press, 2007); Stephen D. Moore, ed., *Divinanimality: Animal Theory, Creaturely Theology* (Fordham University Press, 2014); Whitney Bauman, ed., *Meaningful Flesh: Reflections on Religion and Nature for a Queer Planet* (Punctum, 2015); Catherine Keller and Mary-Jane Rubenstein, eds., *Entangled World: Religion, Science, and New Materialisms* (Fordham University Press, 2017); Eric Daryl Meyer, *Inner Animalities: Theology and the End of the Human* (Fordham University Press, 2018); Mark I. Wallace, *When God Was a Bird: Christianity, Animism, and the Re-Enchantment of the World* (Fordham University Press, 2019); Becker-Lindenthal and Kotva, "Practicing for Death."
42. Keller, *Cloud of the Impossible*, 172.
43. Jeffrey Nealon, *Plant Theory: Biopower and Vegetable Life* (Stanford University Press, 2016), ix–xvii.
44. Michael Marder, *Grafts: Writings on Plants* (University of Minnesota Press, 2016), 38. On critical plant studies, see the series published by Brill, Critical Plant Studies: Philosophy, Literature, Culture, edited by Michael Marder. See also Michael Marder, *Plant-Thinking: A Philosophy of Vegetal Life* (Columbia University Press, 2013); Michael Marder, *The Philosopher's Plant: An Intellectual Herbarium* (Columbia University Press, 2014); and the reader by Giovanni Aloi and Michael Marder, eds., *Vegetal Entwinements in Philosophy and Art: A Reader* (MIT Press, 2023). See also Miller, *Vegetative Soul*; Matthew Hall, *Plants as Persons: A Philosophical Botany* (State University of New York Press, 2011); Irigaray and Marder, *Through Vegetal Being*; Coccia, *Life*

of Plants; Theresa L. Miller, *Plant Kin: A Multispecies Ethnography in Indigenous Brazil* (University of Texas Press, 2019); David Wood, *Thinking Plant Animal Human: Encounters with Communities of Difference* (University of Minnesota Press, 2020); John C. Ryan, Patrícia Vieira, and Monica Gagliano, *The Mind of Plants: Narratives of Vegetal Intelligence* (Synergistic, 2021).

45. Dorothea Keller, *Nutrition and Nutritive Soul in Aristotle and Aristotelianism* (De Gruyter, 2020).
46. Nealon, *Plant Theory*, 107.
47. On the gendering of the vegetative soul, see Miller, *Vegetative Soul*; see also Carolyn Merchant, *The Death of Nature: Women, Ecology, and the Scientific Revolution* (Harper and Row, 1986).
48. Marder, *Plant-Thinking*, 7.
49. Marder, *Plant-Thinking*, 223.
50. Marder, *Grafts*, 47.
51. Marder, *Plant-Thinking*, 134.
52. Marder, *Plant-Thinking*, 134.
53. Marder, *Philosopher's Plant*.
54. Irigaray and Marder, *Through Vegetal Being*, 158–59.
55. Nealon, *Plant Theory*, 113–14. Emphasis in the original.
56. Marder, *Philosopher's Plant*, 220.
57. Marder, *Philosopher's Plant*, 215.
58. Michael Marder, *Green Mass: The Ecological Theology of St. Hildegard of Bingen* (Stanford University Press, 2021), 5, 77.
59. I understand human practices of contemplation to be embodied practices but also practices shared across species. On the relationship between the ecstasy of grace and the ecstasy of nature in Christian mystical theology, see Peter Kwasniewski, *The Ecstasy of Love in the Thought of St. Thomas Aquinas* (Emmaus, 2021), 1–38. I return to Kwasniewski's insightful analysis in chapter 3.
60. A. M. Lawrence, "Listening to Plants: Conversations Between Critical Plant Studies and Vegetal Geography," *Progress in Human Geography* 46, no. 2 (2022): 629.
61. E.g., Daniel Chamovitz, *What a Plant Knows: A Field Guide to the Senses of Your Garden—and Beyond* (Scientific American, 2012); Robin Wall Kimmerer, *Braiding Sweetgrass: Indigenous Wisdom, Scientific Knowledge,*

and the Teaching of Plants (Penguin, 2013); Anthony Trewavas, *Plant Behaviour and Intelligence* (Oxford University Press, 2014); Peter Wohlleben, *The Hidden Lives of Trees*, trans. Jane Billinghurst (William Collins, 2016); Stefano Mancuso, *The Revolutionary Genius of Plants: A New Understanding of Plant Intelligence and Behavior* (Atria, 2018); Suzanne Simard, *Finding the Mother Tree: Discovering the Wisdom of the Forest* (Knopf, 2021).

62. Chamovitz, *What a Plant Knows*, 83.
63. Trewavas, *Plant Behaviour*, 255. Emphasis added.
64. Trewavas, *Plant Behaviour*, 245, 260.
65. For instance, the results of Trewavas's research support rather than undermine the notion of intelligibility in the entities crucial to plant communication: fungi. See Merlin Sheldrake, *Entangled Life: How Fungi Make Our Worlds, Change Our Minds, and Shape Our Futures* (Penguin, 2020), for the relationship between research on plant intelligence and broader discussion of biointelligence.
66. Kevin Corrigan, "Humans, Other Animals, Plants, and the Question of the Good: The Platonic and Neoplatonic Traditions," in *The Routledge Handbook of Neoplatonism*, ed. Svetla Slaveva-Griffin and Paulina Remes (Routledge, 2014), 387.
67. Kevin Corrigan, *Reading Plotinus: A Practical Introduction to Neoplatonism* (Purdue University Press, 2005), 86–188; see also Andrea Nightingale, *Spectacles of Truth in Classical Greek Philosophy:* Theoria *in its Cultural Context* (Cambridge University Press, 2004), 40–71.
68. Clément, *Roots*, 218, citing Pseudo-Dionysius, *Divine Names*, 4.28.
69. Evagrius Ponticus, *The Praktikos and Chapters on Prayer*, trans. John Eudes Bamberger (Cistercian, 1972), 39 (§92).
70. Augustine Casiday, *Reconstructing the Theology of Evagrius Ponticus: Beyond Heresy* (Cambridge University Press, 2013), 153.
71. "So, sitting down in your cell, collect your mind, lead it into the path of the breath along which the air enters in, constrain it to enter the heart together with the inhaled air and keep it." Selo, "Breath and Prayer," 57, citing Nikiphoros the Monk's treatise "On Watchfulness and the Guarding of the Heart," in *The Philokalia*, 4 vols., trans. G. E. H. Palmer, Philip Sherrard, and Kallistos Ware (Faber and Faber, 1979–1995), 4:192.
72. Chamovitz, *What a Plant Knows*, 83.

73. Wood, *Thinking Plant Animal Human*. While I do not engage with it in detail in this book, I have been influenced by Donna Haraway's concept of an ek-centric or out-of-center *anthropos* and by the broader field of multispecies ethics to which it relates; e.g., Donna Haraway, *Staying with the Trouble: Making Kin in the Chthulucene* (Durham University Press, 2016); Sarah Warren, "Haraway's Dream of an Ek-Centric Anthropos: Finding Virtuous Humility in the Age of a Dying Earth," *Environment, Space, Place* 10, no. 2 (2018): 109–27.
74. Gilles Deleuze and Félix Guattari, *A Thousand Plateaus*, trans. Paul Patton (Continuum, 2004), 11, 17.
75. Hannah Stark, "Deleuze and Critical Plant Studies," in *Deleuze and the Non/Human*, ed. Hannah Stark and J. Roffe (Palgrave Macmillan, 2015), 185, 189.
76. Deleuze and Guattari, *Thousand Plateaus*, 266.
77. Nealon, *Plant Theory*, 85, 86.
78. Gilles Deleuze and Félix Guattari. *What Is Philosophy?*, trans. Hugh Tomlinson and Graham Burchill (Columbia University Press, 1994), 212–13.
79. Gilles Deleuze, *Difference and Repetition*, trans. Paul Patton (Columbia University Press, 1994), 75.
80. Nealon, *Plant Theory*, 99. Emphasis in the original.
81. A point also made by Deleuze and Guattari, *What Is Philosophy?*, 213.
82. Nealon, *Plant Theory*, 99.
83. Deleuze, *Difference and Repetition*, 75.
84. Deleuze and Guattari, *What Is Philosophy?*, 212.
85. Nealon, *Plant Theory*, 107.
86. Nealon, *Plant Theory*, 99.
87. See, for instance, D. J. S. Cross, "Furtive Contemplations: Self, Time, and Affect in Deleuze," *New Centennial Review* 17, no. 2 (2017): 157–82. "This contemplation, of course, is not the contemplation readily recognized by the tradition" (157).
88. Jacob Holsinger Sherman, "No Werewolves in Theology? Transcendence, Immanence, and Becoming-Divine in Gilles Deleuze," *Modern Theology* 25, no. 1 (2009): 2.
89. Peter Hallward, *Out of This World: Deleuze and the Philosophy of Creation* (Verso, 2006), 86.
90. Sherman, "No Werewolves in Theology?," 1.

91. See also Jacob Holsinger Sherman, *Partakers of the Divine: Contemplation and the Practice of Philosophy* (Fortress, 2014).
92. Sherman, "No Werewolves in Theology?," 2.
93. Sherman, "No Werewolves in Theology?," 15. Hallward's negative assessment of Deleuze's mysticism has also been addressed from the perspective of Jungian depth psychology, Western esotericism, Hermetic philosophy, and magic; see Joshua Ramey, *The Hermetic Deleuze: Philosophy and Spiritual Ordeal* (Duke University Press, 2013). Ramey, however, is ambivalent regarding contemplation and focuses instead on the language and imagery of ecstatic transformation.
94. *Oxford English Dictionary*, s.v. "contemplate."
95. Jason P. Davies, "Whose Dream Is It Anyway? Navigating the Significance of Dreams in the Ancient World," in *Ancient Divination and Experience*, ed. Lindsay G. Driediger-Murphy and Esther Eidinow (Oxford University Press, 2019), 88: "[The] *possibility* of a significant omen was ever-present because the existence and intervention of the gods was all-pervasive . . . the *templum* of the augurs, for instance, would be a *locus* to isolate and detect a 'current' in reality that was not limited to that designated space." Emphasis in the original.
96. C. Sandilands, "Vegetate," in *Veer Ecology: A Companion for Environmental Thinking*, ed. Jeffrey Jerome Cohen and Lowell Duckert (University of Minnesota Press, 2017), 17–18.
97. Marder, *Grafts*, 15.
98. Tsing et al., *Arts of Living on a Damaged Planet*, M7, M5.

2. A NATURAL HISTORY OF CONTEMPLATION

1. My reading of Plotinus is indebted to Kevin Corrigan, especially his detailed account of nature, contemplation, and the One in *Reading Plotinus: A Practical Introduction to Neoplatonism* (Purdue University Press, 2005), 86–188. See also Kevin Corrigan, "Humans, Other Animals, Plants, and the Question of the Good: The Platonic and Neoplatonic Traditions," in *The Routledge Handbook of Neoplatonism*, ed. Svetla Slaveva-Griffin and Pauliina Remes (Routledge, 2014), 372–90; and John Deck, *Nature, Contemplation, and the One: A Study of the Philosophy of Plotinus* (Toronto University Press, 1967).

2. See Lynn White Jr., "The Historical Roots of Our Ecologic Crisis," *Science* 155, no. 3767 (1967): 1203–7; Carolyn Merchant, *The Death of Nature: Women, Ecology, and the Scientific Revolution* (Harper and Row, 1986); T. LeVasseur and A. Peterson, eds., *Religion and Ecological Crisis: The "Lynn White Thesis" at Fifty* (Routledge, 2017).
3. Plotinus, *The Enneads*, ed. Lloyd P. Gerson (Cambridge University Press, 2018), 3.8.8, 10–20.
4. F. E. Peters, *Greek Philosophical Terms: A Historical Lexicon* (New York University Press, 1967), s.v. *phýsis*.
5. Plotinus, *Enneads*, 3.8.1, 5–9.
6. Plotinus, *Enneads*, 3.8.4, 15–20.
7. Porphyry, *Life of Plotinus*, trans. A. H. Armstrong (Harvard University Press, 1969), 1.1.
8. Michael Marder, *The Philosopher's Plant: An Intellectual Herbarium* (Columbia University Press, 2014), 47, 56.
9. Marder, *Philosopher's Plant*, 49, 50.
10. Deck, *Nature, Contemplation, and the One*, 95.
11. Plotinus, *Enneads*, 3.8.1, 1–7.
12. Plotinus, *Enneads*, 3.8.2, 10–15. A point also articulated by Plotinus earlier in the same passage: "Those, however, who are making this comparison ought to have considered that just as in the case of those who practice such crafts something must remain in them in accordance with which, whilst still remaining in them, they produce their artefact by means of their hands, they must also go back to a similar thing in nature and understand that here, too, all the power that produces not by means of hands must remain and remains entire."
13. Plotinus, *Enneads*, 56.
14. Marder, *Philosopher's Plant*, 50.
15. Anthony Trewavas, *Plant Behaviour and Intelligence* (Oxford University Press, 2014), 93–104.
16. Stefano Mancuso, *The Revolutionary Genius of Plants: A New Understanding of Plant Intelligence and Behavior* (Atria, 2018), 176.
17. Suzanne Simard, *Finding the Mother Tree: Discovering the Wisdom of the Forest* (Knopf, 2021), 228.
18. Trewavas, *Plant Behaviour and Intelligence*, 93.
19. Marder, *Philosopher's Plant*, 56.

20. Luce Irigaray and Michael Marder, *Through Vegetal Being: Two Philosophical Perspectives* (Columbia University Press, 2016), 158.
21. Corrigan, "Humans," 387.
22. Douglas E. Christie, *The Blue Sapphire of the Mind: Notes for a Contemplative Ecology* (Oxford University Press, 2013), 44. See also Douglas Burton-Christie, *The Word in the Desert: Scripture and the Quest for Holiness in Early Christian Monasticism* (Oxford University Press, 1994).
23. Christie, *Blue Sapphire*, 42.
24. *The Anonymous Sayings of the Desert Fathers: A Select Edition and Complete English Translation*, ed. and trans. John Wortley (Cambridge University Press, 2013).
25. Christie, *Blue Sapphire*, 43.
26. Pierre Hadot, *Veil of Isis: An Essay on the History of the Idea of Nature*, trans. Michael Chase (University of Chicago Press, 2008), 183. On the contemplation of nature as a spiritual exercise, see also 182–89, and Pierre Hadot, *Philosophy as a Way of Life: Spiritual Exercises from Socrates to Foucault*, trans. Arnold Davidson (Blackwell, 1995), 251–63.
27. Olivier Clément, *The Roots of Christian Mysticism: Text and Commentary*, trans. Theodore Berkeley and Jeremy Hummerstone (New City, 1995), 215. On *phusike theoria*, see also Thomas Merton, *Mystics and Zen Masters* (Delta, 1967), 91–113; Joshua Lollar, *To See Into the Life of Things: The Contemplation of Nature in Maximus the Confessor and His Predecessors* (Brepols, 2013); Bruce Foltz, *The Noetics of Nature: Environmental Philosophy and the Holy Beauty of the Visible* (Fordham University Press, 2014), 158–74; Norman Wirzba, "Christian *Theoria Physike:* On Learning to See Creation," *Modern Theology* 32, no. 2 (2016): 211–30; Jacob Holsinger Sherman, "Reading the Book of Nature After Nature," *Religions* 11, no. 4 (2020): https://doi.org/10.3390/rel11040205; Andreas Nordlander, "Green Purpose: Teleology, Ecological Ethics, and the Recovery of Contemplation," *Studies in Christian Ethics* 34, no. 1 (2021): 36–55.
28. *Philokalia*, 1:82 (Evagrius of Pontus, *Chapters on Prayer*, 149).
29. Christie, *Blue Sapphire*, 142, 149.
30. Evagrius, *Praktikos*, 15 (*Praktikos*, 2).
31. Peter Brown, *The Body and Society: Men, Women, and Sexual Renunciation in Early Christianity* (Columbia University Press, 1988), 130–31.

32. Evagrius, *Praktikos*, 15 (*Praktikos*, 2).
33. Helen Hunt, *Clothed in the Body: Asceticism, the Body, and the Spiritual in the Late Antique Era* (Routledge, 2012), 85–86, commenting on John Climacus, *The Ladder of Divine Ascent*. Emphasis in the original.
34. Hunt, *Clothed in the Body*, 85–86.
35. Augustine Casiday, *Reconstructing the Theology of Evagrius Ponticus: Beyond Heresy* (Cambridge University Press, 2013), 153.
36. G. W. H. Lampe, *A Patristic Greek Lexicon*, s.v. *anoesia*, "state of being beyond intelligence." See Pseudo-Dionysius, *The Complete Works*, trans. Colm Luibhead (Paulist, 1987), 216–18 (*Celestial Hierarchy*, 3.3.7), 133–42.
37. Pseudo-Dionysius, *Complete Works*, 133–42.
38. Clément, *Roots*, 215. Emphasis added.
39. Elizabeth Theokritoff, "Liturgy, Cosmic Worship, and Christian Cosmology," in *Toward an Ecology of Transformation: Orthodox Christian Perspectives on Environment, Nature, and Creation*, ed. John Cryssavgis and Bruce V. Foltz (Fordham University Press, 2013), 296–97.
40. Christie, *Blue Sapphire*, 366n5.
41. After his death, Evagrius was condemned at the Council of Ephesus, together with Origen, but not on the grounds of Messalianism. On the reputation of Evagrius, see Casiday, *Reconstructing the Theology of Evagrius*, 46–72.
42. Columba Stewart, *"Working the Earth of the Heart": The Messalian Controversy in History, Texts, and Language to A.D. 431* (Oxford University Press, 1991), 10.
43. Hunt, *Clothed in the Body*, 13.
44. Ephrem, *Hymns on Faith*, 22.4, in *The Syriac Fathers on Prayer and the Spiritual Life*, ed. and trans. Sebastian Brock (Cistercian Publications, 1987), 33–34.
45. Kathleen McVey, introduction to Ephrem the Syrian, *Hymns*, trans. Kathleen McVey (Paulist, 1989), 41.
46. Sebastian Brock, introduction to Ephrem the Syrian, *Hymns on Paradise*, trans. Sebastian Brock (St. Vladimir's Seminary Press, 1990), 39–40.
47. Isaac of Nineveh, *Discourses*, 22, in Brock, *Syriac Fathers on Prayer*, 255, 259.
48. Thomas Arentzen, Virginia Burrus, and Glenn Peers, *Byzantine Tree Life: Christianity and the Arboreal Imagination* (Palgrave Macmillan, 2021), 112, 7, 109, 107, 109.

49. Michael Marder, *Grafts: Writings on Plants* (University of Minnesota Press, 2016), 15. Emphasis in the original.
50. Arentzen, Burrus, and Peers, *Byzantine Tree Life*, 139.
51. Marder, *Philosopher's Plant*, 53, citing Plotinus, *Enneads*, 1.4.14, 10–15.
52. Hadot, *Plotinus*, 71, citing Plotinus, *Enneads*, 6. 9.10, 2–3.
53. Hadot, *Plotinus*, 35–47.
54. Hadot, *Plotinus*, 67, citing Plotinus, *Enneads*, 2. 9. 9, 45–60.
55. Hadot, *Plotinus*, 30, 71.
56. Hadot, *Plotinus*, 74, 77.
57. Hadot, *Plotinus*, 86, citing Plotinus, *Enneads*, 5.8.8–20.
58. Hadot, *Plotinus*, 86, 95, 81, 95, 111.
59. Hadot, *Philosophy as a Way of Life*, 281.
60. See, for instance, Daniel Dombrowski, "Asceticism as Athletic Training in Plotinus," *Aufstieg und Niedergang der römischen Welt* 36, no. 1 (1987): 704. Dombrowski summarizes decades of research showing that Plotinian asceticism was about achieving moderation rather than encouraging extreme bodily mortification.
61. Corrigan, "Humans." See also James Wilberding, "Intelligible Kinds and Natural Kinds in Plotinus," *Études Platoniciennes* 8 (2011): 53–76.
62. Clare Carlisle, *On Habit* (Routledge, 2014).

3. VEGETAL MYSTICISM

1. See Bernard McGinn, *The Presence of God: A History of Western Christian Mysticism*, esp. vol. 3, *The Flowering of Mysticism: Men and Woman in the New Mysticism (1200–1350)* (Crossroad, 1998), 26.
2. Louis Cognet, *Post-Reformation Spirituality*, trans. P. Hepburne Scott (Hawthorne, 1959), 54–55. Emphasis added.
3. Michael Marder, *Grafts: Writings on Plants* (University of Minnesota Press, 2016), 38.
4. Luce Irigaray and Michael Marder, *Through Vegetal Being: Two Philosophical Perspectives* (Columbia University Press, 2016), 155–56.
5. Amy Hollywood, *Acute Melancholia and Other Essays* (Columbia University Press, 2016), 144.
6. Matthew Fox, introduction to Hildegard of Bingen, *Book of Divine Works: With Letters and Songs*, ed. Matthew Fox, trans. Robert Cunningham (Bear and Co., 1987), xix. See also Barbara Newman, "'Sibyl

of the Rhine': Hildegard's Life and Times," in *Voice of the Living Light: Hildegard of Bingen and Her World*, ed. Barbara Newman (University of California Press, 1998), 1–29.

7. C. Mews, "Religious Thinker: 'A Frail Human Being' on Fiery Life," in *Voice of the Living Light: Hildegard of Bingen and Her World*, ed. Barbara Newman (University of California Press, 1998), 58.
8. Hildegard of Bingen, *Selected Writings*, trans. Mark Atherton (Penguin, 2001), 5 (Letter to Bernard of Clairvaux).
9. Hildegard of Bingen, *Symphonia: A Critical Edition of the Symphonia armonie celestium revelationum [Symphony of the Harmony of Celestial Revelations]*, trans. Barbara Newman (Cornell University Press, 2015), 127 (*O viridissima virga*).
10. Liz Herbert McAvoy, *The Enclosed Garden and the Medieval Religious Imaginary* (D. S. Brewer, 2021), 127.
11. Hildegard, *Symphonia*, 182 (*O viriditas digiti Dei*). See Barbara Newman, *Sister of Wisdom: St Hildegard's Theology of the Feminine* (University of California Press, 1998), 102.
12. Sara Ritchey, *Holy Matter: Changing Perceptions of the Material World in Late Medieval Christianity* (Cornell University Press, 2014), 67.
13. Hildegard, *Symphonia*, 131 (*O virga ac diadema*).
14. Hildegard, *Symphonia*, 141 (*Spiritus sanctus vivificans vita*).
15. Margaret Berger, *Hildegard of Bingen: On Natural Philosophy and Medicine* (Brewer, 1999); Victoria Sweet, "Hildegard of Bingen and the Greening of Medieval Medicine," *Bulletin of the History of Medicine* 73, no. 3 (1999): 381–403.
16. Hildegard, *Symphonia*, 213 (*Columba aspexit*).
17. McAvoy, *Enclosed Garden*, 128.
18. Bernard McGinn, *The Foundations of Mysticism: Origins to the Fifth Century* (Crossroad, 1991), xvi.
19. Michael Marder, *Green Mass: The Ecological Theology of St. Hildegard of Bingen* (Stanford University Press, 2021), 35.
20. Hildegard, *Book of Divine Works*, 348.
21. Marder, *Green Mass*, 79.
22. Merlin Sheldrake, *Entangled Life: How Fungi Make Our Worlds, Change Our Minds, and Shape Our Futures* (Penguin, 2020), 149–74.
23. Michael Marder, *Plant-Thinking: A Philosophy of Vegetal Life* (Columbia University Press, 2013), 169.

24. Marder, *Green Mass*, 5.
25. Marder, *Green Mass*, 5, 27, 19, 76, 139.
26. Hildegard of Bingen, *Book of Divine Works*, 349. Emphasis added.
27. Marder, *Green Mass*, 95.
28. Daniel Chamovitz, *What a Plant Knows: A Field Guide to the Senses of Your Garden—and Beyond* (Scientific American, 2012), 167–75.
29. Liz Herbert McAvoy, Patricia Skinner, and Theresa Tyers, "Strange Fruits: Grafting, Foreigners, and the Garden Imaginary in Northern France and Germany, 1250–1350," *Speculum* 94, no. 2 (2019): 467–95. The article also focuses on the grafting imagery found in the work of the Helfta mystic Mechthild of Hackenborn (1241–1298), which I do not have space to consider here. Cf. McAvoy, *Enclosed Garden*, 143–94. My thanks to Emily McMillan for drawing this article to my attention; see her forthcoming unpublished work on garden imagery in the Helfta mystics.
30. Gertrude of Helfta, *The Herald of Divine Love*, trans. Margaret Winkworth (Paulist, 1993).
31. McAvoy, Skinner, and Tyers, "Strange Fruits," 472.
32. William Gorrie, *Illustrations of Scripture from Botanical Science* (1854), 77–91.
33. McAvoy, Skinner, and Tyers, "Strange Fruits," 468, 479.
34. Mary Forman, "Gertrud of Helfta: Arbor Amoris in Her Heart's Garden," *Mystics Quarterly* 26, no. 4 (2000): 163–78.
35. Gertrude of Helfta, *Herald of Divine Love*, 176–77.
36. McAvoy, Skinner, and Tyers, "Strange Fruits," 479, 477.
37. McAvoy, Skinner, and Tyers, "Strange Fruits," 474.
38. McAvoy, *Enclosed Garden*, 184–85.
39. McGinn, *Flowering of Mysticism*, 275.
40. McAvoy, *Enclosed Garden*, 5.
41. Marder, *Grafts*, 15.
42. McGinn, *Flowering of Mysticism*, 48, 54–55.
43. Sean L. Field, *The Beguine, the Angel, and the Inquisitor: The Trials of Marguerite Porete and Guiard de Cressonessart* (University of Notre Dame Press, 2012), 234.
44. Marguerite of Porete, *Mirror of Simple Souls*, trans. Ellen Babinsky (Paulist, 1993), 220–21, 99.

45. Marguerite of Porete, *Mirror*, 220. Emphasis added. "Fruition" (*fruition*) is a recurring noun in the *Mirror*.
46. Hollywood, *Acute Melancholia*, 143.
47. Amy Hollywood, *The Soul as Virgin Wife: Mechthild of Magdeburg, Marguerite of Porete, and Meister Eckhart* (Notre Dame University Press, 1985), 106, 112.
48. Hollywood, *Acute Melancholia*, 134, 144, 145.
49. Jacob Erickson, "Irreverent Theology: On the Queer Ecology of Creation," in *Meaningful Flesh: Reflections on Religion and Nature for a Queer Planet*, ed. Whitney Bauman (Punctum, 2015), 58.

INTERLUDE: FRANCIS IN ECSTASY

1. See Marybeth Lorbiecki, *Following in the Footsteps of St. Francis: Pope John Paul II's Call for Ecological Action* (Rizzoli, 2014); and Marybeth Lorbiecki, *On Care for Our Common Home. Laudato Si': The Encyclical of Pope Francis on the Environment*, with commentary by Sean McDough (Orbis, 2016).
2. The painting entered the Frick Collection in 1915 under the title *St. Francis in the Desert*. On the history of the painting and its interpretation, see Marilyn Aronberg Lavin, Jinyu Liu, and Adam Gitner, "The Joy of St. Francis: Bellini's Panel in the Frick Collection," *Artibus et Historiae* 28, no. 56 (2007): 231–56. The interpretation I develop here is indebted to Anthony F. Janson, "The Meaning of the Landscape in Bellini's *St. Francis in Ecstasy*," *Artibus et Historiae* 15, no. 30 (1994): 41–54, and Therese Sjøvoll, "Kunst: Giovanni Bellini, 'Den hellige Frans i ødemarken,'" *St Olav* 3 (2021): 40–43.
3. Peter Kwasniewski, *The Ecstasy of Love in the Thought of St Thomas Aquinas* (Emmaus, 2021), 8. See also Peter Kwasniewski, "The Ecstasy of Love in Aquinas's 'Commentary on the Sentences,'" *Angelicum* 83, no. 1 (2006): 51–93.
4. Kwasniewski, *Ecstasy of Love*, 49–50, 51.
5. *The Earliest Franciscans: The Legacy of Giles of Assisi, Roger of Provence, and James of Milan*, trans. Kathryn Krug (Paulist, 2015), 44.
6. Corrigan, "Ecstasy and Ecstasy," 28, 29, 32.
7. Kwasniewski, *Ecstasy of Love*, 37. Kwasniewski points out that although Aquinas rarely credits Maximus directly, there are "clear resonances" between their thinking on the creaturely nature of ecstasy.

8. Francis of Assisi and Clare of Assisi, *The Complete Works*, trans. Regis J. Armstrong and Ignatius C. Brady (Paulist, 1986), 38.
9. Janson, "The Meaning of the Landscape," 52.

4. LET NATURE BE AROUSED!

1. Georges Bataille, *Erotism: Death and Sensuality*, trans. Mary Dalwood (City Lights, 1962). I do not dismiss the connection between sexual and mystical trance, which recently has been given a nuanced account in *Exploring Sexuality and Spirituality*, ed. P. Shining and N. Michelle Epple (Brill, 2020). However, my argument in this chapter is that the erotic language of arousal in Western Christian mysticism is open to other interpretations, as feminist scholars have also shown. See, for instance, Grace Jantzen, "Power, Gender, and Ecstasy: Mysticism in Post/Modernity," *Literature and Theology* 11, no. 4 (1997): 385–402.
2. Marie-Florine Bruneau, *Women Mystics Confront the Modern World: Marie de l'Incarnation (1599–1672) and Madame Guyon (1648–1717)* (State University of New York Press, 1998), 139.
3. Bruneau, *Women Mystics*, 140.
4. Bruneau, *Women Mystics*, 140.
5. For a comprehensive history of mysticism in this period, the best Anglophone study is now Bernard McGinn, *The Crisis of Mysticism: Quietism in Seventeenth-Century Spain, Italy, and France* (Crossroad, 2021), on which I have relied in what follows. See also Richard Knox, *Enthusiasm: A Chapter in the History of Religion, with Special Reference to the XVII and XVIII Centuries* (Oxford University Press, 1950); Louis Cognet, *Post-Reformation Spirituality*, trans. P. Hepburne Scott (Hawthorne, 1959); J.-R. Armogathe, *Le quiétisme* (Presses Universitaires de France, 1973); and the special edition of *Common Knowledge* 15, no. 1 (2015), in particular 23–38: G. R. Evans, "*Sancta Indifferentia* and *Adiaphora*: 'Holy Indifference' and 'Things Indifferent.'"
6. Interior peace was celebrated famously by Augustine in his *Confessions*. See George P. Lawless, "Interior Peace in the Confessions of St Augustine," *Recherches Augustiniennes* 15 (1980): 80–98.
7. "The Errors of Miguel de Molinos: Apostolic Constitution 'Caelestis Pater' issued by Innocent XI on Nov. 20, 1687," trans. Bernard McGinn, in Miguel de Molinos, *The Spiritual Guide*, trans. Robert P. Baird (Paulist, 2010), 187. Emphasis added.

8. Jacques-Bénigne Bossuet, *Quakerism a-la-mode, or A History of Quietism*, trans. unknown (1698), 53.
9. Bossuet, *Quakerism a-la-mode*, 54.
10. See Charly Coleman, *The Virtues of Abandon: An Anti-Individualist History of the French Enlightenment* (Stanford University Press, 2014), 89–121. As Coleman points out, neither Guyon nor the spiritual tradition she related to were connected to the abuse scandals in question.
11. McGinn, *Persistence of Mysticism*, 156–62.
12. Bo Karen Lee, *Sacrifice and Delight in the Mystical Theologies of Anna Maria van Schurman and Madame Jeanne Guyon* (Notre Dame University Press, 2014), 1–14.
13. Knox, *Enthusiasm*, 247.
14. Jeanne Guyon, *Selected Writings*, ed. and trans. Dianne Guenin-Lelle and Ronney Mourad (Paulist, 2012), 58.
15. In his youth, Ignatius had been suspected of practicing contemplative prayer according to the Alumbrados, "Illuminated ones," or "Illuminati," Spanish heretics condemned in 1623. The Alumbrados predate Quietism but carry many of the same defining features. See Alastair Hamilton, *Heresy and Mysticism in Sixteenth-Century Spain: The Alumbrados* (University of Toronto Press, 1992); and Knox, *Enthusiasm*, 241–42.
16. Bruneau, *Women Mystics*.
17. Fabrizio Bigotti, "Vegetable Life: Applications, Implications, and Transformations of a Classical Concept," in *Vegetative Powers: The Roots of Life in Ancient, Medieval, and Early Modern Natural Philosophy*, ed. Fabrizio Baldassarri and Andreas Blank (Springer, 2021): 383.
18. Natania Meeker and Antónia Szabari, *Radical Botany: Plants and Speculative Fiction* (Fordham University Press, 2020), 7, 6.
19. Meeker and Szabari, *Radical Botany*, 6. The expression "low anthropology" is borrowed from Lee, *Sacrifice and Delight*.
20. Elizabeth Potter, "Modelling the Gender Politics in Science," *Hypatia* 3, no. 1 (1988): 22.
21. Patricia Ward, "Madame Guyon and Experiential Theology in America," *Church History* 67, no. 3 (1998): 486, 485.
22. Marie-Florine Bruneau, "*La vie* de Madame Guyon: Frigidité et masochisme en tant que dispositifs politiques," *French Forum* 8, no. 2 (1983): 101–8.

4. LET NATURE BE AROUSED! ଔ 229

23. There have been many good studies of Guyon's life, politics, role as a woman and writer, and her influence on dissident spirituality (especially Protestantism), but here I will be focusing entirely on her approach to spiritual exercises; in particular, I will not be concerned with determining whether Guyon's views were heretical or with the details of the polemics that engulfed her work during the Quietist controversy of the 1680s. On Guyon, her life and times, see F. Mallet-Joris, *Jeanne Guyon* (Flammarion, 1978); Marie-Louise Gondal, *Madame Guyon (1648–1717): Un nouveau visage* (Beauchesne, 1989).
24. Coleman, *Virtues of Abandon*, 33. See also *Utopia: 16th and 17th Centuries*, ed. David Lee Rubin and Alice Stroup (Rookwood, 1998), 15.
25. Coleman, *Virtues of Abandon*, 54.
26. Coleman, *Virtues of Abandon*, 200, 134.
27. Ryan Hanley, *The Political Philosophy of Fénelon* (Oxford University Press, 2020), 184–85.
28. Coleman, *Virtues of Abandon*, 295.
29. There are different and sometimes conflicting accounts of Guyon's biography. I have found the clearest and most detailed overview to be Bruneau, *Women Mystics*, and I have relied on Bruneau's chronology in this section.
30. Bruneau, *Women Mystics*, 128.
31. See Jeanne Guyon, *The Prison Narratives of Jeanne Guyon*, trans. Dianne Guenin-Lelle and Ronney Mourad (Oxford University Press, 2011).
32. In addition to Guyon, *Selected Writings*, see Jeanne Guyon, *Letters of Madame Guyon*, trans. and ed. P. Upham (1870); and Jeanne Guyon, *Union with God: Including 22 of Madame Guyon's Poems*, ed. and trans. Gene Edwards (SeedSowers, 1981). A comprehensive bibliography of Guyon's works in English translation is included in Guyon, *Selected Writings*, 327–28.
33. Ward, "Madame Guyon," 484–98; Patricia Ward, *Experimental Theology in America: Madame Guyon, Fénelon, and Their Readers* (Baylor University Press, 2009).
34. Bruneau, *Women Mystics*, 147.
35. Guyon, *Selected Writings*, 59 (*Short and Easy Method*).
36. Lee, *Sacrifice and Delight*, 89.

37. Guyon, *Selected Writings*, 69 (*Short and Easy Method*).
38. Louis Cognet, "Le coeur chez les spirituels du XVIIe siècle," in *Dictionnaire de spiritualité ascétique et mystique*, ed. Marcel Viller (Beauchesne, 1937–94), 2303, 2305; quoted in Nicholas Paige, *Being Interior: Autobiography and the Contradictions of Modernity in Seventeenth-Century France* (University of Pennsylvania Press, 2000), 72.
39. Guyon, *Selected Writings*, 72.
40. Molinos, *Spiritual Guide*, 74.
41. Knox, *Enthusiasm*, 260–87.
42. Guyon, *Selected Writings*, 73, 88.
43. Lytta Basset, "Une spiritualité d'enfant," *Transversalités* 115 (2010): 67–91, https://doi.org/10.3917/trans.115.0067. My translation.
44. Jeanne Guyon, *The Way of the Child Jesus: Our Model of Perfection*, trans. Nancy C. James (Madame Guyon Foundation, 2015).
45. Francis de Sales, *Of the Love of God*, trans. H. L. Sidney Lear (1888), 281. On the scriptural imagery that inspires Sales's use of botanical imagery, see William Gorrie, *Illustrations of Scripture from Botanical Science* (1854).
46. Guyon, *Selected Writings*, 190–91 (*Autobiography*).
47. Auguste Saudreau, *Mystical Prayer According to St Jane de Chantal*, trans. A. E. H. Swinstead (Benziger Brothers, 1929), 8.
48. Henri Brémond, *Sainte Chantal 1572–1641* (Lecoffre, 1912).
49. Saudreau, *Mystical Prayer*, 37, 28.
50. Wendy M. Wright and Joseph F. Power, introduction to Francis de Sales and Jane de Chantal, *Letters of Spiritual Direction*, ed. Wendy M. Wright and Joseph F. Power, trans. Péronne Marie Thibert (Paulist, 1988), 80.
51. Jane de Chantal, *Exhortations, Conferences, and Instructions*, ed. Visitandines of Bristol (Loyola University Press, 1928), Conference 34.
52. Jeanne de Chantal, *Sa vie et ses oeuvres*, 8 vols., ed. Religieuses du Premier Monastère de la Visitation Sainte-Marie d'Annecy (1874–1879), 3:285. My translation.
53. In older scholarship one often finds the mysticism of Sales and Chantal described as "abstract," owing to the influence of mystical theology and the *via negativa*.
54. Chantal, *Exhortations, Conferences, and Instructions*, Conference 36.

55. Chantal and Sales, *Letters of Spiritual Direction*, 248–49.
56. Wright and Power, introduction to Chantal and Sales, *Letters of Spiritual Direction*, 77. Before co-founding the order of the Visitation, Chantal had experienced both family life (she gave birth to four children, two of whom survived to adulthood) and the loss of a loved partner: She founded the Visitation order as a widow. This extensive life experience outside the monastery informs her monastic writings and teachings in ways that are quite striking. On Chantal's life, see Elisabeth Stopp, *Madame de Chantal: Portrait of a Saint* (Faber and Faber, 1963).
57. Wright and Power, introduction to Chantal and Sales, *Letters of Spiritual Direction*, 71.
58. Chantal and Sales, *Letters of Spiritual Direction*, 249.
59. Michel de Certeau, *The Mystic Fable*, vol. 1: *The Sixteenth and Seventeenth Centuries*, Trans. Michael B. Smith (University of Chicago Press, 1982), 10.
60. de Certeau, *Mystic Fable*, 176.
61. On the psychological approach to the types of practices I am concerned with in this book, see the exhaustive critique by Ernst Arbman, *Ecstasy or Religious Trance*, 3 vols. (Norstedts, 1963–1970), esp. vol. 1. My thanks to Esaias Järnegard for introducing me to Arbman's remarkable scholarship.
62. de Certeau, *The Mystic Fable*, 9–10, 297.
63. Michel de Certeau, *The Practice of Everyday Life*, trans. Steven Rendall (University of California Press, 1984), 5, 36–38.
64. Bruneau, *Women Mystics*, 7.
65. Bruneau, *Women Mystics*, 150, 149.
66. Jeanne Guyon, *Spiritual Torrents*, trans. A. W. Marston (H. R. Allenson, 1909), 9.
67. Lee, *Sacrifice and Delight*, 1, 125, 124.
68. Lee, *Sacrifice and Delight*, 128.
69. Guyon, *Torrents*, 135. Emphasis added.
70. Jeanne Guyon, [*Selected Poetry*], trans. William Cowper, in *The Poetical Works of William Cowper, with Some of Madame Guyon's Poems in English* (1852), 507–9.
71. Michael Marder, *Plant-Thinking: A Philosophy of Vegetal Life* (Columbia University Press, 2013), 5.

72. Guyon, *Selected Writings*, 71.
73. Guyon, *Selected Writings*, 100, 171.
74. Guyon, *Selected Writings*, 115, 116, 122, 127.
75. Guyon, *Selected Writings*, 100.
76. Bruneau, *Women Mystics*, 156.

5. THE PLANT IN US

1. Elaine P. Miller, *The Vegetative Soul: From Philosophy of Nature to Subjectivity in the Feminine* (State University of New York, 2002), 5.
2. Luce Irigaray, *Elemental Passions*, trans. Joanne Collie and Judith Still (Routledge, 1993), 31.
3. Miller, *Vegetative Soul*, 4, 191.
4. Michael Marder, *The Philosopher's Plant: An Intellectual Herbarium* (Columbia University Press, 2014), 220.
5. Miller, *Vegetative Soul*, 11. Emphasis in the original.
6. Marder, *Philosopher's Plant*, 224. Emphasis in the original.
7. Luce Irigaray and Michael Marder, *Through Vegetal Being: Two Philosophical Perspectives* (Columbia University Press, 2016), 7, 47, 25.
8. Luce Irigaray, *A New Culture of Energy: Beyond East and West*, trans. Stephen Seely, Stephen Pluháček, and Antonia Pont (Columbia University Press, 2021), 79.
9. Irigaray, *New Culture of Energy*, 89.
10. Emanuele Coccia, *The Life of Plants: A Metaphysics of Mixture*, trans. Dylan Montanari (Polity, 2019), 4, 5–6. At stake is the ability to open to the world. Among plants, this is facilitated by the plant's lack of brain-dependent processing; sensory perception, for plants, is not interpreted in the form of images, concepts, and language. It is (following Daniel Chamovitz) "anoetic," rather than "noetic."
11. Coccia, *Life of Plants*, 9, 110.
12. Coccia, *Life of Plants*, 10, 21, 11.
13. Coccia, *Life of Plants*, 15. Emphasis in the original.
14. Coccia, *Life of Plants*, 20, 33, 32, 71.
15. Coccia, *Life of Plants*, 31, 118, 66, 122.
16. Michel de Certeau, *The Mystic Fable*, vol. 1: *The Sixteenth and Seventeenth Centuries*, Trans. Michael B. Smith (University of Chicago Press, 1982), 297.

17. James Arraj, *From John of the Cross to Us* (Inner Growth, 1999), 103–4, passim; *Carmelite Prayer: A Tradition for the Twenty-First Century*, ed. Keith Egan (Paulist, 2003).
18. Simone Kotva, "Habit and the Spiritual Life: Perspectives from Christian Mysticism and the Philosophy of Religion," in *Habit and the History of Philosophy*, ed. Jeremy Dunham and Komarine Romdenh-Romluc (Routledge, 2022), 183–95.
19. Jeanne Guyon, *Spiritual Torrents*, trans. A. W. Marston (H. R. Allenson, 1909), 2.
20. Jeanne Guyon, *Selected Writings*, ed. and trans. Dianne Guenin-Lelle and Ronney Mourad (Paulist, 2012), 57, 59–63, 119.
21. Fabrice Blée, "Transcendance et transformation de soi dans la doctrine du pur amour selon madame Guyon," *Studies in Religion/Sciences Religieuses* 49, no. 4 (2020): 546–63.
22. Guenin-Lelle and Mourad, introduction to Guyon, *Selected Writings*, 31.
23. Guyon, *Selected Writings*, 66, 72, 73, 74.
24. Guyon, *Spiritual Torrents*, 81, 41.
25. Marie-Florine Bruneau, *Women Mystics Confront the Modern World: Marie de l'Incarnation (1599–1672) and Madame Guyon (1648–1717)* (State University of New York Press, 1998), 151.
26. Guyon, *Spiritual Torrents*, 107, 40.
27. Michael Marder, *Plant-Thinking: A Philosophy of Vegetal Life* (Columbia University Press, 2013), 20, 21.
28. Guyon, *Spiritual Torrents*, 119.
29. Guyon, *Spiritual Torrents*, 111.
30. Irigaray, *New Culture*, 14, 21–22, 60.
31. Irigaray, *New Culture*, 34.
32. Irigaray, *New Culture*, 35.
33. Irigaray and Marder, *Through Vegetal Being*, 159.
34. Irigaray, *New Culture*, 54, 55.
35. Irigaray, *New Culture*, 112.
36. Agnes M. F. Selo, "Breath and Prayer in Ancient and Modern Times," *Life of the Spirit* 9, no. 98 (1954): 54. Emphasis added.
37. Patricia Ward, *Experimental Theology in America: Madame Guyon, Fénelon, and Their Readers* (Baylor University Press, 2009), 23.
38. Guyon, *Spiritual Torrents*, 139.

39. Guyon, *Spiritual Torrents*, 129.
40. Marder, *Philosopher's Plant*, 215.
41. Guyon, *Selected Writings*, 73.
42. Guyon, *Torrents*, 144.
43. Jeffrey Nealon, *Plant Theory: Biopower and Vegetable Life* (Stanford University Press, 2016), 99. Emphasis added.
44. Nealon, *Plant Theory*, 87, 98–99, 100, 106.
45. Surprisingly, the same opinion is repeated by commentators focusing on contemplation in Deleuze's philosophy. Thus D. J. S. Cross, for instance, hastens to emphasize how "this contemplation, of course, is not the contemplation readily recognized by the tradition," by which he means the tradition of Western thought. See D. J. S. Cross, "Furtive Contemplations: Self, Time, and Affect in Deleuze," *New Centennial Review* 17, no. 2 (2017): 157.
46. Gilles Deleuze, *Difference and Repetition*, trans. Paul Patton (Columbia University Press, 1994), 75.
47. Cross, "Furtive Contemplations," 157.
48. Kristien Justaert, "Schizoanalysis of the Eucharist: From Oedipal Repetition to Liberating Event," in *Deleuze and the Schizoanalysis of Religion*, ed. Lindsay Powell-Jones and F. LeRon Shults (Bloomsbury, 2016), 42. See also Kristien Justaert, *Theology After Deleuze* (Continuum, 2012).
49. Jacob Holsinger Sherman, "No Werewolves in Theology? Transcendence, Immanence, and Becoming-Divine in Gilles Deleuze," *Modern Theology* 25, no. 1 (2009): 1–20.
50. Joseph Barker, "Against 'Vital Materialism': The Passive Creation of Life in Deleuze," *Mosaic: An Interdisciplinary Critical Journal* 48, no. 4 (2015): 49.
51. Barker, "Against 'Vital Materialism,'" 60.
52. Giorgio Agamben, "Absolute Immanence," in *Potentialities: Collected Essays in Philosophy*, trans. Daniel Heller Roazen (Stanford University Press, 1999), 239.
53. C. Sandilands, "Vegetate," in *Veer Ecology: A Companion for Environmental Thinking*, ed. Jeffrey Jerome Cohen and Lowell Duckert (University of Minnesota Press, 2017), 19.
54. Sandilands, "Vegetate," 17. Emphasis in the original.
55. Sandilands, "Vegetate," 18.

56. Guyon, *Selected Writings*, 57 (*Short and Easy Method*).
57. Michel de Certeau, "Mysticism," *Diacritics* 22, no. 2 (1992): 24.
58. Michael Marder, *Green Mass: The Ecological Theology of St. Hildegard of Bingen* (Stanford University Press, 2021), 5.
59. Irigaray and Marder, *Through Vegetal Being*, 158.

EPILOGUE. ECOLOGIES OF ECSTASY

1. Jeffrey Nealon, *Plant Theory: Biopower and Vegetable Life* (Stanford University Press, 2016), 107.
2. Agnes Arber, *The Manifold and the One* (J. Murray, 1957), 17.
3. Mircea Eliade, *Yoga: Immortality and Freedom*, trans. W. Trask (Pantheon, 1958), 66.
4. See, for instance, Robin Wall Kimmerer, *Braiding Sweetgrass: Indigenous Wisdom, Scientific Knowledge, and the Teaching of Plants* (Penguin, 2013); and Theresa L. Miller, *Plant Kin: A Multispecies Ethnography in Indigenous Brazil* (University of Texas Press, 2019).
5. Mircea Eliade, *Shamanism: Archaic Techniques of Ecstasy*, trans. Willard Trask (Bollingen, 1964).
6. Eduardo Viveiros de Castro, *Cannibal Metaphysics*, trans. Peter Skafish (University of Minnesota Press, 2014).
7. Thomas E. Nevin, *Thérèse of Lisieux: God's Gentle Warrior* (Oxford University Press, 2006).
8. Sara Ritchey, "Spiritual Arborescence: Trees in the Medieval Christian Imagination," *Spiritus* 8 (2008): 64–82.
9. Thérèse of Lisieux, *Collected Poems*, trans. Alan Bancroft (Gracewing, 2001), 212, 213. Ellipsis in the original.
10. Simone Weil, *Waiting on God*, ed. Joseph-Marie Perrin and trans. Emma Craufurd (Routledge and Kegan Paul, 1951), 130.
11. Weil, *Waiting on God*, 55. Simone Kotva, *Effort and Grace: On the Spiritual Exercise of Philosophy* (Bloomsbury, 2020), 131–72.
12. Simone Weil, *On Science, Necessity, and the Love of God*, ed. and trans. Richard Rees (Oxford University Press, 1968), 150, 151.
13. Aliya Say, "Art, Spirit, and Plants: On Botanical Abstraction, Vegetal Ontology, and Mystical States," PhD diss., Aarhus University, 2023. Say's work studies, among others, the vegetal mysticism of the Swedish painter and occultist Hilma af Klint (1862–1944).

BIBLIOGRAPHY

Acta Sanctorum. Ed. J. Bollandus and G. Henschenius. 1863–1940.

Agamben, Giorgio. "Absolute Immanence." In *Potentialities: Collected Essays in Philosophy*, trans. Daniel Heller Roazen, 220–42. Stanford University Press, 1999.

Aloi, Giovanni, and Michael Marder. *Vegetal Entwinements in Philosophy and Art: A Reader.* MIT Press, 2023.

Arber, Agnes. *The Manifold and the One.* J. Murray, 1957.

Arbman, Ernst. *Ecstasy or Religious Trance.* 3 vols. Norstedts, 1963–1970.

Arentzen, Thomas, Virginia Burrus, and Glenn Peers. *Byzantine Tree Life: Christianity and the Arboreal Imagination.* Palgrave Macmillan, 2021.

Armogathe, J.-R. *Le quiétisme.* Presses Universitaires de France, 1973.

Arraj, James. *From John of the Cross to Us.* Inner Growth Books, 1999.

Badiou, Alain. *Deleuze: The Clamor of Being.* Trans. Louise Burchill. University of Minnesota Press, 2000.

Baldassarri, Fabrizio, and Andreas Blank. *Vegetative Powers: The Roots of Life in Ancient, Medieval, and Early Modern Natural Philosophy.* Springer, 2021.

Barker, Joseph. "Against 'Vital Materialism': The Passive Creation of Life in Deleuze." *Mosaic: An Interdisciplinary Critical Journal* 48, no. 4 (2015): 49–62.

Basset, Lytta. "Une spiritualité d'enfant." *Transversalités* 115 (2010): 67–91. https://doi.org/10.3917/trans.115.0067.

Bataille, Georges. *Erotism: Death and Sensuality.* Trans. Mary Dalwood. City Lights, 1962.

Bauman, Whitney, ed. *Meaningful Flesh: Reflections on Religion and Nature for a Queer Planet.* Punctum, 2015.

Beck, B. "Jardin monastique, jardin mystique: Ordonnance et signification des jardins monastiques médiévaux." *Revue d'Histoire de la Pharmacie* 48, no. 327 (2000): 377–94.

Becker-Lindenthal, Hjördis, and Simone Kotva. "Practicing for Death in the Anthropocene: Reading Christian Asceticism After the End of the Human." *Environmental Humanities* 15, no. 2 (2023): 105–23.

Bernard of Clairvaux. *On the Song of Songs.* Trans. Irene M. Edmonds and Kilian J. Walsh. Cistercian Publications, 1979.

Bigotti, Fabrizio. "Vegetable Life: Applications, Implications, and Transformations of a Classical Concept." In *Vegetative Powers: The Roots of Life in Ancient, Medieval, and Early Modern Natural Philosophy*, ed. Fabrizio Baldassarri and Andreas Blank, 383–406. Springer, 2021.

Blée, Fabrice. "Transcendance et transformation de soi dans la doctrine du pur amour selon madame Guyon." *Studies in Religion/Sciences Religieuses* 49, no. 4 (2020): 546–63.

Bossuet, Jacques-Bénigne. *Quakerism a-la-mode, or A History of Quietism.* Trans. Anonymous. 1698.

Brémond, Henri. *Sainte Chantal 1572–1641.* Lecoffre, 1912.

Brintnall, Kent L. "Erotic Ruination: Embracing the 'Savage Spirituality' of Barebacking." In *Negative Ecstasies: Georges Bataille and the Study of Religion*, ed. Jeremy Biles and Kent Brintnall, 51–67. Fordham University Press, 2015.

Brown, Peter. *The Body and Society: Men, Women, and Sexual Renunciation in Early Christianity.* Columbia University Press, 1988.

Bruneau, Marie-Florine. "*La vie* de Madame Guyon: Frigidité et masochisme en tant que dispositifs politiques." *French Forum* 8, no. 2 (1983): 101–8.

———. *Women Mystics Confront the Modern World: Marie de l'Incarnation (1599–1672) and Madame Guyon (1648–1717).* State University of New York Press, 1998.

Bruun, M. B. *A Companion to Bernard of Clairvaux.* Brill, 2011.

Carlisle, Clare. *On Habit.* Routledge, 2014.

Casiday, Augustine. *Reconstructing the Theology of Evagrius Ponticus: Beyond Heresy.* Cambridge University Press, 2013.

Castro, Eduardo Viveiros de. *Cannibal Metaphysics.* Trans. Peter Skafish. University of Minnesota Press, 2014.

Certeau, Michel de. *The Mystic Fable*. Vol. 1: *The Sixteenth and Seventeenth Centuries*. Trans. Michael B. Smith. University of Chicago Press, 1982.

———. "Mysticism." *Diacritics* 22, no. 2 (1992): 11–25.

———. *The Practice of Everyday Life*. Trans. Steven Rendall. University of California Press, 1984.

Chamovitz, Daniel. *What a Plant Knows: A Field Guide to the Senses*. Scientific American, 2012.

Chantal, Jane de. *Exhortations, Conferences, and Instructions*. Ed. Visitandines of Bristol. Loyola University Press, 1928.

———. *Sa vie et ses œuvres*. 8 Vols. Eds. Sisters of the First Monastery of Visitation Sainte-Marie d'Annecy. 1874–1879.

Chantal, Jane de, and Francis de Sales. *Letters of Spiritual Direction*. Ed. Wendy M. Wright and Joseph F. Power. Trans. Péronne Marie Thibert. Paulist, 1988.

Christie, Douglas E. *The Blue Sapphire of the Mind: Notes for a Contemplative Ecology*. Oxford University Press, 2013.

———. "Creation and Revelation." In *The Oxford Handbook of Mystical Theology*, ed. Edward Howells and Mark McIntosh, 529–48. Oxford University Press, 2020.

———. *The Word in the Desert: Scripture and the Quest for Holiness in Early Christian Monasticism*. Oxford University Press, 1994.

Clément, Olivier. *The Roots of Christian Mysticism: Text and Commentary*. Trans. Theodore Berkeley and Jeremy Hummerstone. New City, 1995.

Coccia, Emanuele. *The Life of Plants: A Metaphysics of Mixture*. Trans. Dylan Montanari. Polity, 2019.

Cognet, Louis. *Post-Reformation Spirituality*. Trans. P. Hepburne Scott. Hawthorne, 1959.

Coleman, Charly. *The Virtues of Abandon: An Anti-Individualist History of the French Enlightenment*. Stanford University Press, 2014.

Corrigan, Kevin. "Ecstasy and Ectasy in Some Early Pagan and Christian Mystical Writings." In *Greek and Medieval Studies in Honour of Leo Sweeney, S.J.*, ed. William J. Carroll and John J. Furlong, 27–38. Peter Lang, 1994.

———. "Humans, Other Animals, Plants, and the Question of the Good: The Platonic and Neoplatonic Traditions." In *The Routledge Handbook of Neoplatonism*, ed. Svetla Slaveva-Griffin and Pauliina Remes, 372–90. Routledge, 2014.

———. *Reading Plotinus: A Practical Introduction to Neoplatonism*. Purdue University Press, 2005.
Cross, D. J. S. "Furtive Contemplations: Self, Time, and Affect in Deleuze." *New Centennial Review* 17, no. 2 (2017): 157–82.
Davies, Jason P. "Whose Dream Is It Anyway? Navigating the Significance of Dreams in the Ancient World." In *Ancient Divination and Experience*, ed. Lindsay G. Driediger-Murphy and Esther Eidinow, 87–110. Oxford University Press, 2019.
Deck, John N. *Nature, Contemplation, and the One: A Study of the Philosophy of Plotinus*. Toronto University Press, 1967.
Deleuze, Gilles. *Difference and Repetition*. Trans. Paul Patton. Columbia University Press, 1994.
Deleuze, Gilles, and Félix Guattari. *A Thousand Plateaus: Capitalism and Schizophrenia*. Trans. Brian Massumi. Continuum, 2004.
———. *What Is Philosophy?* Trans. Hugh Tomlinson and Graham Burchill. Columbia University Press, 1994.
Dombrowski, Daniel. "Asceticism as Athletic Training in Plotinus." *Aufstieg und Niedergang der römischen Welt* 36, no. 1 (1987): 701–12.
The Earliest Franciscans: The Legacy of Giles of Assisi, Roger of Provence, and James of Milan. Trans. Kathryn Krug. Paulist, 2015.
Egan, Keith, ed. *Carmelite Prayer: A Tradition for the Twenty-First Century*. Paulist, 2003.
Eliade, Mircea. *Shamanism: Archaic Techniques of Ecstasy*. Trans. Willard Trask. Bollingen, 1964.
———. *Yoga: Immortality and Freedom*. Trans. Willard Trask. Pantheon, 1958.
Engel, Mary Potter, et al. "Roundtable Discussion: Mysticism and Feminist Spirituality." *Journal of Feminist Studies in Religion* 24, no. 2 (2008): 143–87.
Ephrem the Syrian. *Hymns*. Trans. Kathleen McVey. Paulist, 1989.
———. *Hymns on Paradise*. Trans. Sebastian Brock. St. Vladimir's Seminary Press, 1990.
Erickson, Jacob. "Irreverent Theology: On the Queer Ecology of Creation." In *Meaningful Flesh: Reflections on Religion and Nature for a Queer Planet*, ed. Whitney Bauman, 55–80. Punctum, 2015.
Evagrius Ponticus. *The Praktikos and Chapters on Prayer*. Trans. John Eudes Bamberger. Cistercian Publications, 1972.

Evans, G. R. "*Sancta Indifferentia* and *Adiaphora*: 'Holy Indifference' and 'Things Indifferent.'" *Common Knowledge* 15, no. 1 (2009): 23–38.

Field, Sean L. *The Beguine, the Angel, and the Inquisitor: The Trials of Marguerite Porete and Guiard de Cressonessart*. University of Notre Dame Press, 2012.

Foltz, Bruce. *The Noetics of Nature: Environmental Philosophy and the Holy Beauty of the Visible*. Fordham University Press, 2014.

Forman, Mary. "Gertrud of Helfta: Arbor Amoris in Her Heart's Garden." *Mystics Quarterly* 26, no. 4 (2000): 163–78.

Foucault, Michel. "Political Technology of Individuals." In *Technologies of the Self: A Seminar with Michel Foucault*, ed. Luther H. Martin, Huck Gutman, and Patrick H. Hutton, 145–62. Tavistock, 1988.

Francis of Assisi and Clare of Assisi. *The Complete Works*. Trans. Regis J. Armstrong and Ignatius C. Brady. Paulist, 1986.

Gertrude of Helfta. *The Herald of Divine Love*. Trans. Margaret Winkworth. Paulist, 1993.

Gondal, Marie-Louise. *Madame Guyon (1648–1717): Un nouveau visage*. Beauchesne, 1989.

Gorrie, William. *Illustrations of Scripture from Botanical Science*. 1854.

Griffiths, F. J. *The Garden of Delights: Reform and Renaissance for Women in the Twelfth Century*. University of Pennsylvania Press, 2011.

Guyon, Jeanne. *Autobiography of Madame Guyon*. 2 vols. Trans. Thomas Taylor Allen. 1898.

———. *Letters of Madame Guyon*. Ed. P. Upham. 1858.

———. *The Prison Narratives of Jeanne Guyon*. Trans. Dianne Guenin-Lelle and Ronney Mourad. Oxford University Press, 2011.

———. [Selected poetry]. Trans. William Cowper. In *The Poetical Works of William Cowper, with Some of Madame Guyon's Poems in English*, 455–509. 1852.

———. *Selected Writings*. Ed. and trans. Dianne Guenin-Lelle and Ronney Mourad. Paulist, 2012.

———. *Spiritual Torrents*. Trans. A. W. Marston. H. R. Allenson, 1909.

———. *Union with God: Including 22 of Madame Guyon's Poems*. Ed. and trans. Gene Edwards. SeedSowers, 1981.

———. *The Way of the Child Jesus: Our Model of Perfection*. Trans. Nancy C. James. Madame Guyon Foundation, 2015.

Hadot, Pierre. *Philosophy as a Way of Life: Spiritual Exercises from Socrates to Foucault*. Trans. Arnold Davidson. Blackwell, 1995.

———. *Plotinus: Or, the Simplicity of Vision*. Trans. Michael Chase. University of Chicago Press, 1998.

———. *The Selected Writings of Pierre Hadot: Philosophy as Practice*. Ed. and trans. Federico Testa and Matthew Sharpe. Bloomsbury, 2020.

———. *Veil of Isis: An Essay on the History of the Idea of Nature*. Trans. Michael Chase. University of Chicago Press, 2008.

Hall, Matthew. *Plants as Persons: A Philosophical Botany*. State University of New York Press, 2011.

Hallward, Peter. *Out of This World: Deleuze and the Philosophy of Creation*. Verso, 2006.

Hamilton, Alastair. *Heresy and Mysticism in Sixteenth-Century Spain: The Alumbrados*. University of Toronto Press, 1992.

Hanley, Ryan. *The Political Philosophy of Fénelon*. Oxford University Press, 2020.

Haraway, Donna. *Staying with the Trouble: Making Kin in the Chthulucene*. Durham University Press, 2016.

Hildegard of Bingen. *Book of Divine Works: With Letters and Songs*. Ed. Matthew Fox. Trans. Robert Cunningham. Bear and Co., 1987.

———. *On Natural Philosophy and Medicine: Selections from Cause et Cure*. Trans. Margaret Berger. D.S. Brewer, 1999.

———. *Selected Writings*. Trans. Mark Atherton. Penguin, 2001.

———. *Symphonia: A Critical Edition of the Symphonia armonie celestium revelationum [Symphony of the Harmony of Celestial Revelations]*. Trans. Barbara Newman. Cornell University Press, 2015.

Hollywood, Amy. *Acute Melancholia and Other Essays*. Columbia University Press, 2016.

———. *The Soul as Virgin Wife: Mechthild of Magdeburg, Marguerite Porete, and Meister Eckhart*. Notre Dame University Press, 1985.

Hunt, Helen. *Clothed in the Body: Asceticism, the Body, and the Spiritual in the Late Antique Era*. Routledge, 2012.

Irigaray, Luce. *Elemental Passions*. Trans. Joanne Collie and Judith Still. Routledge, 1993.

———. *A New Culture of Energy: Beyond East and West*. Trans. Stephen Seely, Stephen Pluháček, and Antonia Pont. Columbia University Press, 2021.

Irigaray, Luce, and Michael Marder. *Through Vegetal Being: Two Philosophical Perspectives.* Columbia University Press, 2016.

Janson, Anthony F. "The Meaning of the Landscape in Bellini's *St. Francis in Ecstasy.*" *Artibus et Historiae* 15, no. 30 (1994): 41–54.

Jantzen, Grace. *Becoming Divine: Toward a Feminist Philosophy of Religion.* Manchester University Press, 1998.

———. "Feminists, Philosophers, and Mystics." *Hypatia* 9, no. 4 (1994): 186–206.

———. *Power, Gender, and Christian Mysticism.* Cambridge University Press, 1995.

———. "Power, Gender and Ecstasy: Mysticism in Post/Modernity." *Literature and Theology* 11, no. 4 (1997): 385–402.

John of the Cross. *The Collected Works of St John of the Cross.* Trans. Kieran Kavanaugh and Otilio Rodriguez. ICS, 1991.

Justaert, Kristien. "Schizoanalysis of the Eucharist: From Oedipal Repetition to Liberating Event." In *Deleuze and the Schizoanalysis of Religion*, ed. Lindsay Powell-Jones and F. LeRon Shults, 41–58. Bloomsbury, 2016.

———. *Theology After Deleuze.* Continuum, 2012.

Kearns, Laurel, and Catherine Keller, eds. *Ecospirit: Religions and Philosophies for the Earth.* Fordham University Press, 2007.

Keller, Catherine. *Cloud of the Impossible: Negative Theology and Planetary Entanglement.* Columbia University Press, 2015.

Keller, Catherine, and Mary-Jane Rubenstein, eds. *Entangled Worlds: Religion, Science, and New Materialisms.* Fordham University Press, 2017.

Keller, Dorothea. *Nutrition and Nutritive Soul in Aristotle and Aristotelianism.* De Gruyter, 2020.

Knox, Richard. *Enthusiasm: A Chapter in the History of Religion, with Special Reference to the XVII and XVIII Centuries.* Oxford University Press, 1950.

Kotva, Simone. *Effort and Grace: On the Spiritual Exercise of Philosophy.* Bloomsbury, 2020.

———. "Habit and the Spiritual Life: Perspectives from Christian Mysticism and the Philosophy of Religion." In *Habit and the History of Philosophy*, ed. Jeremy Dunham and Komarine Romdenh-Romluc, 183–95. Routledge, 2022.

Kwasniewski, Peter. "The Ecstasy of Love in Aquinas's 'Commentary on the Sentences.'" *Angelicum* 83, no. 1 (2006): 51–93.

———. *The Ecstasy of Love in the Thought of St. Thomas Aquinas*. Emmaus, 2021.

Lamsechi, Guita, and Beatrice Trînca. *Spiritual Vegetation: Vegetal Nature in Religious Contexts Across Medieval and Early Modern Europe*. Brill, 2022.

Lanzetta, Barbara. *Radical Wisdom: A Feminist Mystical Theology*. Fortress, 2005.

Larkin, Ernest. "The Carmelite Tradition and Centering Prayer/Meditation." In *Carmelite Prayer: A Tradition for the 21st Century*, ed. Keith Egan, 202–22. Paulist, 2003.

Lavin, Marilyn Aronberg, Jinyu Liu, and Adam Gitner. "The Joy of St. Francis: Bellini's Panel in the Frick Collection." *Artibus et Historiae* 28, no. 56 (2007): 231–56.

Lawless, George P. "Interior Peace in the Confessions of St. Augustine." *Recherches Augustiniennes* 15 (1980): 80–98.

Ledoux, Arthur. "A Green Augustine: On Learning to Love Nature Well." *Theology and Science* 3, no. 3 (2005): 331–44.

Lee, Bo Karen. *Sacrifice and Delight in the Mystical Theologies of Anna Maria van Schurman and Madame Jeanne Guyon*. Notre Dame University Press, 2014.

LeVasseur, T. and A. Peterson, eds. *Religion and Ecological Crisis: The "Lynn White Thesis" at Fifty*. Routledge, 2017.

Lollar, Joshua. *To See Into the Life of Things: The Contemplation of Nature in Maximus the Confessor and His Predecessors*. Brepols, 2013.

Lorbiecki, Marybeth. *Following in the Footsteps of St. Francis: Pope John Paul II's Call for Ecological Action*. Rizzoli, 2014.

Mallet-Joris, F. *Jeanne Guyon*. Flammarion, 1978.

Mancuso, Stefano. *The Revolutionary Genius of Plants: A New Understanding of Plant Intelligence and Behavior*. Atria, 2018.

Marder, Michael. *Grafts: Writings on Plants*. University of Minnesota Press, 2016.

———. *Green Mass: The Ecological Theology of St. Hildegard of Bingen*. Stanford University Press, 2021.

———. *The Philosopher's Plant: An Intellectual Herbarium*. Columbia University Press, 2014.

———. *Plant-Thinking: Philosophy and Vegetal Life*. Columbia University Press, 2013.

Marguerite of Porete. *Mirror of Simple Souls*. Trans. Elleb Babinsky. Paulist, 1993.

Matter, E. A. *The Voice of My Beloved: The Song of Songs in Western Medieval Christianity*. University of Pennsylvania Press, 1990.

Mayse, Ariel Evan. "Gardens of the Spirit: Land, Text, and Ecological Hermeneutics in Jewish Mystical Sources." *Dibur Literary Journal* 11 (2022): 60–88.

McAvoy, Liz Herbert. *The Enclosed Garden and the Medieval Religious Imaginary*. D. S. Brewer, 2021.

McAvoy, Liz Herbert, Patricia Skinner, and Theresa Tyers. "Strange Fruits: Grafting, Foreigners, and the Garden Imaginary in Northern France and Germany, 1250–1350." *Speculum* 94, no. 2 (2019): 467–95.

McGinn, Bernard. *The Crisis of Mysticism: Quietism in Seventeenth-Century Spain, Italy, and France*. Crossroad, 2021.

———. *The Flowering of Mysticism: Men and Women in the New Mysticism (1200–1350)*. Crossroad, 1998.

———. *The Foundations of Mysticism: Origins to the Fifth Century*. Crossroad, 1991.

———. *The Persistence of Mysticism in Catholic Europe: France, Italy, and Germany 1500–1675*. Crossroad, 2020.

McFague, Sallie. *The Body of God: An Ecological Theology*. Fortress, 1992.

Meeker, Natania, and Antónia Szabari. *Radical Botany: Plants and Speculative Fiction*. Fordham University Press, 2020.

Merchant, Carolyn. *The Death of Nature: Women, Ecology, and the Scientific Revolution*. Harper and Row, 1986.

———. *Earthcare: Women and the Environment*. Routledge, 1996.

Merton, Thomas. *Mystics and Zen Masters*. Delta, 1967.

Mews, C. "Religious Thinker: 'A Frail Human Being' on Fiery Life." In *Voice of the Living Light: Hildegard of Bingen and Her World*, ed. Barbara Newman, 52–69. University of California Press, 1998.

Meyer, Eric Daryl. *Inner Animalities: Theology and the End of the Human*. Fordham University Press, 2018.

Miller, Elaine P. *The Vegetative Soul: From Philosophy of Nature to Subjectivity in the Feminine*. State University of New York, 2002.

Miller, Patricia Cox. *In the Eye of the Animal: Zoological Imagination in Ancient Christianity*. University of Pennsylvania Press, 2018.

Miller, Theresa L. *Plant Kin: A Multispecies Ethnography in Indigenous Brazil*. University of Texas Press, 2019.

Molinos, Miguel de. *The Spiritual Guide*. Trans. Robert P. Baird. Paulist, 2010.

Moore, Stephen D., ed. *Divinanimality: Animal Theory, Creaturely Theology*. Fordham University Press, 2014.

Nealon, Jeffrey. *Plant Theory: Biopower and Vegetable Life*. Stanford University Press, 2015.

Nevin, Thomas E. *Thérèse of Lisieux: God's Gentle Warrior*. Oxford University Press, 2006.

Newman, Barbara. *God and the Goddesses: Vision, Poetry, and Belief in the Middle Ages*. Pennsylvania University Press, 2005.

———. *From Virile Woman to WomanChrist*. University of Pennsylvania Press, 1995.

———. "[Review:] Liz Herbert McAvoy, *The Enclosed Garden and the Medieval Religious Imaginary*." *Speculum* 97, no. 4 (2022): 1226–27.

———. "'Sibyl of the Rhine': Hildegard's Life and Times." In *Voice of the Living Light: Hildegard of Bingen and Her World*, ed. Barbara Newman, 1–29. University of California Press, 1998.

———. *Sister of Wisdom: St. Hildegard's Theology of the Feminine*. University of California Press, 1998.

———. *Voice of the Living Light: Hildegard of Bingen and Her World*. University of California Press, 1998.

Nightingale, Andrea. *Spectacles of Truth in Classical Greek Philosophy: Theoria in its Cultural Context*. Cambridge University Press, 2004.

Nordlander, Andreas. "Green Purpose: Teleology, Ecological Ethics, and the Recovery of Contemplation." *Studies in Christian Ethics* 34, no. 1 (2021): 36–55.

On Care for Our Common Home. Laudato Si': The Encyclical of Pope Francis on the Environment. Commentary by Sean McDonagh. Orbis, 2016.

Paige, Nicholas. *Being Interior: Autobiography and the Contradictions of Modernity in Seventeenth-Century France*. Pennsylvania University Press, 2000.

Perkinson, J. W. *Political Spirituality in an Age of Eco-Apocalypse: Communication and Struggle Across Species, Cultures, and Religions*. Palgrave Macmillan, 2015.

Peters, F. E. *Greek Philosophical Terms: A Historical Lexicon*. New York University Press, 1967.
The Philokalia. 4 vols. Ed. and trans. G. E. H. Palmer, Philip Sherrard, and Kallistos Ware. Faber and Faber, 1979–1995.
Plotinus. *The Enneads*. Ed. Lloyd P. Gerson. Cambridge University Press, 2018.
Porphyry. *Life of Plotinus*. Trans. A. H. Armstrong. Harvard University Press, 1969.
Potter, Elizabeth. "Modeling the Gender Politics in Science." *Hypatia* 3, no. 1 (1988): 19–33.
Prevot, Andrew. *The Mysticism of Ordinary Life: Theology, Philosophy, and Feminism*. Oxford University Press, 2023.
Pseudo-Dionysius. *The Complete Works*. Trans. Colm Luibhead. Paulist, 1987.
Ramey, Joshua. *The Hermetic Deleuze: Philosophy and Spiritual Ordeal*. Duke University Press, 2013.
Richard of St. Victor. *The Twelve Patriarchs, The Mystical Ark*. Ed. and trans. Grover Zinn. Paulist, 1979.
Ritchey, Sara. *Holy Matter: Changing Perceptions of the Material World in Late Medieval Christianity*. Cornell University Press, 2014.
———. "Spiritual Arborescence: Trees in the Medieval Christian Imagination." *Spiritus* 8 (2008): 64–82.
Rubin, David Lee, and Alice Stroup. *Utopia: 16th and 17th Centuries*. Rookwood, 1998.
Ruymann, Mallory A. "Nuns as Gardeners: Using and Making Enclosed Gardens." *Athanor* 35 (2017): 41–47.
Ryan, John C., Patricía Vieira, and Monica Gagliano. *The Mind of Plants: Narratives of Vegetal Intelligence*. Synergistic, 2021.
Sales, Francis de. *Of the Love of God*. Trans. H. L. Sidney Lear. 1888.
Sandilands, C. "Vegetate." In *Veer Ecology: A Companion for Environmental Thinking*, ed. Jeffrey Jerome Cohen and Lowell Duckert, 16–29. University of Minnesota Press, 2017.
Saudreau, Auguste. *Mystical Prayer According to St. Jane de Chantal*. Trans. A. E. H. Swinstead. Benziger Brothers, 1929.
Say, Aliya. "Art, Spirit, and Plants: On Botanical Abstraction, Vegetal Ontology, and Mystical States." PhD diss., Aarhus University, 2023.

Selo, Agnes M. F. "Breath and Prayer in Ancient and Modern Times." *Life of the Spirit* 9, no. 98 (1954): 53–62.

Sheldrake, Merlin. *Entangled Life: How Fungi Make Our Worlds, Change Our Minds, and Shape Our Futures*. Penguin, 2020.

Sherman, Jacob Holsinger. "Beyond the Greening of Faith: Contemplative Practice in the Anthropocene." *Toronto Journal of Theology* 38, no. 2 (2022): 214–27.

———. "No Werewolves in Theology? Transcendence, Immanence, and Becoming-Divine in Gilles Deleuze." *Modern Theology* 25, no. 1 (2009): 1–20.

———. *Partakers of the Divine: Contemplation and the Practice of Philosophy*. Fortress, 2014.

———. "Reading the Book of Nature after Nature." *Religions* 11, no. 4 (2020). https://doi.org/10.3390/rel11040205.

Shining, P., and N. Michelle Epple, eds. *Exploring Sexuality and Spirituality*. Brill, 2020.

Simard, Suzanne. *Finding the Mother Tree: Discovering the Wisdom of the Forest*. Knopf, 2021.

Sjøvoll, Therese. "Kunst: Giovanni Bellini, 'Den hellige Frans i ødemarken.'" *St Olav* 3 (2021): 40–43.

Stark, Hannah. "Deleuze and Critical Plant Studies." In *Deleuze and the Non/Human*, ed. Hannah Stark and J. Roffe, 180–96. Palgrave Macmillan, 2015.

Steinmann, Andrea E. "He Is Like a Tree: Arboreal Imagery for Humans in Biblical Wisdom Literature," *Religions* 12, no. 10 (2021): 804. https://doi.org/10.3390/rel12100804.

Stewart, Columba. *"Working the Earth of the Heart": The Messalian Controversy in History, Texts, and Language to A.D. 431*. Oxford University Press, 1991.

Stopp, Elisabeth. *Madame de Chantal: Portrait of a Saint*. Faber and Faber, 1963.

Sweet, Victoria. "Hildegard of Bingen and the Greening of Medieval Medicine." *Bulletin of the History of Medicine* 73, no. 3 (1999): 381–403.

Theokritoff, Elizabeth. "Liturgy, Cosmic Worship, and Christian Cosmology." In *Toward an Ecology of Transformation: Orthodox Christian Perspectives on Environment, Nature, and Creation*, ed. John Cryssavgis and Bruce V. Foltz, 295–306. Fordham University Press, 2013.

The Syriac Fathers on Prayer and the Spiritual Life. Ed. and trans. Sebastian Brock. Cistercian Publications, 1987.

Thérèse of Lisieux. *Collected Poems.* Trans. Alan Bancroft. Gracewing, 2001.

Trewavas, Anthony. *Plant Behaviour and Intelligence.* Oxford University Press, 2014.

Tsing, Anna, Heather Swanson, Eliane Gan, and Nils Bubandt. *Arts of Living on a Damaged Planet.* University of Minnesota Press, 2017.

Tsur, Reuven. *On the Shore of Nothingness: A Study in Cognitive Poetics.* Imprint Academic, 2003.

Virenque, Naïs. "Dendrites' and Preachers' Trees: A Literary and Iconographic Study of Mnemonic Images." In *Spiritual Vegetation: Vegetal Nature in Religious Contexts Across Medieval and Early Modern Europe*, ed. Guita Lamsechi and Beatrice Trînca, 27–48. Brill, 2022.

Wallace, Mark I. *When God Was a Bird: Christianity, Animism, and the Re-Enchantment of the World.* Fordham University Press, 2019.

Ward, Patricia. *Experimental Theology in America: Madame Guyon, Fénelon, and Their Readers.* Baylor University Press, 2009.

———. "Madame Guyon and Experiential Theology in America." *Church History* 67, no. 3 (1998): 484–98.

Warren, Sarah. "Haraway's Dream of an Ek-Centric Anthropos: Finding Virtuous Humility in the Age of a Dying Earth." *Environment, Space, Place* 10, no. 2 (2018): 109–27.

Weil, Simone. *On Science, Necessity, and the Love of God.* Ed. and trans. Richard Rees. Oxford University Press, 1968.

———. *Waiting on God.* Ed. Joseph-Marie Perrin. Trans. Emma Craufurd. Routledge and Kegan Paul, 1951.

White Jr., Lynn. "The Historical Roots of Our Ecologic Crisis." *Science* 155, no. 3767 (1967): 1203–7.

Wilberding, James. "Intelligible Kinds and Natural Kinds in Plotinus." *Études Platoniciennes* 8 (2011): 53–76.

Winston-Allen, Anne. "Gardens of Heavenly and Earthly Delight: Medieval Gardens of the Imagination." *Neuphilologische Mitteilungen* 99, no. 1 (1998): 83–92.

Wirzba, Norman. "Christian *Theoria Physike:* On Learning to See Creation." *Modern Theology* 32, no. 2 (2016): 211–30.

Wood, David. *Thinking Plant Animal Human: Encounters with Communities of Difference.* University of Minnesota Press, 2020.

Wortley, John, ed. *The Anonymous Sayings of the Desert Fathers: A Select Edition and Complete English Translation*. Cambridge University Press, 2013.

Yountae, An. *The Decolonial Abyss: Mysticism and Cosmopolitics from the Ruins*. Fordham University Press, 2016.

INDEX

Acute Melancholia and Other Essays (Hollywood), 103–104
affections, 10–11, 138, 142–144, 150–151, 174, 204; arousal of in mysticism, 123–128, 142, 144, 146, 185, 201, 203
Agamben, Giorgio, 191
agency, 3, 12–13, 20–22, 26, 34, 68, 128, 130, 147, 152, 157, 160–161, 173, 188, 190–192
air, xx, 139, 155, 165–166, 177, 179–182, 184
Alumbrados, 228n15
amour propre (self-love), 138
animal life, xiii–xv, xvii, 3, 22–23, 27, 32–33, 35, 41, 50–54, 57, 69, 108–109, 128, 132, 142, 160, 168, 179, 191
anthropotechnics, 39
anti-individualism, 131
Arber, Agnes, 201
Arbman, Ernst, 231n61
Arentzen, Thomas, 3, 67–72
Aristotle, xii–xiii, 15–16, 51–52, 78

annéantisement (annihilation), 122, 138. *See also* self-annihilation
anoesia (without ratiocination), 25
anoetic consciousness, 25–26, 94, 166, 232n10
anoetic prayer, 25–26, 61, 82
anthropocentrism, 84, 157, 170, 202
apatheia, 60, 65
Apophthegmata, 58
asceticism, 4, 11, 61, 74–70, 71–79, 223n60; *ascesis*, 66, 72–73
Asia Minor, 57
attention, xiv–xix, 28, 34–35, 40–42, 46–49, 79, 83–84, 108–109, 111, 137, 152, 164–166, 175–182, 190–195, 205; in Carmelite mysticism, 172–173; as an epistemology, 13; in Evagrian monasticism, 59–64; in Guyon's mysticism, 147–152, 183–187; in Plotinus' asceticism, 74–76; unconscious and vegetal, 18–20, 55
atmosphere. *See* air

Aquinas, Thomas, 226n7
Augustine, 227n6
austerities, 138–139, 144–145
Autobiography (Guyon), 136, 142

Bastille, 135–156
Bataille, Georges, 119, 227n1
Beguines, 101
Bellini, Giovanni, xviii–xix, 84, 111–117, 226n2
Benedictines, 95
Bernard of Clairvaux, 4–5, 85, 95–96
Bible, 4–5, 10, 85, 88–89, 92, 97, 108, 135, 155–158, 189, 204. *See also specific books*
Blée, Fabrice, 175
Blue Sapphire of the Mind, The (Christie), 58
Boehme, Jacob, 201
Bonaventure, 114
Bossuet, Jacques-Bénigne, 125–126, 133, 136
breathing, xx, 1, 20, 25, 27, 41–42, 69, 137–138, 148, 151, 160–195, 217n71
Brintnall, Kent, 12
Brock, Sebastian, 66
Brown, Peter, 60
Bruneau, Marie-Florine, xx, 123–124, 136, 149–154, 158, 171, 177
Buddha, 164
Buddhist practices, 19, 25, 175, 183–184, 202
Burrus, Virginia, 3, 67–72
Byzantine Christianity, 47, 67–72
Byzantine Tree Life (Arentzen, Burrus, and Peers), 67–72

Carmelites, Discalced, xix, 141–144
Casiday, Augustine, 25, 60–61
Catholicism, xi, xix, 4–5, 11, 40–41, 81, 111, 119–158, 198–203
Centering Prayer, 199
Certeau, Michel de, xx, 130, 147–150, 158, 170, 178, 193–194
Chamovitz, Daniel, 22–26, 94, 166, 232n10
Christian Library, A (Wesley), 136
Christie, Douglas, xvii, 11, 58–63, 72, 194–195
Cistercians, 95
Clément, Olivier, 59
Cloud of the Impossible (Keller), 14
Coccia, Emanuele, xxi, 2, 42, 140, 161, 166–171, 187–182
coeur (heart), 138, 143
cogito (I think), 147
Coleman, Charly, 131–132, 228n10
Columba aspexit (Hildegard of Bingen), 88
Commentary on the Song of Songs of Solomon (Guyon), 155–157
Confessions (Augustine), 227n6
contemplation, xi–xxi, 2–3, 9–11, 45–48, 80–85, 102, 159–161, 201–206; *ascesis* and, 72–79; birds and, xiv, 10, 17, 39, 141; breathing as, 179–183; creation as, 187–195; cross-species, 25–26;

Deleuze on, 28–39, 234n45;
ecstasy and, 92, 116; embodied,
216n59; etymology of, 39; Guyon
on, 120–146, 171–179; freedom
and, 155; gravity and, 139; habit
as, 172–173; infants and, 45,
138–139; infused or acquired,
214n29; Marguerite of Porete
on, 103; of nature (*phusike
theoria*), 57–64, 221n27, 221n26;
passivity and, 161–171, 173–174;
pure sensation as, 32–33; in
Syriac asceticism, 66–67;
Plotinus on, 48–57; vegetal life
and, 18–19, 24, 40–43, 68–71, 89,
114, 168–169, 183–187
contemplative ecology, xvii, 9–15,
40, 58, 195
consciousness, xv, 1, 9, 13, 17–18,
23–26, 35, 40, 50, 82, 94, 144,
166–167, 178
Corrigan, Kevin, 24, 57, 115, 219n1
cosmism, 3–4, 81, 123, 141, 211n4
Council of Ephesus, 64–65
critical plant studies, xvi, xx, 2, 14,
28–31, 37, 161, 187, 193, 215n44
Cross, D. J. S., 234n45

Darwin, Charles, 22
David of Thessaloniki, 68
Deck, John, 50–52
decolonial theory, 12
Deleuze, Gilles, xvi, xxi, 2, 14,
28–29, 42, 47, 161, 187–191, 205
dendrite saints, 4, 67–71
Desert Fathers, 8, 184

Difference and Repetition (Deleuze),
33, 187–190
Disibodenberg, 85
dispossession, 131
Dombrowski, Daniel, 223n60

ecstasy, xviii, 2, 9, 21, 81–84, 92–97,
103, 108–109, 120–121, 181, 186,
193, 200–201; ecologies and,
39–43; *ekstasis*, 13, 115–116;
exstasis, 114; of nature, 111–117
Ecstasy or Religious Trance
(Arbman), 231n61
Eden, Garden of, 4, 89
Edigna of Puch, 4
Egypt, 17, 57–58, 64–65
Elemental Passions (Irigaray), 162
elements, the four, 27, 41, 155,
158, 177
Eliade, Mircea, 202–203
embodiment, xii, xx, 7, 12, 69, 81,
84, 92–94, 100, 105–107, 120–121,
143–151, 175–178;
transcorporeality, 128–134
Enclosed Garden, The (McAvoy),
97–98
Enneads (Plotinus), 33, 50–54,
71–74, 78, 188–189
Ephrem the Syrian, 65–71
Erickson, Jacob, 108
Erotism (Bataille), 227n1
Evagrius of Pontus, 25, 57–65, 71,
222n41
evolution, 23, 129
Exploring Sexuality and Spirituality
(Shining and Epple), 227n1

feminist theory, xix, 5, 7, 12–13, 46, 92, 97, 130, 136, 146, 149, 162, 227n1
Fénelon, François, 132–136
Foltz, Bruce, 11
Foucault, Michel, 39, 59
France, 100–105, 119–158, 203–205
Francis (pope), 111
Franciscans, 84, 111–117
Francis de Sales, xix, 10, 230n53
Francis of Assisi, 111–117, 122
freedom, 157
fruitio Dei (enjoyment of God), 125
fungi, xiv, 1, 55, 90, 217n65

gardens, 95, 164; in Christian mysticism, 4–5, 86, 88, 95, 96, 99, 106, 108, 156
gemma (bud, gem), 88
gender, 6–9, 86–88, 162–163
Geneva, 134–135
Gertrude the Great of Helfta, xviii, 83, 95–100
Gex, 134
gift, 62
God, xviii–xx, 3–4, 62, 86–87, 102–109; abandonment to, 145; air as, 20, 165; creatures contemplating, 24, 62, 66, 99; enjoyment of, 11, 56, 65, 119, 120, 125, 137, 143–146, 151, 158, 177, 185–186; dialogue with, 142, 200; nature and, 3, 61–66, 70, 92, 98–99, 114–115, 123, 131; perceiving, 25, 75, 82, 93, 135, 139, 166, 173–176, 193; present everywhere, 153, 156–157; in the present moment, 47, 126; rethinking of, 64, 193; spontaneous striving toward, 133, 184; soul's presence in, 179; sun as, 205–206; union with, xviii, 7, 43, 94, 97, 102, 122, 141, 152, 158, 167; self and, 101, 107; vegetal life and, 64, 88, 100, 106, 108, 122, 129–130, 154–155, 178, 185–186; as weak, 154–155
gods, xii, 52, 189; plants and, 17–18
Gondal, Marie-Louise, 130
Gorrie, William, 212n6
grafting, 42, 69–70; in mysticism, xviii, 95–100; in the New Testament, 70–71
Grafts (Marder), 99
Gregory the Great, 85
Green Mass (Marder), 7, 20–21, 89–94
Grenoble, 135
Guattari, Félix, 29–35
Guyon, Jeanne, xix–xxi, 8, 10, 27, 40–42, 79, 109, 111, 122–123, 141–143, 160, 169, 197–206, 229n23, 229n29, 229n32; on attention, 147–152, 183–187; Bruneau on, 149–158; Certeau and, 147–149; Chantal and, 142–146; on contemplation, 138–140, 161–162, 171–179, 191–195; life of, 134–137; on nature, 131, 137, 180; on prayer, 179–187; on trees, 153–154; Quietism and, 124–142. *See also specific works*

INDEX 255

habit, 33, 38, 41–42, 64, 73, 76–78, 159, 172–173, 175–180, 186, 195, 200; *ethoi*, 40
Hadot, Pierre, 2, 59, 72–78, 188, 190
Hallward, Peter, 219n93
Hanley, Ryan, 133
Haraway, Donna, 218n73
Helfta, nuns of, 95–100, 194, 197
Herald of God's Loving-Kindness (Gertrude the Great of Helfta), 95
heresy, xvii, xix, 11, 56, 64, 101–102, 107, 124, 213n27, 214n29, 228n15
Hermetic Philosophy, 219n93
Hildegard of Bingen, xvii–xviii, 5, 7, 20, 83–94, 105, 107–108, 122, 186, 194, 197
Hilma af Klint, 235n13
Hindu practices, 184, 202
Holy Matter (Ritchey), 86–87
Hollywood, Amy, xviii, 84, 103–108, 128, 194
Hunt, Helen, 65
Hymn of the Sun (Francis of Assisi), 116–117
Hymn to Faith (Ephrem the Syrian), 66

Ignatius of Loyola, 11, 124, 127, 228n15
Illuminati. *See* Alumbrados
indifference, 144, 170
indigenous traditions, xv, 48, 198, 202
infants, 7, 45, 138–139, 141, 176, 185
intra-action, 8, 88, 99

Irigaray, Luce, xx, 2, 5–7, 19, 42, 140, 161–170, 180–187, 190–195
Isaac of Nineveh, 66–67

Jane de Chantal, xix, 123, 140–147, 184, 230n53, 231n56
Janson, Anthony, 116
Jantzen, Grace, 5–6
Järnegard, Esaias, 231n61
Jesus Christ, xviii, 10, 96–97, 141, 165
John of the Cross, 124, 141, 172, 214n29
John Paul II (pope), 111
Judea, 57
Justaert, Kristien, 189
Justifications (Guyon), 136

Kant, Immanuel, 20
Keller, Catherine, 13–14
Kingdom of Heaven, 60, 63–64
Kwasniewski, Peter, 114–115, 216n59

Lacombe, Father, 134
landscape painting, 112
Lee, Bo Karen, xx, 129, 151, 155, 158
Life of Antony (Athanasius of Alexandria), 58
Life of Plants, The (Coccia), 2, 169–171, 179
Life of Plotinus (Porphyry), 50
liturgy, 88, 160
Louis XIV (king), 131, 135
love, 88; compared to vegetal life, 92; divine, 146, 174, 199; ecstasy of, 115; Marguerite of Porete on, 101–108; selfless and nonvicious, 133

low anthropology, 129, 228n19
Low Countries, 101

Madame de Maintenon, 135
magic, 219n93
Maimonides, Moses, 98
Malaval, François, 135
Mancuso, Stefano, 54
Marder, Michael, xiv–xviii, 2, 42, 68–73, 76, 82–83, 99–104, 121, 128–129, 137, 140, 150, 158–159, 167, 169, 177–178, 188–190, 200, 211, 213, 215, 216, 219–225, 231–235, 237, 243–244; on grafting, 69–70; on Hildegard of Bingen, 89–95; Hollywood and, xviii, 84, 105–109; Irigaray and, 6–7, 19, 163–166, 183–185, 193–195; on Miller, 162–163; on the plant in us, 50, 106, 159; on Plotinus, 48–57; on plant-thinking, xiii, 15–17, 54, 90–92, 94, 195; on practical contemplation, 19, 21, 26–27, 162–165; on vegetalizing, 18–20, 155; on vegetal mindfulness, 18–19, 47, 54–56, 93. *See also specific works*
Marguerite of Porete, xviii–xix, 8, 84, 100–109, 111, 123–124, 128, 138
Marseilles, 135
Mary (mother of Jesus), 4, 85, 91, 145, 165, 180
Matthew (6:26–30), 10, 141, 189
Maximin of Trier, 88
Maximus the Confessor, 226n7

McAvoy, Liz Herbert, xviii, 7–8, 83, 86, 88, 94–100, 105–107, 194
McFague, Sallie, 13
McGinn, Bernard, xvi, 81, 81, 89, 99, 101
McMillan, Emily, 212n11, 225n29
Mechthild of Hackenborn, 225n29
meditation, 9–10, 67, 102, 139, 174; Buddhist and Hindu, 19, 25, 183–184, 202; informal, 199–201
Meditations (Roger of Provence), 114–115
Meeker, Natania, xix, 129, 132, 177
Meister Eckhart, xviii, 11, 124
Messalianism, 64–65, 222n41
Metaphysics (Aristotle), 52
Methodists, 136
Miller, Elaine, 2, 50, 129, 162–163
Mirror of Simple Souls, The (Marguerite of Porete), xviii, 102–107
Molinos, Miguel, 125, 139
monasticism, 57–71, 86–89, 140–146. *See also specific religious orders*
morphe (form), 60
mṣallyānā (one who prays), 64
multispecies ethics, 30, 49, 57, 218n73
mystical union, xii, 2, 9, 21, 82–83, 95–100, 114–115, 120–121, 130, 141, 155–156, 170, 194
Mystic Fable, The (Certeau), 147–148

mysticism, xi–xxi, 1–3, 45–49, 81–84, 119–123, 157–158, 187–195; abstract, 230n53; antimysticism, 125; antinomianism and, 56–57; breathing and, 179–184; Carmelite, 140–141; Certeau on, 147–149, 193; cosmism and, 3–4, 81, 123, 141; critical reading and, 105; critical theory and, 12–14; Deleuze and, 36–39; democratizing, 141; early Christian, 24–25, 57–71; early modern, 128–134; ethics of, 40–42; of French spiritual reformers, 140–146; gender and, 5–9, 86–88; of Guyon, 134–140, 147–158, 171–179; heresy and, 11, 100–102, 107, 123–128; Jewish, 5; in landscape painting, 111–117; Marder on, 20–21, 89–95; of medieval women, 81–107; monsters and, 42–43; multispecies, 39; nature and, 177–178; non-Western, 201–203; passivity and, 162; plant biology and, 23, 26; Plotinian, 75–69; psychological approaches to, 39, 231n61; silence and, 186; of Thérèse of Lisieux, 203–205; vegetal metaphors in, 26–27, 95–100

mystique (mystics), 147–148

nature, xiii–xiv, 4, 77–79; affirmed, 11, 13, 46; arousal of, 123–126; as book, 25, 63; contemplation of, vii, 11, 67–71, 193, 221n27; as contemplation, 24, 52–53, 77, 114–117, 188–190, 193; contranatural, 46, 60, 98, 102; Deleuze and Guattari on, 30–31; early modern views of, 122, 126–134; gendering of, 6, 8, 162–163; Guyon on, 131, 137, 174, 177, 180; human, 10, 140; Irigaray on, 183; Marder on, 16–17; in medieval mysticism, 83–84, 101–107; Plotinus on, 49–54, 190; renounced, 46–47, 78; symbolized, 163. See also *phusis*

Nealon, Jeffrey, xiii, xvi, 2, 16, 17, 19, 30, 31, 32, 33

Neoplatonism, 24, 47–57, 72, 77, 150, 190

New Culture of Energy, A (Irigaray), 165–166, 180

Newman, Barbara, 6, 86

Nikiphoros the Monk, 217n71

noemata (thoughts, representations), 25

noesis (thinking), 49

nonconformism, xix, 11, 41, 30, 133, 136, 140

nothingness, 12–13

Nous (thought, mind), 24, 49

Pantheism, 14, 101, 130, 177

Paris, 135

passivity, xix–xx, 6–8, 28–38, 94, 116, 120, 133, 139, 157–171, 173–174

Paul (saint), 69–70, 96–98

Peers, Glenn, 3, 67–72
Perkinson, James, 13
Philosopher's Plant, The (Marder), 19, 50, 54, 162
philosophy, 14–16, 42, 45, 47, 69, 82, 99, 166, 180, 191–192, 206; Coccia on, 167–171; contemplative turn in, 12; Deleuze and Guattari on, 28–39, 187; environmental, 46; Hellenistic, 59–60; Marder on, 90–91, 162–164; Neoplatonic, 24, 49–57, 71–77; political, 19
Philosophy as a Way of Life (Hadot), 59
phuo (to grow), 49
phusike theoria (contemplation of nature), vii, 11, 67–64, 221n27
phusis (nature), xiii, 16–17, 27, 49–51, 53–54, 58, 62–65, 72–73, 75–79, 116, 186, 191
phutike noesis (growth-thought), 49
phuton (plant), xiii, 17
Plant Behaviour and Intelligence (Trewavas), 23
Plant Theory (Nealon), 15–16, 19, 37, 187–189
plants, xii–xv, 1–8, 16, 19–21, 35, 41, 45, 69, 120, 137, 142, 159, 201–202; in the Bible, 212n6; Coccia on, 166–171; Deleuze and Guattari on, 29–30; early modern views of, 128–129, 132; gendering of, 162–163; and gods, 17–18; intelligence of, 22–23, 54–55, 94, 217n65; Irigaray on, 164, 180; Marder on, 69–70, 83, 90–91, 108, 163, 185; in mysticism, 27, 85–100, 155–158, 195, 204–205; Plotinus on, 50–57, 78; soul of, 15. *See also* trees; vegetal life
plant-thinking, xiii, 15, 38, 54, 63, 90–94, 103, 195
Plant-Thinking (Marder), 16, 18, 54, 90
Plotinus, 48–54, 71–76, 219n1, 223n60
politics, 19, 37, 132–133, 148, 157–158
Porphyry, 50, 73–75
Power, Joseph, 144
Practice of Everyday Life, The (Certeau), 148
practices, 18–20, 28, 35, 39, 109, 148–149, 179, 190, 206
Praktikos (Evagrius), 60
prayer, xi–xv, 26, 67, 103, 119–122, 125–127, 133, 159, 197–206; amorphous, 60; attentiveness as, 59; anoetic, 25–26, 61, 82; breathing and, 160–195, 179–187, 217n71; continuous, 64; Chantal's method of, 142–146; Guyon's method of, 138–140, 160, 171–183; Hadot on, 74; mystical, 119, 124, 142, 146, 159–160; wordless, xi, 23, 101, 124, 127, 134–135, 201, 203
Prison Narratives (Guyon), 136
Protestantism, 11, 41, 134, 229n23
Pseudo-Dionysius, 25, 61, 82
psukhe (soul), 192. *See also* soul

Quakers, 11, 136
queer plants, xviii, 9, 83–89, 91–100, 107–108
queer theory, 12
Quietism, xix, 124–125, 136, 139, 142, 227n5, 228n15

Radical Botany (Meeker and Szabari), 132
Ramey, Joshua, 219n93
rhizome, 29–35
Richard of St. Victor, xiii, 9–10
Ritchey, Sara, xviii, 4, 86, 94
Roger of Provence, 114–115
Roman Catholic Church. *See* Catholicism
Roman Empire, late, 58, 64–65

Saint-Cyr, 135
samādhi (absorption), 181
Sandilands, Catriona, 191–192
Say, Aliya, 234n13
scala naturae (scale of nature), 128
self-annihilation, xviii–xix, 12, 26, 84, 89, 101–109, 122, 134–139, 143, 150
Selo, Agnes, 184, 217n71
sensation, xv, 21, 32–35, 138, 142, 147, 178, 186, 193, 201
sexuality, xviii, 7–8, 16, 69, 87, 88, 95–98, 107–108, 119, 121, 156, 162–163, 165, 227n1; asexuality, xviii, 7, 29, 96
sexuate difference, 6–8, 163
Shamanism (Eliade), 202
Sheldrake, Merlin, 217n65

Sherman, Jacob Holsinger, 11, 36–37, 189
Short and Easy Method of Prayer, A (Guyon), xx, 42, 126, 140, 155, 160, 171–179, 199
skin, xi–xii, xiv, 18–20, 34, 55, 69, 137, 182, 185, 201
Skinner, Patricia, 95–96, 99
silence, xix–xx, 41, 21, 13, 55, 173–186, 176–177; of plants, 35
Simard, Suzanne, 55
Sloterdijk, Peter, 39
Song of Songs, 4–5, 88, 92, 135, 155, 158, 204
soul, 15–16, 24–25, 33, 39; in Christian mysticism, 60, 65, 96, 99–105, 120–121, 125, 132, 139, 142, 156, 168, 173, 176, 178–179, 205; Marguerite of Porete on, 101–105; vegetative or vegetable, xiii, xv, 16, 33, 82, 120, 131, 133, 159, 162, 188, 200
Soul as Virgin Wife (Hollywood), 103
species extinction, 39–40
speciesism: critique of, 17, 38, 90, 100, 157–158; in Plotinus' philosophy, 50, 53
Speculum of the Other Woman (Irigaray), 164
Spinozism, 132
Spirit, xvii, 5, 66, 75, 86–87, 89, 93, 130, 147, 157, 168, 183–187; *spiritus*, 1, 165, 179–183
spirit possession, 202
spiritual arborescence, 4

spiritual exercises, xi–xv, 54, 59, 127, 140, 147, 159, 174–175, 188, 198; across species, 1–45; physics as, 59; Buddhist, 19, 25, 164, 183–184, 202; Yoga, 164–165, 180–183, 202. *See also specific topics*

Spiritual Exercises (Ignatius of Loyola), 127, 174

Spiritual Guide (Miguel Molinos), 125

spiritual life, 39, 41, 64, 72, 81, 120, 126, 130, 153, 175, 180

Spiritual Torrents (Guyon), 134, 138, 152, 154, 173

spontaneity, xiv, 53, 77–78, 133, 138, 140–143, 155, 174, 184, 204

Stark, Hannah, 29

St. Francis in Ecstasy (Bellini), 84, 111–117, 226n2

strategies, 41, 131; Certeau on, 148–158

suavis (sweet), 88

swarm intelligence, 54–57, 62, 188

Syria, 57, 65, 68

Syriac asceticism, 17, 47, 64–71

Szabari, Antónia, xix, 129, 132, 177

tactics, xix, 41; Certeau on, 148–171, 193

Telemachus (Fénelon), 132–133

templum (space, sanctuary), 39

Teresa of Ávila, 11, 124, 141, 172

Theokritoff, Elizabeth, 62

theoria (contemplation), 17, 24, 28–40, 42, 47, 51–52, 58–59, 66–67, 72, 76–77, 79, 187, 190, 191. *See also* contemplation

Thérèse of Lisieux, 203–205

Thousand Plateaus, A (Deleuze and Guattari), 29–32

Through Vegetal Being (Irigaray and Marder), 6–7, 18, 55–56, 164

trance, 202, 227n1

tranquility, 124, 139, 176, 227n6

Treatise on the Love of God (Francis de Sales), 141–142

trees, 23, 27, 55, 90–91; Bellini and, 84; Buddha and, 164–165; in Christian mysticism, 4–5, 25, 40; Deleuze and Guattari on, 29, 33; Guyon on, 153–154; hermits and, 67–71; in Neoplatonism, 53, 73, 77; Thérèse of Lisieux on, 204

tree sitting. *See* dendrite saints

Trewavas, Anthony, 22–24, 35, 54, 217n65

Tyers, Theresa, 95–96, 99

Veer Ecology (Cohen and Duckert), 191

vegetable contemplation, 28–39, 47, 188, 191

vegetal anarchy, 55–56, 64, 70, 74

vegetalizing, 8, 18, 20, 47, 53, 84, 87, 105, 140, 154, 158, 183, 193–194

vegetal life, xii–xxi, 15–28; contemplation and, 40–43, 68–71, 89, 114, 168–169, 183–187; contemporary philosophies of, 2–9, 83, 137–140, 149–150,

158–161, 171–173, 197–198; God and, 64, 88, 100, 106, 108, 122, 129–130, 154–155, 178; theology and, 17
vegetal mindfulness, xiii, 18–19, 47, 55–57, 93, 104, 175, 197
vegetal modernity, 19, 129–133, 177, 188
vegetal mysticism, xvii–xx, 49, 81–110, 111, 120, 137, 140, 198, 203–204, 235n13
vegetative soul, xii–xiii, 15–16, 82, 120, 159, 216n47
Vegetative Soul, The (Miller), 162–163, 216n47
Verna, Mount La, 111
Veil of Isis, The (Hadot), 59
via negativa (negative way), 11, 13, 20–21, 93–94, 100, 121, 126–127, 137, 155, 230n53
via vegetativa (vegetal way), 89–95, 100, 106, 121
virginity, 19, 25, 119, 202; Irigaray on, 165; *virginitas*, 86–101

viriditas (greenness), xvii–xviii, 83, 85–94, 106
Visitandines (Sisters of the Visitation of Mary), 231n56
vitalism, 29; contemplative, 190–191

Waiting for God (Weil), 205
Ward, Patricia, 184–185
Weil, Simone, 13, 197, 205–206
Wesley, John, 136
Western Esotericism, 206, 219n93
What a Plant Knows (Chamovitz), 22
What Is Philosophy? (Deleuze and Guattari), 32–35
Wibert of Gembloux, 90–93
Women Mystics Confront the Modern World (Bruneau), 149
Wright, Wendy, 144–145

Yoga, 164–165, 180–183, 202
Yoga (Eliade), 202
Yoga Sūtras (Patañjali), 181

GPSR Authorized Representative: Easy Access System Europe, Mustamäe tee
50, 10621 Tallinn, Estonia, gpsr.requests@easproject.com

www.ingramcontent.com/pod-product-compliance
Lightning Source LLC
Chambersburg PA
CBHW022041290426
44109CB00014B/936